ROYAL BLOODLINE

ROYAL BLOODLINE: ELLERY QUEEN,
AUTHOR AND DETECTIVE

by

FRANCIS M. NEVINS, JR.

Bowling Green University Popular Press
Bowling Green, Ohio 43403

Cover design: Frank McSherry, Jr.

FOR BOB WASHER

ACKNOWLEDGMENTS

During the five years this book has been inching toward completion, a small army of friends and acquaintances and correspondents, Queen lovers every one, helped in countless ways. My thanks go to Robert C. S. Adey, Michael Avallone, Jon L. Breen, Robert E. Briney, Ray Browne, Lianne Carlin, J. R. Christopher, William J. Clark, Edward Connor, J. Randolph Cox, Constance DiRienzo, Norman Donaldson, Stanley Ellin, Pat Erhardt, Ira Fistell, Estelle Fox, David L. Godwin, Edward D. Hoch, Allen J. Hubin, Harold Knott, Marvin Lachman, W. O. G. Lofts, Frank D. McSherry Jr., John J. Newton, John Nieminski, Otto Penzler, Hans Stefan Santesson, Scott Meredith Literary Agency, Larry Shaw, Charles Shibuk, Eleanor Sullivan, Julian Symons, Bill Thailing, Robert E. Washer, Donald A. Yates, and my deepest thanks of all to FREDERIC DANNAY and the late MANFRED B. LEE without whom there would have been nothing to write this book about.

Francis M. Nevins, Jr.
St. Louis, Missouri
May 6, 1973

INTRODUCTION

ONE DAY IN THE FALL OF 1928 TWO YOUNG NEW YORKERS, first cousins, decided to write a detective novel. The occasion was a newly announced $7500 prize contest, sponsored jointly by *McClure's* Magazine and the publishing house of Frederick A. Stokes. The work consumed the young men's nights and weekends for about three months, then they mailed in the manuscript and awaited the verdict. Eventually they received unofficial word that they had won the prize. They bought each other Dunhill pipes in celebration and made plans to quit their jobs and settle down to the literary life in the south of France.

Then *McClure's* Magazine went bankrupt and its successor awarded the prize to someone else.[1]

In the normal course of events, Frederic Dannay and Manfred B. Lee would probably have remained with their jobs in advertising and publicity. They would probably by now have been executives near retirement age, holding down corner suites on Mad Avenue, with perhaps several hundred radio and TV commercials to their credit; Dannay after all, with his poetic ambitions,

1

might have penned some catchy jingles on the merits of this or that deodorant.

Fortunately for tens of millions of readers, the normal course of events did not come about. Even though the cousins' novel was no longer the prizewinner, Stokes decided to publish it anyway. It was called *The Roman Hat Mystery*, and both its spine and its sleuth bore the same name: Ellery Queen.

What were these two young men like who were about to launch the most successful collaboration in the history of prose fiction? Both were born in 1905, nine months and five blocks apart, of immigrant Jewish stock, in a crowded Brooklyn tenement district. Dannay, the younger of the two, was born Daniel Nathan, and Lee's name at birth was Manford Lepofsky. Both cousins' mothers used the same family physician, who seems to have stepped straight out of a Philip Roth novel, for he took it upon himself to register the babies' birth certificates under the names David and Emanuel. As young men they changed their names to the forms under which the world knows them. Daniel Nathan took the name of Frederic out of admiration for Chopin, while Dannay is simply a combination of the first syllables of his birthname. Manford Lepofsky truncated and de-ethnicized his last name to Lee, and although he never publicly explained the reason for his slight alteration of his first name, it may not be insignificant in view of his lifelong belief in nonviolence that etymologically Manfred means man of peace.

Lee's family stayed in Brooklyn and Lee grew up in what he called a typical sidewalks-of-New-York atmosphere, but it was a far more brutal atmosphere than the allusion to the old ballad suggests and Lee early in life performed an "inner emigration," turning to books as a refuge from the battleground of the streets. Many years later he said that he had known he was going to be a writer from the time he was eight. His ambition while attending Boys High School and New York University (where he led a five-piece jazz band as a student) was to be "the Shakespeare of the twentieth century."

Dannay's parents, however, moved upstate to Elmira in 1906, when he was less than one year old, and his boyhood was closer to the Tom Sawyer and Huck Finn models than was Lee's. He roamed through woods and fields, took part in elaborate business adventures with his playmates, and, as the town liquor dealer's son, enjoyed the prestige of being the only boy in the community who was admitted to saloons. In the summers his cousin from Brooklyn would come up to visit, and the boys would compete against each other in games of one-upmanship that would continue in different form over their joint lifetime. All in all, Dannay looks back on his childhood as a precious gift, and on the heartaches of his childhood as a part of that gift.

In 1917 the Nathan family returned to New York City and it was in the winter of that year, while twelve-year-old Danny was in bed suffering from an abscess of the left ear, that an aunt walked into the sickroom and handed him a book she had borrowed from the neighborhood library, thereby giving him his first introduction to the literature of crime. The volume was Conan Doyle's *Adventures of Sherlock Holmes,* and it so fired the boy's imagination that next morning he stole out of the house, wangled a library card, and stripped the shelves of all the Holmes books he could lay his hands on. That was the beginning, and when Dannay retells the story today in reflective twilight, the encounter with the Master still seems almost a religious experience.

Dannay like his cousin attended Boys High, but he did not go on to college. While in school he too developed literary ambitions, although his lay in the direction of poetry. By the late 1920's both cousins were out of school, Dannay working as a copywriter and art director for an advertising agency, Lee writing publicity for the New York office of a movie company. They met almost every day for lunch, and among the subjects they discussed over their meals was the possibility of collaborating on a detective story of their own. (This was the heyday of S. S. Van Dine, whose Philo Vance novels proved that hyperintellectualism and deduction could catapult a mystery onto the best-seller lists.) Among the suggestions they tossed around for their sleuth's name were James Griffen and Wilbur See—hardly inspired inventions. But their plans and dreams remained unfulfilled until the announcement of the $7500 prize contest catalyzed them into serious action.

And so Ellery Queen, author and detective, came into being. The cousins had agreed that their protagonist's name should be slightly unusual, easy to remember and rhythmic in sound, and after several false starts they came up with that superb combination of syllables. Dannay's poetic bent may have contributed to the creation of the magic name, but the exact process by which it was conjured up is now lost in the mists of memory. We do know, however, that Ellery was the name of a boyhood friend of Dannay's; and its derivation, from an Anglo-Saxon word meaning "on the island where the alders grow," struck Dannay in later years as having a poetic quality, as of a place where one might want to go. The choice of Queen for the detective's last name was probably for its sound alone. Dannay and Lee have pointed out in interviews that in their youthful innocence they had had no idea of the word's homosexual connotation.

Of course the most original feature of the name Ellery Queen is that the cousins decided to use it for their own joint pseudonym as well as for their detective. They knew that casual readers of mystery fiction tend to remember the names of fictional sleuths but not of their creators, and reasoned brilliantly that employing the same name in both functions would make it doubly difficult for readers to forget. No mystery writer had thought of such a simple device before, and it must have contributed significantly to the cousins' success. Within the Queen novels, the fictional character Ellery Queen is also a writer of detective stories, and these fictions-within-fictions seem themselves (at least some of the time) to center around the exploits of a certain Ellery Queen. One may suspect that Dannay and Lee had read some Pirandello as well as poetry.

The Roman Hat Mystery was issued by Stokes in 1929. Since the Depression confronted the public at roughly the same time as *Roman Hat*, the cousins prudently decided to keep their jobs awhile longer and to continue writing as a sideline. It was only after the publication and success of two more Queen novels, one each in 1930 and 1931, that they were persuaded by their agent to take the plunge and make it as professionals or bust. (Read any history of the Depression and ask yourself whether you would have had the self-confidence to quit a secure job in 1931.) Needless to add that they made it. Between 1932 and 1935 they published six more Ellery Queen novels, four additional detective novels under the byline of Barnaby Ross, and a book of Ellery Queen short stories, besides editing the short-lived but now legendary *Mystery League* magazine.

By 1932 "Queen" had attained such eminence in

the field that Columbia University School of Journalism
invited "him" to deliver a lecture on mystery writing.
The cousins flipped a coin to see who would do the
honors; Lee lost, and gave the lecture wearing a black
mask. During the following year he had many more
opportunities to wear the mask, sitting at tables in department stores autographing Ellery Queen novels. Later
a lecture bureau sent both cousins on cross-country
speaking engagements, with Dannay posing as Barnaby
Ross and Lee playing Queen, both still masked. Their
"act" on the lecture platform involved challenging each
other's skill as detectives, with one tossing off the clues
in an imaginary murder case and defying the other to
solve it on the spot. These little games brought considerable publicity in their wake, and rumors began to
circulate that Queen was really another pen name of S. S.
Van Dine and Ross was the pseudonym of Alexander
Woollcott. A brief paragraph in *Publishers' Weekly* for
October 10, 1936, finally revealed the true identities
behind both Queen and Ross.

The books Dannay and Lee were turning out during these early years, from *Roman Hat* through *The
Spanish Cape Mystery* (1935), are generally bracketed
together as Queen's First Period. The obvious hallmark
of this period is the recurrence of adjectives of nationality in the titles. Another, more significant but less
obvious, is the overpowering influence of Van Dine,
which began to melt away around 1932 and had almost
totally vanished (as had Van Dine's appeal to readers) by
1935. The Ellery of these first "Problems in Deduction"
is a polysyllabic literatus wreathed in classical allusions
and pince-nez—in short, a close imitation of Philo Vance
or, as Manfred Lee in recent years called him, the biggest
prig that ever came down the pike. For those who don't

like First Period Queen—a group that apparently includes the authors themselves, to judge from interviews near the end of Lee's life—these novels are sterile, lifeless, relentlessly intellectual exercises, technically excellent but unwarmed by any trace of human character nor by any emotion other than the "passions of the mind." For those who love Period One, including myself and most Queenians, these books are splendid *tours de force* of the artificer's art and are nowhere near totally devoid of interest in human character or concern with fundamental issues. I cover the ground in Chapters One through Three and let readers judge for themselves.

It's convenient to date the beginning of Queen's second period from *Halfway House* (1936) since this is the first of Ellery's cases not to contain an adjective of nationality in the title. But the new title format is merely symptomatic of changes in substance. The main influences on Dannay and Lee in this period were the women's slick magazines, to which they began to sell around the middle of the decade, and Hollywood, where they worked as script writers for Columbia, Paramount and M-G-M in the late Thirties.[2] Compared with the early masterworks, the novels of Period Two suffer from intellectual thinness, an overabundance of feminine emotion, and characters cut out of cardboard with the hope that they would be brought to life by movie performers. On the other hand, with the broader perspective that accompanies the passage of time we can see the entire second period as a series of steps in the progressive humanization of Ellery and the Queenian universe and as the necessary preparation for the great synthesis of Period Three. In Chapter Four I cover the second period, which ends with *The Dragon's Teeth* (1939) although the short stories of the period were not collected until the following year.

By the late Thirties Dannay and Lee were putting in twelve hours' work a day in their respective homes and meeting once a week in a bare little office in the Fisk Building near Columbus Circle—an office on whose floor they kept a large brown envelope labeled "Ideas." Despite these long hours, between the end of 1939 and 1942 Queen published no new fiction at all, although beginning in 1940 the Barnaby Ross novels were reissued under the Queen byline. One reason for the three-year silence was a literary accident: the cousins had to abandon a novel-in-progress when they discovered that Agatha Christie in *And Then There Were None*, which was being serialized in a national magazine, had anticipated their plot. Another factor was an automobile accident in 1940 that came close to taking the life of Frederic Dannay. Contributing causes included the time and energy the authors were investing in building up the world's finest private library of short crime fiction, laying the groundwork for *101 Years' Entertainment* and *Ellery Queen's Mystery Magazine,* and in writing a script a week for the Ellery Queen radio show. Queen's radio work will be considered in Chapter Five and his contributions as editor, scholar and anthologist in Chapter Six.

Queen's third period, which many would judge the crown of his career, opens with *Calamity Town* (1942) and embraces twelve novels, two books of short stories and sixteen years. In this period there was nothing Queen would not dare. We find complex deductive puzzles; achingly full-drawn characterizations; the detailed evocation of a small town and of a great city, each of which comes to life on the page; the creation of a private, topsy-turvy, Alice-in-Wonderland otherworld; explorations into the historical, psychiatric and religious dimensions; hymns of hate directed at McCarthyism and other brands of political filth; a gently sketched middle-age love story; a nostalgic re-creation of Ellery's young manhood. We find all this and so much more within a sequence of strict detective stories, whose delights we shall taste in Chapters Seven through Ten.

These Period Three years, 1942-58, saw Dannay and Lee at the peak of their powers and popularity, selling millions of copies a year, praised as highly by critics and their fellow writers as by their immense audience. The very name Ellery Queen, like that of Holmes before him, entered common parlance as virtually a synonym for detective. But spectacular as was the success of their creation, the authors' lives remained, in Anthony Boucher's words, "unspectacular and irrelevant," except in one sense which we shall shortly explore. Manfred Lee settled down in suburban Connecticut, first in Westport, later on a 63-acre estate in Roxbury, where he and his wife, a former actress who often played roles on the Queen radio show, raised a total of eight children. Lee declared his property a game preserve, added to his stamp and record and medal collections, beat a playwright neighbor named Arthur Miller in an election to the Roxbury library board, and served as the small community's Justice of the Peace during 1957-58. Meanwhile Frederic Dannay and his family settled in Larchmont, New York, about 90 minutes from Roxbury and half an hour from New York City. In whatever moments he could spare from his multitudinous Queenly duties he continued to write poetry, none of it published (one editor said it was too highly personal in nature), and to collect stamps and first editions, and all in all to give the appearance of a well-to-do gentleman of high cultivation, living a busy but essentially tranquil existence.

The reality was harsher. Personal tragedy stalked Dannay through the years and caught him more than once, the decisive blow being the birth of his youngest son, Stephen, with incurable brain damage which led to his death at the age of 6. The birth-death motifs in such diverse novels as *Cat of Many Tails, Inspector Queen's Own Case, The Finishing Stroke,* and *A Fine and Private Place* can probably be attributed at least in part to Stephen's short and unhappy life, but none of these novels was the most direct literary outgrowth of the tragedy. Shortly before the child's death Dannay for therapeutic reasons began work on a completely personal book, uncontributed to in any way by Manfred Lee. The novel was called *The Golden Summer* and was published by Little, Brown in 1953 under Dannay's birth-name, Daniel Nathan.

Dannay's therapeutic strategy was to evoke the contentment of his own blissful, vanished childhood—"the lovely past"—as a means of at least partially erasing from his mind the anguish of his middle life. *The Golden Summer* is set in Elmira and tells how ten-year-old Danny spent the summer of 1915. Although Danny is slight, skinny, shy, bespectacled and physically the weakest in his peer-group, he is shrewd and nimble-witted enough to think or talk himself out of any spot, and to manipulate his playmates to his own advantage. Most of the novel consists of a series of unrelated "business adventures" in each of which Danny winds up with a few coins net profit. He displays the ghost of Long John Silver for a two-cent admission fee, raffles off a damaged copy of the brand-new Sherlock Holmes novel *The Valley of Fear,*[3] organizes the Great Lolla paloosa Bi-Plane Company, and even adds a dime to his hoard through a splendiferous one-upmanship contest with his city cousin Telford (a thinly disguised Manfred). Thus *The Golden Summer* turns out to be a book-length *double entendre*: the season of incredible innocence and security and peace, the season the precocious little entrepreneur Danny Nathan made $4.73 from his playmates. And to most of its reviewers this double meaning seemed to be a basic flaw in the novel's purpose and structure—we are supposed to delight in Danny's adventures as in the exploits of Tom Sawyer or Penrod, but these adventures portray him as little more than a money-hungry wheeler-dealer, junior division. Whether the reviewers were right or wrong, *The Golden Summer* was a thumping failure commercially.[4] But even if as an independent work the book suffers from the conflict between nostalgia and brutal honesty, as a product of the same mind that shaped the Queenian universe it is not only not a failure but in many senses the key to the entire structure.   The intellectual games Queen has always played with readers, the recurrent theme of "the lovely past," the origin of the names Ellery and Barnaby and a host of other elements of Queenland are dazzlingly illuminated by *The Golden Summer,* which also contains the only specimens of Dannay's poetry ever published anywhere. Whoever has savored even a few Ellery Queen novels should haunt the second-hand bookstores for a copy of this impossibly rare volume. And now that literary nostalgia has again become a highly marketable commodity, we may perhaps even hope someday for a new and better-selling edition.

After *The Finishing Stroke* (1958) Queen seemed to have closed the circle of his work and hung up the gloves. Dannay spent a semester teaching creative writing at the University of Texas and ended up selling the

University his entire collection of priceless first editions of books of detective short stories. But after five years of silence Queen in 1963 inaugurated a fourth period, which will be examined in Chapters Eleven and Twelve. The hallmarks of Period Four are, on the one hand, an undiminished zest for radical experiment within the strict deductive tradition, and on the other hand, a retreat from attempts at naturalistic plausibility coupled with a reliance on stylization of plot and character and the repetition of dozens of motifs from the earlier periods. The risks of such an approach are obvious and the audience for recent Queen novels seems to have diminished. Only time will tell whether the death of Manfred Lee in April 1971 marks the end of Period Four. But Dannay has announced that he will carry on, and millions of grateful readers hope as I do that he will never retire.

Suppose we cover the remaining items of business through an imaginary interview.

WHAT'S DANNAY LIKE IN PERSON? WHAT WAS LEE LIKE?

The photos in this book describe their physical appearance better than I can. I'd say that Fred Dannay projects something of the popular image of a professor—very precisely spoken, a lover of books and the finer things, a trifle absent-minded over practical matters but gifted with one of the most razor-sharp intellects I've seen in action in my life. Manny Lee was sturdier, more sharp-tongued and robust, though his health had been poor for several years before his death. He seemed to relate more to nature and the things of nature than to books and the things of the mind. I can't conceive of Manny Lee writing poetry, nor of Fred Dannay digging his fingers into freshly turned earth.

WHO CONTRIBUTED WHAT TO A QUEEN NOVEL?

That, friend, is the secret of the ages, and only one or two people know the full story. Dannay and Lee said in several interviews that they tried every conceivable method of collaboration before they hit on one that was exactly right for them. For further details I refer you to Jorge Luis Borges, who said: "If you collaborate, you have to forget you have an identity. If you are to work successfully in collaboration, you shouldn't think whether you said that or whether I said it." And W. H. Auden says something very similar: "If you collaborate with someone at all, you form a third person who is entirely different. Critics like to play the game of what is by me and what is by him with a collaboration and they're wrong 75 per cent of the time."

COME ON, NEVINS, YOU CAN DO BETTER THAN THAT.

Okay. As a general principle the conceptual work on a Queen novel—themes, plotting, basic characters, deductions, clues, etc.—is by and large the creation of Dannay, while the detailed execution, the fleshing out of character and incident and the precise choice of words, was by and large the creation of Lee.

HOW ABOUT *ELLERY QUEEN'S MYSTERY MAGAZINE*?

EQMM has always been the work of Dannay alone, and likewise the Queen anthologies and scholarly works.

WHAT STORIES ARE QUEEN'S BEST?

Everyone has his own favorites. From Period One I'd nominate the four novels of 1932 (The Greek Coffin Mystery, The Egyptian Cross Mystery, The Tragedy of X, The Tragedy of Y); and two short stories, "The Bearded Lady" and "The Glass-Domed Clock"; and that great 1935 novelet "The Lamp of God." From the second period I'd pick "Man Bites Dog" and "Mind Over

Matter," two sports shorts of 1939. From the Forties,
Calamity Town *and* Cat of Many Tails, *plus the short
story "The Dauphin's Doll." From the Fifties,* The Glass
Village, Inspector Queen's Own Case, *and the short-short
"Snowball in July." From the Sixties,* The Player on the
Other Side, *"Abraham Lincoln's Clue," and* Face to
Face.

HOW ABOUT *AND ON THE EIGHTH DAY,* **THE ONE EVERY-
BODY DISLIKED?**
    *That's a special case we'll reach in time. And every-
body didn't dislike it. A friend of mine insists it's the
greatest Queen of all.*

DOES QUEEN AGREE WITH WHAT YOU SAY IN THIS BOOK?
    *Of course not. Queen didn't even agree with him-
self, as anyone knows who has heard of the legendary
arguments between Dannay and Lee. What creator has
ever agreed with his commentators? When you've spent
almost forty-five years building your own universe, you
can't stand apart from it and treat it like an observer.*

**WILL QUEEN EVER WRITE HIS OWN BOOK OF "MEMORIES
AND ADVENTURES," HIS OWN ACCOUNT OF
HIMSELF?**
    God, how I hope so.

CHAPTER ONE

BEFORE WE BEGIN TO DISCUSS THE FIRST QUEEN NOVELS WE must take a brief detour and consider a certain obscure art critic named Willard Huntington Wright.[1] Wright (1888-1939) was an erudite aesthete whose faith in the values of Western civilization was destroyed by the carnage of World War I. He withdrew into a shell of detachment, but the combination of overwork and despair drove him into a nervous breakdown in 1923. Forbidden to read "serious" literature during his two-year convalescence, he amassed and devoured a huge library of mystery fiction, studied the aesthetics of the genre, and amused himself by creating a fictional detective of his own, who would carry erudition and cerebration—and ironic detachment from the obscene mess of man's struggles—to undreamt-of heights. Finally Wright arranged a luncheon date with the legendary Maxwell Perkins, editor at Scribner's, and gave Perkins his lengthy outlines for three novels about the projected sleuth. Perkins agreed to publish the novels, and they proceeded to make history, putting Wright's criminous pseudonym, S. S. Van Dine, on the best-seller lists and turning his hyper-

15

cerebral hawkshaw, Philo Vance, into a household name.

Van Dine's novels—*The Benson Murder Case* (1926), *The "Canary" Murder Case* (1927), *The Greene Murder Case* (1928), *The Bishop Murder Case* (1929) and others —were consumed by the public of the Twenties and early Thirties with incredible gusto; but they are not very highly regarded today. The many technical gaffes in plotting, the wooden characterizations and leaden prose, Vance's infuriating mannerisms and his encyclopedic footnoted disquisitions on intellectual trivia which interrupt the already snail-paced story every few pages— all these flaws make it almost an act of penance to read Van Dine today, even when one realizes the significance of his books as studies in the possibility and varieties of emotional solipsism. The many weaknesses of the Philo Vance novels make it too easy for us to forget that Van Dine almost singlehandedly created the skeletal structure of that most noble specimen of mystery fiction, the formal deductive puzzle, which during the Thirties would be fleshed out and perfected by the giants of the Golden Age, such as Carr, Christie, Gardner, Blake, Innes—and Ellery Queen.

And what, you may ask, is the formal deductive puzzle? In these days when the type is near extinction, few remember what a crackle of intellectual excitement filled the best detective stories of those years. What delectable frustration consumed both reader and detective as both discovered an entanglement wrapped inside every complication and a conundrum within every enigma! And still with unshakable determination the detective would continue to sift through masses of bizarre circumstances and conflicting testimony, knowing full well that much of what he was being told was flat lies and the rest of it even at best "shaped by the teller, reshaped by the listener, concealed from both by the dead man of the tale." How the blood would leap in our veins when the detective, at the most perplexing point in the investigation, would look up, the fever slowly dying in his eyes, and announce: Now I see. Few today have experienced the sense of awe evoked in the reader as the detective unfolded his solution, setting each fact and clue in its logical niche and, inexorably as death, giving a name to the murderer. That, friends, is the formal deductive puzzle. That is the kind of book Van Dine wrote, and influenced Ellery Queen to write even better. In Dannay's words: "He influenced us because he made so much money; and then, the kind of thing he did appealed to us in those days. It was complex, logical, deductive, almost entirely intellectual."

Just as Van Dine's titles followed a strict pattern— *The* Six-Letter-Word *Murder Case*—so did Queen's: *The* Adjective-of-Nationality Noun *Mystery.* Just as Philo Vance's exploits were narrated by a characterless attorney named S. S. Van Dine, so those of Ellery Queen were put before the public by a characterless acquaintance known as J. J. McC. (Queen's stroke of genius was to use the same name for author and detective, a much wiser move than adopting the same name for author and Watson as Van Dine did.) Indeed both the narrator Van Dine and the introducer McC informed their readers in Prefaces that the names Philo Vance and Ellery Queen were merely pseudonyms adopted to protect the identities of the respective sleuths, *both* of whom were alleged to be living in retirement in Italy.[2] Philo and Ellery are both scholarly dilettantes who tend to talk like books as well as about them; both are tall and aristocratically slim, though Vance must be at least ten years older. Vance entered the domain of crime detection through the good offices of his friend John F. X. Markham, District Attorney of New York County, while Ellery's connection is of course his long-suffering father, Inspector Richard Queen, NYPD. The doughty but uninspired Sergeant Heath would inevitably come up with erroneous theories for Vance to demolish, and likewise the bulky and rather blockheaded Sergeant Velie (rhymes with mealy) is always around to register amazement at the deductions of Ellery, whom he calls Maestro. Wherever there is a murder, there must also be an irate Medical Examiner to be pulled out of a warm bed or a hot poker game for the post-mortem—a service performed in Van Dine's books by Dr. Emanuel Doremus, in Queen's by Dr. Samuel Prouty. The personal needs of Vance are seen to by his butler, Currie, and those of the Queens by the impish gypsy boy Djuna (named, Dannay told me, for the novelist Djuna Barnes).

In short, no major mystery writer anywhere was more influenced by S. S. Van Dine than was Queen. But in several significant respects Queen altered the Van Dine structure for the better. First of all, even in his earliest novels Queen proved himself far more skillful at drawing character, writing vividly, and plotting with finesse. Second, Queen dropped the first-person narrative employed by Van Dine and thereby gained the flexibility of being able to write scenes at which no official is present. But most important of all was Queen's innovation of fair play, of providing the reader with all the information needed to solve the case along with or ahead of the detective. Fair play was not a ground rule of the game as Van Dine played it, and in fact most of Vance's solutions depend on intricate, and often debatable, psychological analyses of the suspects. Ellery's solutions on the other hand are based on rigorous logical deductions from empirical evidence, which, unlike the mental data from which Vance proceeded, was as accessible to the reader as to the detective, a point emphasized by Queen's famous "Challenge to the Reader" device.

With this background we can now enter Queenland, Period One, beginning with the novel that won and then lost the $7500 prize, *The Roman Hat Mystery* (1929). It is the evening of Monday, September 24.[3] A romantic gangster melodrama entitled *Gunplay* is playing to a well-filled house at the Roman Theater, on 47th Street west of Broadway. Near the end of the second act a scream tears through the audience and the lights snap on. The occupant of LL32, the leftmost seat in the rear aisle, has been found poisoned in his seat. The police are summoned.

> There was nothing remarkable in either the physique or the manner of Inspector Richard Queen. He was a small, withered, rather mild-appearing old gentleman. He walked with a little stoop and an air of deliberation that somehow accorded perfectly with his thick grey hair and mustaches, veiled grey eyes and slender hands. . . .
>
> Ellery Queen towered six inches above his father's head. There was a square cut to his shoulders and an agreeable swing to his body as he walked. He was dressed in oxford grey and carried a light stick. On his nose perched what seemed an incongruous note in so athletic a man—a rimless pince-nez. But the brow above, the long delicate lines of the face, the bright eyes were those of a man of thought rather than action.

Almost at once the Queens and the rest of Richard's team begin to unearth bizarre facts. The body is identified as that of Monte Field, an unsavory criminal lawyer. The seven seats nearest to the dead man are all strangely vacant, although box-office records show all had been paid for. Field is wearing evening clothes but his top hat is missing. There is a woman's evening bag in his pocket and a half-empty ginger ale bottle under his seat. An usher has been standing at each exit since the beginning of the play and the ticket seller swears no one left by the front door, so the murderer must still be in the theater. Unfortunately the theater seems to be filled with people who might have had reason to want Monte Field dead, including a former underworld client, a former law partner, and a society girl engaged to one of the actors in the play. When the investigators leave the theater and turn to Field's apartment and office, the plot grows murkier still with the addition of an angry mistress, a suspicious valet, a set of books on handwriting analysis, intimations of mass blackmail, several more missing toppers, and a succession of lies in which various suspects are caught. The solution, when it comes, is distinctively Queenian: fair to the reader, utterly surprising, and so complex as to consume roughly 9% of the book's wordage. The debut of Ellery Queen, author and detective, is a wondrous specimen of sustained technique, as readable today as it was almost forty-five years ago.

When you are trying to write a book that is "almost entirely intellectual," what do you do when you are confronted with an existential issue? Consider the following words of Inspector Queen to District Attorney Sampson and his assistant, Cronin. The individual concerned,

". . . to make it short and ugly, has a strain of negroid blood in his veins. He was born in the South of a poor family and there was definite documentary evidence . . . to prove that his blood had the black taint. . . . I needn't explain what it would have meant to (him) to have the story of his mixed blood become known to his (Social Register in-laws-to-be) . . ."

"Black blood, eh?" murmured Cronin. "Poor devil."

"You would scarcely guess it from his appearance," remarked Sampson. "He looks as white as you or I."

"(He) isn't anywhere near a full-blooded Negro," protested the Inspector. "He has just a drop in his veins—just a drop, but it would have been more than enough (to ruin his forthcoming marriage)."

This passage is representative of the young Queen's perspective: detached, intellectualized, unprejudiced but not outraged or even upset by the racism of the society, stoically accepting as unalterable (in Richard's words to Ellery) that "there's little justice and certainly no mercy in this world." As we shall see when we reach the novels of the Forties and Fifties, the outlook of the mature Queen is considerably more attractive.

Queen's second novel, *The French Powder Mystery* (1930), is technically even more dazzling than *Roman Hat.* We open on the morning of Tuesday, May 24, with a high-level police conference at the Queens' apartment, on the top floor of a three-family brownstone house on West 87th Street, "a man's domicile from the piperack over the hearth to the shining sabers on the wall." Subject of the conference is what strategy to adopt against a certain large drug ring. But soon after the meeting adjourns, the Queens are diverted from narcotics (or so at first it seems) and confronted with murder. The body of Winifred Marchbanks French has tumbled out of a concealed wall bed in the display window of the fabulous French's Department Store, seriously disconcerting both the model demonstrating the furniture inside the window and the crowd watching from outside. Thus Ellery and Richard Queen are propelled into the intrigues within tycoon Cyrus French's family—his wife, his daughter, his mysteriously absent stepdaughter, the wife's first husband and her brother—and into the rather different intrigues within the old man's business family (the store's board of directors, the security staff, and others). One of this book's most rewarding aspects is its evocation of such a family and such a store, which is virtually a character in its own right; and the integration of the store and its functions into the plot is even more satisfying.

But if French's Department Store is huge, the physical clues to the murder in its show window are minute. There is a lipstick in the dead woman's purse that does not match the color of her lips. A piece of green felt protecting the underside of an onyx bookend is not the same shade as that on the matching bookend. A hat and a pair of shoes are not quite where they should be, and a few grains of powder are where they should not be. Out of such minutiae Ellery forges a chain of iron logic in a climactic scene which Anthony Boucher has praised as "probably the most admirably constructed denouement in the history of the detective story." Queen keeps the name of the murderer concealed throughout thirty-five closely printed pages of explanation, right up to the very last two words of the novel—a feat that has almost never been equalled in the genre.

In his third book, *The Dutch Shoe Mystery* (1931), the milieu is again as vivid a character as the human beings, the setting this time being that most fitting stage for murder, a hospital. On a raw Monday morning in January, Ellery drops into the Dutch Memorial Hospital in the East Sixties to obtain some information from a medical friend. Dr. Minchen tells Ellery that emergency surgery is about to be performed on Abigail Doorn, the hospital's multimillioned foundress and principal support, and invites Ellery to observe the operation from the upstairs gallery. As the Doorn family and retainers converge on the hospital to await the outcome, a mysterious visitor insists on seeing the operating surgeon, Dr. Janney, even though surgery is about to begin. When Janney returns to the operating theater and Mrs. Doorn's stretcher is wheeled in from the anteroom, the patient is dead, but not from organic causes. She has been strangled with picture wire while lying on her stretcher in the anteroom. And the testimony of several witnesses seems to establish that only Janney, who was well remembered in Mrs. Doorn's will, could have committed the crime. Janney swears that he was with his mysterious visitor at the time of the murder, charges that someone entered the anteroom disguised as him and strangled the old lady, but refuses to say who his elusive visitor was.

These are only a few of the dilemmas plaguing Ellery and Richard Queen in the Doorn case. Is it coincidence that a loanshark with strong reason to want Mrs. Doorn dead was having his appendix removed in the Dutch Memorial Hospital at the time of the murder? Is it relevant that several doctors and several members of the Doorn family have motives of hatred or gain, and no alibis? What is the secret connection between the hospital diagnostician and Mrs. Doorn's fanatically religious companion? What was in the papers the family lawyer destroyed shortly after the murder? And could Janney have impersonated himself?

After a second strangulation in the hospital, Ellery presents his solution, based on a pair of starched white trousers and a pair of white canvas shoes. It's a stunning and beautifully fair solution, and accounts brilliantly for all but one little fact.[4] Thus for the third year in a row Queen both fulfilled and helped to promote the highest standards of criminous professionalism. It must be confessed, however, that the highest bibliophilic standards were not well served by the fourteen-page "Interlude" chapter, which Queen had printed on pages with extra-wide margins "for the use of the reader in jotting down his personal notes about the solution." The reverent book-lover that Queen was soon to become would have eaten the pages rather than have them published in such form!

CHAPTER TWO

HAVING PUBLISHED THREE SUPERB NOVELS DEALING WITH Ellery and Richard Queen, Dannay and Lee in 1932 proceeded to adopt a second pseudonym, Barnaby Ross,[1] and to create a second world, which existed for the length of four novels and then was terminated irrevocably. But even though the last novel of the quartet was published in 1933, the series has never been forgotten. At least two of the four are among the best of Queen's books ever—which automatically ranks them among the supreme specimens of the American detective novel.

At the center of the quartet, aged but erect, stands Mr. Drury Lane, the world-renowned Shakespearean actor who was driven from the stage by total deafness and was inspired by his love for Shakespeare to create his own Elizabethan village community on his estate above the Hudson. The village is dominated by Lane's private castle, The Hamlet, and is populated by down-and-out theatrical folk who live on Lane's bounty, wearing period costumes and sporting Shakespearean names. But, unsatisfied with having recreated Shakespeare's physical

world, and incapable of creating dramatic worlds like
the master, Lane turns to intervening in (and thereby in
a sense rewriting) the dramas of real life. "From obey-
ing the jerk of the master's strings, I now have the
impulse to pull the strings myself, in a greater author-
ship than created drama." Thus the leitmotif of Lane's
existence is power—to stir audiences with his perform-
ances, to control his villagers' lives down to their very
names, to change the outcome of life-and-death dramas
by his presence. In short, he wants to be more powerful
in his own way than William Shakespeare.

The Tragedy of X (1932) opens with a biographical
sketch of Lane and a letter which he sends to the New
York City police, offering the solution to an unsolved
murder case. (These introductory elements are unac-
countably omitted from the 1961 reissue of Lane's first
three cases under the Queen byline, The XYZ Murders.)
The solution having proven correct, Inspector Thumm
and District Attorney Bruno pay a visit to The Hamlet
to meet Lane, thank him, and solicit his help on an even
more bewildering crime problem.

It had begun four days earlier, when an aging,
lecherous and sadistic stockbroker named Harley Longstreet threw a cocktail party to celebrate his engagement
and to make his guests squirm. Among the invitees are
his browbeaten partner, his ex-mistress, a man who is in
love with a woman he wants to make his mistress, a
former lover of his present fiancee, and a market-playing
politician who blames the brokers for his ruinous losses.
After cocktails Longstreet insists that everyone accom-
pany him to a dinner party in New Jersey. But as the
group reaches the street a sudden thunderstorm erupts,
making it impossible to get a taxi for the ride to the
ferry, and so the party clambers onto the crosstown trol-

ley. The packed streetcar is lurching west towards the
ferry slip when Longstreet reaches into his pocket and
suddenly collapses dead in the aisle, his hand pricked
and bleeding in a dozen places. Called to the scene,
Inspector Thumm searches the dead man's pockets and
finds a ball of cork riddled with dozens of needles, each
one coated at both ends with pure nicotine poison. But
there are too many suspects with motive and opportunity, and Thumm's investigation gets nowhere. When he
and Bruno have recounted these facts to Drury Lane,
the actor announces that he believes he knows the murderer; but for his own reasons, based partly on his
analysis of the facts and at least in equal part on his
desire to exercise power in the case, he refuses to say
more. The next evening there is a second murder, the
victim being thrown from the upper deck of a ferry and
crushed to pulp as the boat pulls into the Weehawken
slip. Later we witness a spectacular murder trial, an un-
cannily disturbing conversation aboard a New Jersey
local train, a third murder carried out within a few feet
of Lane himself, and finally, during another train ride,
the unmasking of the murderer.

   The Tragedy of X must be ranked among the
supreme masterpieces of the Golden Age of detective
fiction, a book of staggering complexity, stunning inge-
nuity and dazzling fairness to the reader. Queen used
this novel to introduce two motifs that were to become
hallmarks. First is a distinctive murderer-victim relationship whose exact nature I can't specify lest I spoil several
early Queen novels for those who haven't yet read them;
the *locus classicus* of this motif being Conan Doyle's
The Valley of Fear, I will refer to it as the Birlstone
Gambit. As we shall see, Queen employed the motif
over and over during the early Thirties, then dropped it

at the end of Period One. The second motif introduced in *X* was left virtually untouched for almost two decades but became literally synonymous with the Queen canon during the Fifties and Sixties: I mean, of course, the classic Queenian device of the Dying Message. Riding in the Weehawken local during the small hours of the morning, Drury Lane and several others, one of whom will be dead within minutes, discuss the last moments of life in a conversation which is as central to Queen's work as is the famous locked-room lecture in *The Three Coffins* to the understanding of John Dickson Carr. (The Vienna dying-message story which Lane tells his companions was reworked by Queen twenty-odd years later into the short-short "A Lump of Sugar.") The discussion culminates in Lane's words: "There are no limits to which the human mind cannot soar in that unique, godlike instant before the end of life." That statement suggests that beneath the criminous surface of *X* Queen is seriously concerned with power and the love of power, and indeed these themes recur in the book in several forms, such as the murderer's silent intimate relationships with his victims over the years in which he is shaping their destruction, Longstreet's sadistic lust for power over the men and women in his milieu, the motives behind Lane's own investigations, and the god-like power of the dying. And if we prescind from serious literary intent and simply look at the large number of sharply etched characterizations, and the vivid evocations of time and place (and especially of the transportation network made up of the streetcar, the ferry and the short-line passenger train, all three near extinction today), and the integration of the milieu into the plot and of each of the plot's myriad details into a rationally harmonious mosaic, we will find so many more reasons why *The*

Tragedy of X must appear in any listing, however short, of the supreme achievements of crime fiction, and why it will be read with awe long after our grandchildren are dust.

The *Tragedy of Y* (1932) is no less dazzling than *X* in perfection of structure and technique and in its blending of serious intent with the deductive puzzle. In it Queen created a milieu fully worthy of the doom-haunted Eugene O'Neill to whom he had referred in the very first paragraph of *Roman Hat*. Emily Hatter, the ruthless old millionairess of Washington Square, is rumored to have something evil in her blood which has cursed her entire family. Her first husband died mysteriously long ago. Her daughter by that first marriage, Louisa Campion, was born blind and mute and became totally deaf the day she turned eighteen, "as a sort of birthday gift from the dark gods who seemed to rule her destiny." Throughout thirty-seven years of marriage to the unworldly chemist York Hatter she has made her second husband's life one long hell. One child of Emily's second marriage is a hopeless alcoholic, another is a vicious and frigid playgirl. Her grandchildren, the sons of the alcoholic, aged 13 and 4, are wilful sadists. "Mad as a Hatter" is not a humorous expression in this milieu.

The book opens with a fishing trawler off the Atlantic coast discovering a shapeless body identified as York Hatter, who had vanished several weeks before. A suicide note is found, but the autopsy proves that the cause of death was poison. Emily identifies the body without hesitation and without a tear. On a Sunday afternoon two months later, the nightmare begins. Someone adds strychnine to Louisa Campion's egg nog, which is snatched and gobbled up by the 14-year-old grandson who at once falls to the floor, screaming. Inspector Thumm solicits the advice of Drury Lane, who warns him that the poisoner will probably try to strike at Louisa again. Two more months pass, then Lane is summoned to Washington Square; someone has used York Hatter's mandolin to bludgeon old Emily to death in her bed. Even though Louisa Campion, who slept in the same room with her mother, witnessed the crime and even touched the murderer's face, the detectives make no progress. But such clues as a box of spilled talcum powder and some tiptoeing footprints put Lane on the trail, which he refuses to share with Thumm. Slowly we experience a sense of the imbecility of these crimes which matches our growing understanding of the filth and perversion eating away at the Hatters. For this doomed family is not merely a group of figures in a detective novel but a paradigm of American society, its members rotting with greed and sadism and inertia, consenting for the sake of expected legacies to be dehumanized in love-hate relationships with each other and with the bitch goddess of wealth and property who rules the roost. But the sickness in the Hatters is not curable by surgery or social revolution; it is not some naturalistic venereal disease but a disease of human nature and the human condition, the gift of a dark god. "Good God," Bruno gasps when he learns the identity of the murderer. "Not a very good God," Lane replies. "Not to that poor . . . creature."

The Tragedy of Y is, like its predecessor, one of the most stunning detective novels ever written, and also like *X* it introduces two motifs that have come to be distinctively identified with Queen. One is distrust and despair of human nature, which will reappear throughout the Canon but with especial force during the McCarthy-haunted Fifties in such books as *The Origin of*

Evil and *The Glass Village.* The other is the motif of manipulation.   In this case the manipulation is un-intended and the manipulator is dead before the story begins, but the principle is the same one that will inform such later Queen novels as *Ten Days' Wonder* and *The Player on the Other Side* (which is an almost conscious reworking of certain elements from *Y*). And over and above the brilliance of *Y* as a detective novel stands the power of its black vision, which is as haunting in its own way as the nightmare stories of Cornell Woolrich. Al-though rooted in a genre that has traditionally been oriented to reason, order and optimism, *Y* evokes depths of tragic despair that are virtually without parallel in the history of crime fiction.

In the third Drury Lane novel, *The Tragedy of Z* (1933), the impersonal and somber narrative of the earlier cases is replaced by the more sprightly first-person storytelling of a newcomer. Miss Patience Thumm, the Inspector's lovely and brainy daughter, who had spent her childhood and adolescence in Europe, returns to New York ten years after the *X* and *Y* cases and rejoins her father, now retired from the force and running his own detective agency.[2] Patience is no slouch as a sleuth herself, as she demonstrates when she is taken to meet Drury Lane and former District Attorney Bruno, now the Governor of New York. From The Hamlet the Thumms proceed to upstate New York's Tilden County, the Inspector having been retained by the part-owner of a local marble quarry to find out why the firm has been awarded so many state building contracts. The investiga-tion is soon interrupted by the fatal stabbing of a state senator in his study and such clues as a piece of a carved toy chest, a footprint trodden in ashes, a jagged scratch on a forearm, and a blackmail demand from a recently released ex-convict. It is this convict, a one-eyed and one-armed derelict named Aaron Dow, whom the police seize upon as the obvious murderer. Although Patience insists that proper interpretation of the evidence proves Dow's innocence, the local prosecutor, who stands to gain considerable political advancement by the senator's death, proceeds to put the wretch on trial for murder. Patience enlists the aid of Drury Lane in saving Dow's life, but the race against time is complicated by a prison break, a second murder (whose victim also received a section of a carved toy chest before being stabbed to death), and a chain of events originating in Viet Nam at the turn of the century. The novel climaxes in one of the most chilling denouements in the history of the genre, as Lane reconstructs the case and unmasks the killer in the execution chamber of the prison only seconds before the electrocution of Aaron Dow is to take place.

Z is by no means one of Queen's greatest achievements, being far less dazzling and full-bodied than the masterworks. Except for one brief scene, Lane is kept offstage until almost halfway through the book, and the presence and first-person narration of Patience Thumm are woefully inadequate substitutes. Compared with the great novels of 1932, Z's plot is both simplistic and flawed; it presupposes, for example, that a dedicated and incorruptible warden discovers a message smuggling system within his prison and does absolutely nothing about it, for no other reason than that the plot requires the system to be still operational later in the book. But the faults are more than compensated for by the bone-chilling bizarrerie of the two sequences in the death house (which are both suspenseful and effective as outcries against capital punishment), and by the unobtrusively brilliant planting throughout the book of clues to be collated by Lane at the denouement. Though not one of Queen's most distinguished novels, *Z* is a highly intriguing work that repays more than one reading.

Which is more than can be said for the last of the Barnaby Ross tetralogy. *Drury Lane's Last Case* (1933) has some excellent ideas but is marred by haste, disorganization, coincidence, artificiality, incredible motivation, and a staggering number of holes in the plot. The book is set in the near future and opens when a mysterious man sporting a blue and green beard pays Inspector Thumm one thousand dollars for holding a manila envelope in which the client claims is a clue to a secret worth millions. Three weeks later Thumm becomes entangled in the case of a guard who vanished from the Britannic Museum while a sightseeing-busload of Indiana schoolteachers were being given a guided tour by the curator. It soon turns out that there were two extra men in the sightseeing group, one of whom returned from the museum and one of whom didn't. Evidence also indicates that one of the two extras broke into one of the museum's glass cases, removed a valuable Shakespeare folio, replaced it with another that is absolutely priceless, and next day returned the stolen edition to the museum. By this time Drury Lane, a financial patron of the Britannic, is in the case alongside Thumm, Patience, and a young Shakespeare scholar who has fallen in love with Patience at first sight. Eventually they discover that the man with the dappled beard and his envelope are also involved in the Britannic mystery. Although murder doesn't rear its head until the final quarter of the book, there is so much intellectual puzzlement throughout that no one cares.

Unfortunately not all the puzzlement is dissipated

at the end. We never learn, for example, how the museum thief found out about the unscheduled bus trip to the Britannic, nor how the planter of the time bomb got into Dr. Ales' house undetected, nor how dozens of other plot elements came into being. Those explanations that are provided are all too often absurd, such as the far-out motives behind the antics of the bibliomaniac Sedlar brothers. Equally damaging is Queen's disastrous decision to put almost the entire deductive burden on Patience Thumm, who sometimes gives one the unpleasant impression that "she" is Ellery Queen in drag.[3] Finally, the climax of the novel depends on a staggeringly silly Shakespearean fantasy and on a murderer whose identity is a stunt rather than a logical outgrowth of the plot.[4] This is the single early Queen novel which one might wish had remained unwritten, and it is a shame that the two finest sequences in the book (the deductions from the Saxon Library notepaper and the matter of the ax wielder and the alarm clock) were not instead used as springboards for Ellery Queen short stories.

We've spent long enough with one of Queen's awesomely rare weak books. Let us return to Ellery and his father and the beginning of 1932.

CHAPTER THREE

THE GREEK COFFIN MYSTERY *(1932) BEGINS WITH THE DEATH* of an old man. Georg Khalkis, the prominent blind art dealer and connoisseur, dies of heart failure in the library of his West 54th Street brownstone. Three days later the coffin is borne to the church graveyard next door and lowered into the family crypt. When the burial party returns to the house, the attorney for the estate discovers that the steel box which contained Khalkis' will is missing from the wall safe. The police are called in, but after two days the box is still missing. Among those present at a police conference called to discuss the case are Inspector Richard Queen and a rather young and self-confident Ellery, who has just begun to apply his talents to crime problems. Ellery deduces that the box must be in the coffin of Georg Khalkis, an exhumation order is obtained, and the coffin is opened. Inside is not the will but the putrefying corpse of a second man, strangled, lying on top of Khalkis' body.

Inspector Queen and his staff soon unearth a bewildering array of counterplots inside the Khalkis household and an assortment of intrigues outside the old brownstone as well, many of them originating out of the theft of a Leonardo from a British museum. About one-third of the way through the novel, Ellery offers a solution, a devilishly ingenious one based on the amount of tea water in a percolator and the color of a dead man's tie. But the case is nowhere near being solved, and Ellery soon becomes aware that the "player on the other side" in this game is his equal and perhaps even his master. Ellery's analysis is merely the first of four solutions to the Khalkis case, each one radiating outward from its predecessors and accounting for more of the total picture. The fourth and final explanation alone embraces the entire brain-numbing network of plot and counterplot, and reveals, with complete fairness to the fully alert reader, a murderer whose identity is one of the most stunning surprises in the genre.

During Solution Four Ellery characterizes the murderer's plot (and by implication the overall structure of this book) as "a complex plan which requires assiduous concentration for complete comprehension." In less Elleryesque terminology, *Greek Coffin* may blow your mind, especially if you're unfamiliar with the complexities of the formal deductive puzzle. Although it's not perfectly flawless in all its thousands of details, the flaws are virtually imperceptible without several careful readings.[1] In short, *The Greek Coffin Mystery* is probably the most involuted, brain-crushing, miraculously well constructed detective novel published in the United States during the Golden Age.

Ellery's second adventure of the year, besides being a brilliant puzzle, reveals further evidence of Queen's concern with larger meanings. *The Egyptian Cross Mystery* (1932) opens on a chill Tuesday between Christmas and New Year's, as Ellery and his father arrive at a muddy West Virginia crossroads where the branch road leading to the village of Arroyo forms a T with the main highway. At the junction is another T, a signpost with a crossbar. A few hundred feet away is a third T, smeared in blood on the front door of Andrew Van, the hermit-like schoolteacher of Arroyo. And on Christmas morning a fourth T had been found, a beheaded and crucified body nailed to the signpost and identified as the atheistic schoolmaster; a T that had once been a man. It is this crime that has brought the Queens to Arroyo. At the inquest there is evidence that a limping foreigner was searching for Van's house on Christmas Eve, and that a local medicine man calling himself Ra-Harakht the Sun God had employed a limping foreigner named Velja Krosac until the man vanished on Christmas Eve. The case dies, six months pass, then Ellery reads that the maker of T's has returned. The body of Thomas Brad, wealthy rug merchant and checkers enthusiast, has been found beheaded and lashed to a totem post on his own Nassau County estate. And only a few miles away is an island nudist colony run by a man calling himself Harakht. But there are also many suspects in Brad's own house and neighborhood, including his wayward wife, his lovelorn daughter, his ex-convict chauffeur, his ambitious business manager, and his often absent partner. The only clues are a red checker, a pipe filled with the wrong tobacco, a misplaced rug, the remnants of a checker game and the remnants of a Montenegro blood feud. And more beheadings are to come before Ellery's deductions unmask the sequential crucifier.

There is more abundant carnage in *Egyptian Cross* than in any other deductive novel by Queen or anyone else, but the bloodbath, far from being gratuitous, serves two purposes. Within the deductive framework, the profusion of headless and crucified bodies is a precondition to the ingenious variations of the Birlstone Gambit on which the solution rests. Looking outward to the experiment with larger meanings, the physical horror of the murders is necessary to Queen's analogies between the Tvar-Krosac vendetta and its equivalent in macrocosm, war. If we look at the parallels Queen draws between the fugitive Tvars and nation-states (each brother's alias, for example, is the name of a city in a distant country), and at the fratricidal elements of the plot, and at the staggeringly vague and inadequate motives for the carnage, we will appreciate that buried within *Egyptian Cross* are the aborted remains of what might have become a powerful anti-war novel.

Technically the book is less than perfect, with much of the counterplotting in the middle chapters only distantly related to the story as a whole—a defect I call the Hollow Center. There are also a few unplugged holes at the end; for instance, it seems impossible that the hapless Kling did not starve when his captor wasn't with him, and that there were no signs of captivity on Kling's body. But with an exceptionally large and well-handled cast and a richly involuted plot and the vivid evocation of several socially, economically and geographically disparate milieus, *Egyptian Cross* must be ranked one of the better Queen novels of Period One.

Although Ellery's next case may seem a tame and lightweight exercise when compared with its two predecessors, *The American Gun Mystery* (1933) is even today as readable and re-readable as any other Queen novel. The setting is a gigantic rodeo, "ripped up from its alkaline soil and transplanted bodily—horses, lariats, steers, cowboys and all—to the stony soil of the East" or, more precisely, to the Colosseum, New York's newest

and largest sports arena. The star attraction of Wild Bill
Grant's rodeo during its New York engagement is Buck
Horne, the legendary Westerner, star of countless silent
cowboy films until age and the talkies laid him low.[2]
That his old friend Grant is staking Horne to a comeback
is due not only to friendship and hope of profit but
also to the likelihood that his son Curly Grant will soon
be married to Horne's adopted daughter Kit.   Among
the twenty thousand spectators at the rodeo's opening
night are Ellery and Richard Queen.   In the first event
Horne is supposed to lead forty riders in a hell-for-
leather chase around the arena.   But when the riders
draw their pistols and shoot as one man into the air, the
aged horseman thirty feet ahead of them suddenly falls
to the tanbark and is crushed under the hoofs of forty-
one horses.   Ellery and the Inspector leap into the arena,
open their investigation at once, and quickly establish
that the victim was shot with a .25 automatic.   But after
a bone-numbing search of the Colosseum and every person in it, the weapon remains invisible.   Frustrations and
false leads breed like rabbits as Ellery and Richard pursue
separate lines of inquiry, and it is only after a second
murder at the rodeo, under almost identical circumstances including the vanished .25, that the truth is revealed.

The solution of *American Gun* is eminently fair to
the reader, but once again depends on the Birlstone
Gambit.   Furthermore the killer's motive is a woefully
weak one, and Ellery never explains how he managed to
get his first victim into the position required for his
plan.   The novel also suffers from a Hollow Center, with
the boxing counterplot that fills out the middle chapters
unrelated to the basic storyline.   And last but not least,
Queen's unfamiliarity with film history and technique

leads to the incorporation of several sizable cinematic gaffes into the plot structure.[3]   But despite its flaws *American Gun* is still a richly rewarding detective novel; if it does not strike one as an untouchable masterpiece, this is largely because Queen's own best work has helped raise the standards so high.

In *The Siamese Twin Mystery* (1933) Queen again attempted to infuse a philosophic dimension into the formal deductive puzzle, with notable success on both levels. Ellery and his father, returning from a Canadian vacation, are trapped by a forest fire on the side of Arrow Mountain. Their only hope of survival is to drive up to the mountain top. Long after nightfall they discover a house on the peak of the forsaken mountain. That the mountain's entire base is now ablaze makes the Queens grateful for the hospitality of Dr. John Xavier, the eminent retired surgeon, and his strange family; but it soon becomes evident that something is wrong. Who is the vicious fat man wandering around the mountain? Why were several rings stolen from the household in the past week? Who is the extra woman hiding in an upstairs bedroom? And who or what is the crablike creature that scuttles through the corridors at night? The next morning Dr. Xavier is found shot to death in his study, a game of solitaire laid out in front of him, a torn half of the six of spades clenched between his fingers. It's up to the Queens alone to solve the crime, for the fire has by now sealed off the mountaintop. Despite the steadily nearing flames a second murder soon follows, this time with half a jack of diamonds in the victim's hand.

The climax comes when the fire reaches the house and all the members of the Xavier menage take their last refuge in the cellar and wait for the flames to eat them.

Previously Ellery had determined to preserve some remnants of civilized tradition at the brink of chaos; he had told the male and female firefighters "Get as much of your clothing off *as you decently can*" (emphasis mine) and he had harangued the abject Smith with the words: "You're the type, old friend, who loses his head at the last moment and goes about bashing his brains out against the nearest wall. I'll thank you to remember that you've a certain amount of sheer pride to live up to." Now, in the basement, Ellery undertakes to keep his companions' minds from the terrible death that is minutes away by deducing the identity of the double murderer among them—a completely pointless exercise whose only purpose is to "lighten the last hour with a game of wits." He is fully aware of the inanity of what he's doing, and wishes "with fierce yearning that at this moment, when their attention was wholly caught, when for the fluttering instant they turned their faces away from death, that death would come crashing and smoking upon them through a collapsed ceiling, so that their lives might be snuffed out with no warning and no pain." Yet he will not betray his ideal of human excellence as long as a thread of life is in him; like a French aristocrat, he will face Madame Guillotine calmly. Queen balances perfectly the nobility and the lunacy in this confrontation of Enlightened Man and death.

The Siamese Twin Mystery is not as richly plotted as the earlier Queen novels; were it not for the fire sequences the book would be no more than a novelet. But Queen does not pad. The detection and the fiery background are necessary to each other and to Queen's theme of the power and emptiness of reason in the face of death. Purely on the puzzle level, Queen supplies some truly dazzling variants on the false confession gambit, and sets out (for the first time in a novel about Ellery and his father) a series of magnificently involuted Dying Message devices. *Siamese Twin* is by far Queen's best book of 1933 and one of the best of all his Period One works.

His single novel of the following year was a considerable letdown by comparison. *The Chinese Orange Mystery* (1934), like a Chinese dinner, is exotic in the eating but leaves one empty and unsatisfied soon after the meal is over. Most of it takes place on the twenty-second floor of Manhattan's Hotel Chancellor, which houses both the office of Donald Kirk—wealthy young publisher, socialite, jewel and stamp collector—and the apartment where Kirk resides with his sister, his wheel-chair-bound father, and the fiery old philologist's private nurse. At 5:44 p.m. of a brisk fall day, a stout middle-aged man of excruciatingly ordinary appearance steps out of the elevator and asks Mrs. Shane, the floor clerk, to direct him to Kirk's office. Asking to see Kirk on confidential business, the man is informed by Osborne, Kirk's secretary, that Mr. Kirk is out. Osborne ushers the stranger into a luxurious waiting room where the stranger sits down, alone. During the next hour several of Kirk's acquaintances drop into the office looking for him, including his future brother-in-law, a female novelist and an international adventuress, but Mr. Kirk is still out. When he arrives, at 6:45, he is accompanied by Ellery Queen. As they enter the waiting room they find it has been transformed into an almost comic horror. The rug has been turned upside down, the pictures and the clock are facing the walls, the floor lamps stand on their shades. Every movable article in the room is inside-out or backside-front. And lying on the overturned rug, his brains splattered from a blow with the fireplace poker, is Mr. Nobody from Nowhere, the nameless visitor on nameless business. His every article of clothing is on him backwards: collar, shirt, coat, trousers, shoes. No necktie is on the body or in the room, but the peelings of a tangerine are found in a fruit bowl. Two ornamental African spears have been thrust up the dead man's trouser legs, out at the waist and under his reversed suit jacket, with the blades sticking out of his lapels like horns growing on the back of his neck.

If the entire story of the man who was backwards even approached the craftsmanship and bizarrerie of the early chapters, this would be one of the greatest detective novels of the century. Unfortunately most of the remainder consists of a series of excursions into philately, sex, Chinese culture, blackmail and missing Hebrew biblical commentaries, none of which has any relevance to the murder case except that by amazing coincidence each involves some element that is, in one or another of the many senses of the word, backward. Despite the Challenge to the Reader, the solution can't be called completely fair, since it hinges on physical manipulations so outlandish that not one reader in ten thousand could even conceive of them. Even more damaging is that the manipulations must have left physical traces that the simplest laboratory examination of the two spears under magnification would have disclosed, although for obvious reasons the police technicians never bother to make such an examination. Finally, Queen never explains why the murder victim had told his associates so much about his own plans when nobody in the victim's circumstances would have confided in anyone. It must be regretfully concluded that *The Chinese Orange Mystery* is one of the weakest novels of Queen's first period.

Queen's next book was not a novel but a collection

of short stories, *The Adventures of Ellery Queen* (1934). At the instigation of his agent he had branched out into the short form late in 1932, hoping to break into the high-priced slick-paper magazines at once. But Ellery's first short adventure wound up printed in a short-lived pulp (alongside stories by Dorothy Sayers, Earl Derr Biggers and Sax Rohmer) and paying a mere $35 which had to be shared by Dannay, Lee and the agent. Yet even though the eleven tales collected in the *Adventures* paid Queen far less than his stories of later periods, as a whole they make up what may well be the best of his many volumes of short fiction. The quality of the *Adventures* ranges from the superb to the substandard, but even the least distinguished items are enviably meaty, and all of them demand more than one reading. "The Adventure of the African Traveler" (no prior magazine publication) rests on an intriguing premise which Queen regrettably used only once: Ellery as Professor of Applied Criminology, taking his students to the scene of a murder his father is investigating, and later arguing alternative solutions with the class. The hotel-room bludgeoning of a lecherous salesman turns up a neat variant on the cliché of the watch that stopped at the victim's death, but there are far too many coincidences and implausibilities (the two torn-out photographs, the victim wearing the maid's watch, the maid's unexplained preference for a man's timepiece), and the case is far below Queen's capabilities.

In "The Adventure of the Hanging Acrobat" (*Mystery*, May 1934, as "The Girl on the Trapeze"), Ellery and the Inspector probe the backstage murder of a promiscuous trapeze star, and learn much about the sociology of vaudevillians and the art of knot-making before Ellery deduces which of the victim's amorous coworkers put the rope around her neck. The unique vaudeville milieu and the tightly constructed puzzle merge into an excellent story. Ellery's closing statement, "I'm not really interested in the moral aspects of crime," will be retracted in principle with *The Spanish Cape Mystery* and in practice with *Calamity Town* and its successors.

Queen's ill-paying first short story, "The Adventure of the One-Penny Black" (*Great Detective*, April 1933), offers a neat blend of the classic Six Napoleons and Purloined Letter situations. A stamp initialed by Queen Victoria and worth $30,000 is stolen from a dealer; the thief is chased into a bookstore but escapes; during the next few days everyone who purchases from the store a copy of a certain best-seller is visited by a thief who steals nothing but that book. Ellery employs a battery of psychological deductions to wrap up the case in this auspicious debut.

"The Adventure of the Bearded Lady" (*Mystery*, August 1934, as "The Sinister Beard") is the earliest and one of the best of Queen's many Dying Message short stories. The murderee is a doctor and amateur painter, embroiled in an intra-familial war over legacies, whose last act before being stabbed to death in his studio was to paint a beard on a portrait of Rembrandt's wife. The gruesome family of suspects bears a distinct resemblance to the mad Hatters in *The Tragedy of Y* but the solution and Ellery's reasoning are brilliantly original, capping one of the finest short works in the entire Queen canon.

In "The Adventure of the Three Lame Men" (*Mystery*, April 1934) Ellery and the Inspector are confronted with some bizarre evidence indicating that a trio of cripples kidnapped a prosperous banker from his love nest and left his mistress to suffocate to death on her gag. Ellery's more rational interpretation of the evidence vindicates the prime suspect and deftly exposes a surprising murderer. At the conclusion Richard comments: "I feel sorry for (the killer's wife)." Ellery replies: "You always were a sentimentalist."

"The Adventure of the Invisible Lover" (*Mystery*, September 1934, as "Four Men Loved a Woman") brings Ellery to somnolent Corsica, a New York hamlet of 745 souls, to solve the murder of the artist who was staying in the local boardinghouse and romancing his landlord's lovely daughter. An attorney engaged to the girl had made threats, the fatal bullet came from the fiancee's gun, and the lawyer admits that no one could have taken the weapon from him during the crucial period. Ellery rearranges the boardinghouse furniture and unearths a meticulously wrought frame-up, the frustration of which somehow convinces him (though it would not impress a trained philosopher or theologian) that there is a God.

"The Adventure of the Teakwood Case" (*Mystery*, May 1933, as "The Affair of the Gallant Bachelor") begins when Ellery is asked to look into a series of jewel thefts in an exclusive apartment house. On the scene he finds his father trying to solve a strangulation that has just occurred in the same building, the only object missing from the victim being the titular cigarette case. After a second murder committed almost under the Queens' noses, Ellery solves both the thefts and the killings, but his reasoning and the whole story are based on the unacknowledged premise that the murderer is clairvoyant.

In "The Adventure of 'The Two-Headed Dog' " (*Mystery*, June 1934) Ellery stops over at a remote New

England inn whose proprietor tells him of some weird events that took place there several months before, involving a vanishing red-bearded stranger and a murdered dog. The host insists that unearthly noises have come ever since from the cabin where the redbeard had stayed. A few hours later another guest of the inn is found in his cabin with his throat slashed. A worn spot on a rug leads Ellery to a peculiarly inhuman murderer in this most atmospherically chilling of the *Adventures.*

"The Adventure of the Glass-Domed Clock" (*Mystery League,* October 1933) is the most elaborate Dying Message short story Queen ever wrote, and very probably the best. A curio dealer is found bashed to death in his shop, and the evidence indicates that with his last ounce of strength he had smashed a glass jewel-case, clutched at a large amethyst with his left hand, crawled over to a pedestal, knocked the titular clock to the floor and died with his right hand resting on it. The case is further complicated by a silver loving-cup, an exiled Russian nobleman, a poker game and five birthday messages. Ellery follows the tangled trail of a dying man's last thoughts and ends up with a magnificent solution, probably the earliest specimen of that Queenian specialty, concealing the obvious answer right under the reader's nose by mesmeric but completely fair misdirection.

"The Adventure of the Seven Black Cats" (*Mystery,* October 1934, as "The Black Cats Vanished") opens when Ellery visits a pet shop on a routine errand and hears about an eccentric and miserly old invalid lady who phones in an order once a week for a black green-eyed tomcat, although it is known that she hates all cats. Intrigued, Ellery goes to the apartment shared by the invalid and her sister, and finds both women vanished and the black cat beaten to death in the bathtub. Before the end of the day he has also found a vicious murderer of people. The alert reader may notice, however, that he never does find an acceptable motivation for the murder of the cat or of the second human victim.

The first short story Queen managed to sell to a high-priced slick is "The Adventure of the Mad Tea-Party" (*Redbook,* October 1934), in which Ellery is invited to a Long Island houseparty featuring a private performance of *Alice in Wonderland.* Festive spirits are dampened when the host disappears the morning after Ellery's arrival. Soon there begins to turn up a mystifying array of packages, containing such items as pairs of shoes, cabbages and chessmen. Ellery's solution of the mad events is astoundingly simple (though it presupposes a secret closet without a *raison d'être*), and his psychological war against the adversary is a more sophisticated variant of Poe's "Thou Art the Man." The influence of Lewis Carroll, always a favorite author of Dannay's, is manifest on every page of this first "Ellery in Wonderland" story and last of the eleven *Adventures,* which Dannay has picked as his own favorite among the early short tales.

The requirements of the slick-paper medium, in which "The Mad Tea-Party" first appeared, had much to do with a radical change in the direction of Queen's fiction that began to emerge about this time. In his next novel we can see his dissatisfaction with the strict chess problem in the Van Dine mold, and we can infer that the end of Period One is in sight. *The Spanish Cape Mystery* (1935) is set on a private peninsula thrusting out into the Atlantic. At the far end of the cape is the sprawling hacienda of a hermit-like Wall Street pirate named Walter Godfrey, who putters around his beloved rock gardens in filthy overalls, with lordly indifference to the guests his young wife has invited to the Cape. Among these guests are an overweight overwrought matron, a savage cowboy millionaire, a former musical comedy star, a young man in love with Godfrey's daughter, and a ruthless professional lover known as John Marco. It is Marco who is found one morning on the private beach terrace, strangled by a coil of wire. His hat is on his head, his ebony stick is in his right hand, a black opera cloak is draped about him, but beneath the cloak he is stark naked. Ellery, visiting in the area and enlisted by the local police, has other questions to answer beside who is guilty. Why did a one-eyed giant kidnap Walter Godfrey's brother-in-law shortly before the murder? Why did Mrs. Godfrey invite as house guests people who were complete strangers to her? Why did the guests accept the invitations as though nothing unusual were happening? Why is every woman in the house terrified by Marco's death? And most puzzling of all, why did the murderer take every stitch of clothing from his victim except for hat, stick and cloak?

Ellery's solution is relentlessly logical and scrupulously fair, but one can sense Queen's realization that he is fast exhausting the possibilities of the formal deductive puzzle. For this is the fourth of his novels since 1932 that rests on another version of the Birlstone Gambit, and the wary reader of earlier Period One work should be able to spot the gambit, and the murderer it entails, before he has finished fifty pages. A more significant pointer to Queen's dissatisfaction is the beginning of a change in Ellery's world-view that parallels a shift in Queen's view of his craft. In Chapter 15 Ellery expresses his credo up to this point: "My work is done with symbols . . . not with human beings. . . . I choose to close my mind to the human elements and treat it as a problem in mathematics. The fate of the murderer I leave to those who decide such things." This of course is the classic stance of the scientist who develops Cyclon B or napalm and leaves the practical consequences of his brainwork to the practical men. But at the end of the book Ellery realizes that he has exposed a murderer whose act was justified if any crime ever was. "I've often boasted that the human equation means nothing to me. But it does, damn it all, it does!" But at this point Ellery's new perception costs nothing to anyone, since he and we are assured that on the known facts no local jury will find the murderer guilty. We have not yet reached the later and more somber novels like *Ten Days' Wonder* where the misuse of Ellery's mind kills people. Nevertheless, with *The Spanish Cape Mystery* Queen closes out Period One—one of the greatest sustained endeavors in the history of crime fiction—and begins the movement away from the pure problem of deduction and in the direction of the novel that incorporates such a problem.

CHAPTER FOUR

QUEEN'S OUTPUT FROM LATE 1935 TO 1939 IS SO DIFFERENT IN content, style, form and motifs from the work of 1929-1935 as to make up a second period in his career, which with our usual gift for *le mot juste* we will call Period Two. S. S. Van Dine, the major influence on Queen's first period, had plummeted abysmally in both critical and commercial esteem by late 1935. His place was taken over not by another person but by media: the high-priced women's slick magazines and Hollywood.[1] In some respects the influence of these media was unfortunate, for none of Queen's novels of this period and only two of his short stories are even in the same league with the works of Period One. In the long perspective, however, we can see the whole of Period Two as a transitional stage, as a series of steps in the progressive humanization of Queen's universe. Under the guidance of his two new markets he learned to infuse greater life and warmth into his characters, including Ellery himself; to master the presentation of a woman's viewpoint, whose difficulties he had not completely overcome when he had written about Patience Thumm; and to develop a skill with character and relationship approximating his finesse with clue and counterplot. In short, Queen in Period Two worked at "opening up" the formal deductive puzzle, making room within its intellectual rigor for more of the virtues of mainstream storytelling. His experiments of the late 1930's were to come to full fruition, integrated into the most devious of puzzle plots, with the great novels of Period Three.

It's convenient, and conventional, to regard *Halfway House* (1936), the first Queen novel to break the chain of nationality-titles, as the beginning of the second period. However, this novel preserves both the subtitle "A Problem in Deduction," which had appeared in all of Ellery's book-length adventures of Period One, and the Challenge to the Reader, which had appeared in most of them. Further, Ellery himself in the Foreword to *Halfway House* points out to that mainstay of Period One, J. J. McC., that there is no reason why the book could not have been called something like *The Swedish Match Mystery*. But as long as the movement away from the work of 1929-1935 is recognized as a gradual evolution and not a sudden change of course, there's no harm in considering *Halfway House* the first novel of Period Two.

The book opens in a restaurant in Trenton, New Jersey, where Ellery has stopped off for dinner on his way back to New York. In the dining room he happens to encounter Bill Angell, a long-unseen college friend who is now practicing law in Philadelphia and protesting the fact of one law for the rich and another for the poor. Ellery learns that Bill's sister Lucy has been married for several years to a traveling salesman named Joe Wilson, who is on the road most of the time, and who has asked Bill to meet with him privately, for undisclosed reasons, that very evening. Bill drives out to the deserted and dilapidated shack where he is to meet his brother-in-law.   As he approaches, a scream tears the silence, and he sees a female figure rush out the front door of the shack, into a huge cream Cadillac, and away. Bill enters the shack, a shabbily furnished hovel except for its rich fawn wall-to-wall carpet. On the center table is a chipped plate containing twenty burnt paper-match stubs.   Near the plate lies a blood-bathed paperknife, with a tiny cone of cork impaled on its point. Behind the table lies Joe Wilson, who with his last breath tells Bill that he was stabbed by a veiled woman. Bill phones Ellery as well as the police.

Ellery observes that although the suit worn by the dead man is of very poor quality, several other suits in the house bear the label of the most exclusive private tailor in New York. The shack contains neither food nor a bed, but in the boathouse at the river's edge is a sailboat with an outboard motor. A rusty nude figurine, part of an automobile's radiator cap, is discovered in the muddy driveway.   But the most astonishing discovery comes when Ellery realizes that he knows the dead man— not as Joe Wilson the lower-middle-class peddler, but as Joseph Kent Gimball of Park Avenue, husband of socialite Jessica Borden Gimball and stepfather of the lovely Andrea Gimball. The murder of the man with two wives and two lives, in the halfway house between New York and Philadelphia where he was both of his identities and neither, seems on all the evidence to be the work of Lucy Wilson. Not only does she have motive and no alibi, but the rusty figurine and some tire-tracks in the mud place her car on the scene, although she denies even knowing of her husband's double life. As Bill Angell prepares to defend Lucy in court, Ellery goes off on investigative paths of his own, and after many weeks he returns to Halfway House to lay an elaborate psychological trap for the person he now knows to be the killer.

The middle portions of Queen's earlier books had been, with few exceptions, packed with involution and counterplot organically related to the main storyline, but what occupies the center of *Halfway House* is the straightforward and relatively uncomplicated account of Lucy Wilson's trial and of Ellery's attempts to pry Andrea Gimball's hidden knowledge out of her. Queen apparently decided to loosen and simplify his structure and add a greater measure of "human interest," so as to satisfy readers for whom the austere brain-bruising webwork of *Greek Coffin* and *The Tragedy of X* might have been too rich. Unfortunately we are never told how the murderer even knew that Wilson/Gimball would be at Halfway House on the fatal night, nor why he so planned the crime that the dead man's double life had to be exposed to the world although the killer had every reason *not* to want Jessica's bigamous marriage publicized. However, aside from these and a few other snags, the plot is intriguing (though unworkable in these days of the mini-skirt), the solution closely reasoned, and the clues brilliantly planted; note how unobtrusively subtle, for example, is the crucial incident of Pierre the obliging tobacconist. And Queen handles both the New Jersey setting and the courtroom scenes skillfully enough to satisfy even a Garden State lawyer. His transition novel into Period Two is, all things considered, an enviably smooth one.

If *Halfway House* was not vastly different from the works of 1929-1935, Queen's next novel is so unlike its predecessors as hardly to seem the product of the same author. In *The Door Between* (1937) deduction takes a

back seat to intuition, the stress is on characterization
and relationships, and for the first time in the Queen
canon one finds "love interest" on every page. The
explanation: the book first appeared in *Cosmopolitan*
(December 1936). And yet, against all human expectation, it's probably the best Queen novel of Period Two.

Karen Leith had come to the United States from
Japan in 1927, after her expatriate father's death, and
had sequestered herself in a house in Greenwich Village,
from which thenceforward came forth a series of incredibly beautiful novels. Upon her winning the major
American prize in literature, her publisher arranges a
celebration in the Japanese garden behind her prim house
in Washington Square. Among the lesser guests is a mystery writer named Queen, who meets both Miss Leith
and the eminent physician to whom she is engaged. Dr.
John MacClure, worn out by years of search for a cancer
cure, has come to treat money and fame and life with
detached scientific aloofness. (Could Queen have modeled him on Van Dine?) Ellery does not get to meet
MacClure's lovely niece Eva, but Eva meets a young
society doctor named Richard Scott and is soon engaged
to him. While the exhausted Dr. MacClure is away on an
ocean voyage, Eva and Dick decide to get married right
after his return, and Eva dashes downtown to share the
news with Karen Leith. The maid tells her that Karen is
busy writing, and Eva waits in the sitting room next to
Karen's bedroom-study. But after a long and unaccount-
able silence from within, Eva steps into the inner room—
and finds Karen lying on the dais behind her desk,
stabbed in the throat with a half-scissors. Being no more
blessed with brains than most other heroines of women's
mystery fiction, Eva fingers the weapon, gets the dead
woman's blood on her hand, and all in all presents a

perfect picture of a murderess caught in the act to the strange young man she suddenly sees observing her from the doorway. Being as much of a witling as most other male leads in women's mystery fiction, private detective Terry Ring concludes on the spot that the girl is innocent and immediately sets out to rearrange the evidence so as to suggest an outside assailant. Terry's and Eva's attempts to deceive Inspector Queen and Ellery consume as much of the novel as the gradual revelation of skeletons in the Leith and MacClure family closets. Among the puzzling elements of the mystery are the rock that broke Karen's window while she lay dying, the pet jay that vanished from the death room and reappeared downstairs, the woman with the short right leg whom Karen had been keeping in her attic, and a twenty-year-old "accident" in Japan. At the denouement Ellery explains the crime to the satisfaction of everyone but himself, then later reveals, to the murderer alone, a second and even more stunning solution. This two-solutions device is employed here for the first time in a Queen novel, evoking intellectual, moral, and sheerly human ambiguities with an intensity worthy of Simenon.

As a formal puzzle *The Door Between* can't stand up against the best novels of Period One. Queen quite rightly omitted the usual Challenge to the Reader this time, since Ellery's solution is so intuitive as to suggest Maigret rather than the logical successor to Sherlock Holmes. A huge technical flaw in the plot is that the murderer's plan would have gone up in smoke if Karen Leith had done the natural thing and written prior to her death the kind of note that Ellery produces at the denouement. But as a simultaneous imitation and parody of the Rinehart/Eberhart "women's mystery novel" it's an excellent job, full of strokes of satiric genius like putting a hard-boiled private eye in the traditional role of idiot hero. As a study of character and atmosphere the book breaks little new ground (in fact the triangle Eva/Terry Ring/Richard Scott is almost identical with the triangle Andrea Gimball/Bill Angell/Burke Jones in *Halfway House*), but it's more vivid and convincing in these respects than many of Queen's earlier efforts. *The Door Between* is not in itself major Queen but it is a major stride forward on the road to Period Three.

One step forward, two steps back. Among all Queen's experiments his next novel, *The Devil to Pay* (1937), is one of the least successful, its characters mere molds to be filled by movie actors and its plot more suitable to a novelet than a full-length novel. The setting is a Hollywood hilltop development called Sans Souci which consists of four pseudo-Spanish mansions and a central swimming pool. The middle-aging millionaire sportsman Rhys Jardin occupies one of the houses, along with his daughter Valerie and his confidant/athletic trainer Pink and a small army of servants. Across the pool lives the fat and ruthless tycoon Solomon Spaeth, with his "protegee" Winni Moon and—when he hasn't stormed out of the house after a political argument—his left-wing cartoonist son Walter. Despite his proletarian principles Walter is in love with that daughter of economic royalism, Val Jardin. Solly Spaeth had persuaded Rhys Jardin to join him in the gigantic Ohippi Hydro-Electric Development project but had sold out his own interest at a huge profit just before floods ruined the Ohippi machinery and plants. Mobs of ruined investors converge on Sans Souci, while the now-bankrupt Rhys Jardin has two violent arguments with Solly and Walter threatens to take any action necessary to make his father restore Ohippi. Meanwhile an acquaintance of Walter's

named Queen arrives in town to write screenplays for
Magna Studios, his language bereft of polysyllables and
his face sporting a luxuriant beard. Shortly thereafter
Solomon Spaeth is found in his study dead of a stab
wound with a molasses stain at its edge, and a 17th-
century Italian rapier is missing from the collection on
the study wall. The gatekeeper tells Inspector Glücke
that he saw Rhys Jardin enter the grounds just before
the murder, but Val knows the visitor was Walter Spaeth,
wearing Rhys' torn camel's hair coat. Walter does not
admit the truth, refuses to explain why he will not, and
asks Val to trust him and keep silent. Soon they discover
Rhys' bloodstained coat and the missing rapier, both
planted in the Jardin closet, but the police discover the
same objects immediately afterwards. Ellery enters the
case to help Val clear her arrested father, but he must
break down the interconnecting lies of Val, Rhys and
Walter before he can tie together the two-fingered handprint, the Indian club dropped down a sewer, the tear in
the terrace awning and the pair of cracked binoculars,
and deduce the identity of the murderer.

The plot is nowhere near Queen's best and nowhere
near complex enough for a Queen novel, although it's
competent and adequate in most respects. The characterization and dialogue, however, are somewhat less
than adequate. Even Ellery becomes no more than a
mold for a B-picture leading man; change his name to
Charlie Brown and, except for the denouement scene,
you'd never know he was supposed to be the detective
of Queen's earlier novels. Hollywooden misunderstand-
ings abound between the male and female leads, the un-
masked killer aims a weapon at the detectives and snarls
"Don't move," True Love triumphs at the fadeout.
Although the agony of the Depression is supposedly a

central theme of the book, Queen permits no more real pain or despair to intrude than the most timid and reactionary front office would consent to. Instead, the tears are reserved for the oh-so-tragic plight of the Jardins, reduced from wealth to the penury of a five-room apartment, one car and one measly quasi-servant!

"It's like a movie, thought Walter gloomily," Queen writes in Chapter II; and that's precisely the problem. Queen attempted to reduce his rich world to Hollywood's dimensions in hopes of a movie sale. Result: poor book, no movie (at least not officially). However, insofar as it gave Queen additional practice at integrating other types of fiction with the detective novel, *Devil* can be accepted as another step towards Period Three.

A rather larger stride in the same direction was taken the following year when Queen published his next novel. *The Four of Hearts* (1938) is a potpourri of diverse styles and elements that tend to get in each other's way, but at its center is one of Queen's better Period Two plots. Ellery has been sitting around Magna Studios for several highly paid weeks of doing nothing, when finally the vice-president and reigning boy wonder, Jacques Butcher, gives the great man a screenwriting project fitted to his talents. Ellery is to collaborate on a blockbuster biographical film dealing with Magna's own leading star families, the Royles and the Stuarts, whose highly publicized feud has cheered the hearts of Hollywood gossip columnists for two decades. While researching the project Ellery meets and promptly falls madly in love with one such columnist, the lovely recluse Paula Paris, who provides him with inside information on the debonair Jack Royle and his son Ty, and on the gorgeous Blythe Stuart and her equally gorgeous daughter Bonnie. But while Ellery is tagging along after his subjects, Jack and Blythe discover, and admit to each other, that despite twenty years of feuding they are and always have been in love. The Magna publicity office goes into ecstasies and makes plans for the stars to have a gigantic public wedding at an airfield, to be followed by a flight in Ty Royle's plane to an equally public island honeymoon. The only cloud on the lovers' horizon is the strange series of playing cards that Blythe Stuart is receiving in the mails. One card is even delivered to her at the airfield, just before the wedding. The ceremony is performed, everyone drinks toasts to the happy couple, and the red and gold monoplane takes off. Shortly after the take-off, Ty Royle, who supposedly is piloting the plane, is found bound and gagged in the hangar. Whoever is at the controls, the plane never reaches the honeymoon island. When it is located that night, on a plateau not far from the remote mountain estate of Blythe Stuart's hypochondriac father, the substitute pilot is gone, and Jack and Blythe are found in the plane's cabin, dead of morphine poisoning. Ellery's informal investigation of the murders alienates the harried Inspector Glücke but unearths some intriguing clues, including a set of filed-down typewriter keys, a threatening letter written to a dead woman, a frightened old man running around in a thunderstorm wearing a flying helmet, and an unobtrusive glass of iced tea. In addition to analyzing the evidence and bemoaning the snail's progress of his own romance with Paula Paris, Ellery must also find a way of sabotaging the budding love affair between Ty Royle and Bonnie Stuart, which he believes is a source of extreme danger to them both. Finally, knowing the murderer's identity but lacking evidence to convict him, Ellery devises a gigantic charade to make him attempt another double murder.

The Four of Hearts boasts a number of skillfully planted clues, an exceptionally well-concealed murderer, and a gorgeous plot bristling with legal points that are best discussed in the learned obscurity of a footnote.[2] On the negative side, a great deal of the material in the book is not strictly relevant to the grand design. Here more than in any other single novel, Queen threw every conceivable ingredient into the mixture: a wacky-humor opening, three separate and distinct love stories, a barrage of movieland patter, and a quite serious multiple murder scheme. Queen's attitude toward the Hollywood milieu varies from chapter to chapter, and he makes us see the movie capital as in turn absurd (the initial chapter), sick (the funeral sequence), and warmly wonderful (the Paula Paris aspects). The abrupt changes of tone from farce to grief to light romance to rigorous rationality are grating at times, and there's a certain meant-to-be-made-into-a-movie aura about the book that prevents one from taking it with full seriousness. But the disunity of tone is functional at least to the extent that it enables Queen to plant clues unobtrusively in the chapters one is most tempted to read with a relaxed mind; re-reading those chapters, we can learn a great deal about the murderer's reactions to unforeseen developments by taking a close look at dialogue which, the first time around, we passed off as Hollywood banter. *The Four of Hearts* is by no means the apex of the Queen canon, but it provides us with a divertingly cockeyed view of the big movie studios of the Thirties and with a wild roller-coaster ride through the celluloid Wonderland.

The main setting of Queen's next novel is New York rather than Hollywood, but the tone of *The Dragon's Teeth* (1939) still comes straight out of movie-land, specifically from the screwball comedy films of the late Thirties, the kind that Carole Lombard used to star in. The book is something of a quickie, the chapter titles are atrocious puns as they were in *The Devil to Pay*, and Ellery is still little more than a receptacle for the personality of a movie actor; but there are plenty of fascinations herein for the Queen addict, and if you don't expect a *Greek Coffin* or a *Cat of Many Tails* you can have a lot of fun with it. The first half deals hardly at all with the Queens but introduces a new central character, Beau Rummell, lawyer, ditchdigger, and aspiring sleuth. He and Ellery meet and decide to form their own detective agency. A few months later trouble knocks at the door of Ellery Queen, Inc. in the form of an eccentric retired millionaire named Cadmus Cole, who retains the firm to perform a task after his death whose nature he refuses to disclose now. Six weeks pass, and Cole is reported to have been buried at sea after suffering a heart attack on his yacht. His will reveals that his mission for the Queen firm is that of locating his two long-lost nieces, who inherit his entire fortune if (a) they are and forever remain unmarried, and (b) they agree to live together for a year on his Tarrytown estate. Beau—who for his own good reasons temporarily adopts the name of Ellery Queen—locates the younger of the cousins, Kerrie Shawn, and they promptly proceed to fall in love. Margo Cole, the other heiress, is located in France, comes to New York, and also begins to cast eyes at "Ellery." The girls' sojourn at the Tarrytown estate is complicated by a series of near-fatal "accidents" aimed at Kerrie; and, the survivor cousin taking all under the Cole will, Margo quickly becomes chief suspect. When she is herself shot to death in front of Kerrie's eyes, the false Ellery frantically contacts his partner to bail out his beloved. Making all sorts of deductions from a series of toothmarks on a pen-and-pencil set, Ellery succeeds in unmasking the evil one and bringing the lovers and the Cole millions together.

As an exercise in logic *The Dragon's Teeth* is full of cavities. The obvious explanation of the evidence in the case is wrong, but you'll never figure out why it's wrong unless you happen to be a dentist. Attorneys who pick up the book will give short shrift to Queen's premise that a will would be probated where (a) the only available witness to its execution is also a principal beneficiary, and (b) it contains an anti-marriage clause that the court would declare unenforceable as against public policy even if a dozen competent witnesses swore to the will's authenticity. Those who have read one or two Perry Mason novels will be aware, as Queen apparently was not when he wrote Chapter II, that you don't need a body to establish a *corpus delicti.* Both the attempted asphyxiation of Kerrie Shawn and the murder of Margo Cole are possible only because the killer, in Raymond Chandler's phrase, had God sitting in his lap. But the reader with sense enough to tolerate the less than perfect will find a multitude of incidental rewards here. The love and money problems of the people in the white hats are funny enough to qualify as (unintended?) farce. There is a set-piece with the heroine trapped and being asphyxiated in a locked garage which is almost an object lesson to female writers on how the "woman's mystery novel" should be written. Queen has a field day playing with variants of the Birlstone gambit before he settles on a brilliant resolution of the problem. In short, even though it's a slight and minor diversion, *The Dragon's Teeth* is an acceptable light entertainment.

Queen had begun work on another novel, but the project ran aground halfway through its course when one

of the cousins picked up a well-known national magazine
and discovered that a new book by Agatha Christie being
serialized therein, *And Then There Were None,* was
based on exactly the same plotline. So it came about
that there was no new Queen novel to open up the new
decade, leaving *The Dragon's Teeth* with the dubious
honor of being the last novel of Period Two. Queen's
second collection of short fiction, *The New Adventures
of Ellery Queen* (1940), recapitulates his development
from the end of Period One to the end of 1939. The
book as a whole lacks the unity of style and content of
the first volume of *Adventures* or the later *Calendar of
Crime,* and the individual stories range from the magnificent to the indifferent, but the best tales in *New Adventures* rank with Queen's greatest work at less than novel
length, and more than that no one can ask from a book
of short fiction.

　　Crown of the collection is that peerless classic "The
Lamp of God" (*Detective Story,* November 1935, as
"House of Haunts"). Having never written a detective
novelet before in his life, Queen calmly turned out here
one of the half dozen greatest works of all time in that
form, then dropped the form for almost a quarter of a
century. The story begins with a desperate phone call
from an attorney friend, which brings Ellery out into
the raw January snowscape of Long Island. The patriarch of the decayed and maniacal Mayhew family is
believed to have hidden a fortune in gold somewhere in
the nightmarish old mansion where he lived and recently
died, and attorney Thorne suspects that certain of the
old tyrant's relatives are determined to uncover and appropriate the treasure before it can be turned over to
the old man's long-lost daughter. After a raw-nerved
evening with an obscenely fat doctor, a demented old

lady, and a mysterious young hired man, Ellery and the others go to bed, and wake up to an event that convinces them the world has gone mad. The entire huge black house of old Sylvester Mayhew has disappeared during the night.

"The Lamp of God" is the second stunning example of a Queen specialty we have seen before at short-story length in "The Adventure of the Glass-Domed Clock" and shall see again at book length in *The King Is Dead*: titanic misdirection concealing a blindingly simple solution.[3] It is also one of the finest pieces of atmospheric writing in the mystery genre, evoking a physical and a metaphysical chill that rise off the page into the reader's bones. Queen here proved himself a genius at summoning up the howling fear that the world has been abandoned to the demonic, and then at exorcising the panic of chaos through the rigorous exercise of reason—which is, I submit, the fundamental ritual underlying detective fiction.

The religious dimension of the story deserves some comment. Queen significantly describes Ellery as "that lean and indefatigable agnostic," and Ellery says of himself: "If I were religiously inclined . . . if I, poor sinner that I am, possessed religious susceptibilities, I should have become permanently devout in the past three days." And elsewhere in the tale he comments: "No riddle is esoteric . . . unless it's the riddle of God; and that's no riddle—it's a vast blackness." Finally, Ellery speaks of "chance, cosmos, God, whatever you may choose to call it," giving him the instrument for understanding the truth: on one level, human reason, on the other, its analogue the sun, the light, the lamp of God. This novelet, then, is Queen's most explicit treatment of a theme that is central to several of his later masterpieces, including *Ten Days' Wonder, The Player on the Other Side* and *And On the Eighth Day*: theomachy, the battle of (in a non-literal sense) gods, of light against darkness as in Zoroastrianism, of sun against cold, of reason against the absurd.

After the soul-pounding intensity of "The Lamp of God" it's a welcome relief to enter the light and bantering world of the collection's first short story. Ellery's mission in "The Adventure of the Treasure Hunt" (*Detective Story*, December 1935) is to find the rope of pearls that one of retired General Barrett's house guests filched from his daughter's bedroom, and to identify the thief. Ellery devises a treasure hunting game as a psychological trap and solves the case neatly and quickly.

In "The Adventure of the Hollow Dragon" (*Red-Book*, December 1936), the theft of a soapstone doorstop brings Ellery to the home of a wealthy Japanese importer in financial straits, and a few deductions from an almanac (which is not furnished the reader) lead him not only to the thief and his motive but to an unsuspected murder as well. Ellery is again described as a "notorious heretic," and stands up for respect for others' beliefs as against the vilifications of Eastern religion indulged in by Miss Letitia Gallant, one of the most obnoxious specimens of Christian upbringing in the Queen canon.

"The Adventure of the House of Darkness" (*American Magazine*, February 1935) is one of the three subtlest, most tightly plotted shorts in the collection. When murder is committed in a surrealistic amusement park to which Ellery has taken his houseboy Djuna for the day, the great man must deduce not only who did it but also how the killer was able to put four lethal bullets into his victim's back in total darkness. Students of

Queen should note the motif of red-green colorblindness, which harks back to *The Greek Coffin Mystery*, is used here in a different but no less ingenious way, and will be seen again.

"The Adventure of the Bleeding Portrait" (*American Cavalcade*, September 1937, as "The Gramatan [sic] Mystery") is the least characteristic and dullest Queen short story of the Thirties. Ellery, vacationing in the artists' summer colony of Natchitauk, becomes entangled in the amorous problems of the lovely Mimi Gramaton, the jealous rages of her husband Mark, and the legend of the fourth Lord Gramaton's portrait, which is said to bleed when a Gramaton woman has been unfaithful. There is no action, a scintilla of desultory deduction, and a slick-magazine aura that hangs over the tale like thin smog.

The final four stories in *New Adventures* were conceived and written as a series. In each of them Ellery solves a crime—homicide, attempted equicide, jewel theft—that is connected with a major sporting event. To appreciate just how far the character of Ellery has evolved since his debut a decade earlier, try to visualize Philo Vance, originally the model for Ellery, enjoying a baseball game or, God save us, a boxing match.

"Man Bites Dog" (*Blue Book*, June 1939) is set in the Polo Grounds during a Yankees-Giants world series game.[4] In a box near that of Ellery and Richard Queen, a baseball great of yesteryear drops dead after mistakenly picking up and eating the frankfurter of his estranged wife. Ellery's frantic desire to get back to his seat for the final innings does not keep him from brilliantly analyzing a tight-packed and devious plot. This is one of the two finest stories of any length that Queen wrote during Period Two.

In "Long Shot" (*Blue Book*, September 1939, as "The Long Shot") Ellery visits craggy old John Scott's horse-breeding ranch in order to do research on a racing screenplay he's been assigned, and becomes ensnared in the love problems of the old man's daughter, who wants to marry a stablehand, and in a plot to kill or maim Scott's prime thoroughbred, Danger. Unfortunately too many of the characters are just silly, and the puzzle is less than completely fair (why weren't we told that there were powder burns around that wound?), and the solution is a less than subtle variation on the "Hollow Dragon" story.[5]

"Mind Over Matter" (*Blue Book*, October 1939) is the equal of "Man Bites Dog" in fairness, subtlety and interest. Ellery attends the world heavyweight championship boxing match, later discovers the stabbed body of the vicious dethroned champ in a parking lot, but seems much more concerned to find his missing camel's hair coat than to find the killer—because he knows that when he has gotten the one he will have the other. It's a superb tight-knit plot with not a word wasted, and a pure joy to read even if you've never gone to a boxing match in your life.

The collection closes with "Trojan Horse" (*Blue Book*, December 1939, as "The Trojan Horse"), in which the theft of eleven matched sapphires from a wealthy old grad and football buff mars the traditional New Year's Day Rose Bowl game. Ellery deduces the thief and the gems' hiding place without leaving his box seat. Like "The Treasure Hunt" this tale runs on a single track, free of complexity and involution. But though unspectacular, it's a not unpleasant coda to Queen's second collection of short fiction, and to the second period of his criminous career.

CINEMATIC INTERLUDE

"*(A) BENEDICTION UPON THE HEAD OF WHOEVER INVENTED THE* cinema. May he be thrice blessed!" exclaimed Ellery in Chapter 21 of *The American Gun Mystery.* If Queen could have foreseen how the movie industry would maul his material over the next several years, he might not have been so enthusiastic. The sad but undisputed truth is that every single one of the films based on Queen's novels or characters is completely irrelevant to the Queenian universe, and all but one or at most two are cinematic messes considered independent of their source. Dannay and Lee had nothing whatever to do with any aspect of these films, and Dannay told me that if he is watching TV in bed at night and a Queen movie comes on, he ducks under the covers.

The sad history of the attempts to transfer Queen to celluloid began when the newly formed Republic Studios released *The Spanish Cape Mystery* (1935), based on Queen's novel of the same name. The film was directed by Lewis D. Collins from a screenplay by Albert DeMond, and starred Donald Cook as Ellery and Guy Usher as his father who didn't appear in the book at all.

DeMond added a romance between Ellery and the female lead, played by Helen Twelvetrees, and deleted large chunks of Queen's plot and Ellery's reasoning. The critics complained about weak adaptation, wobbly direction, and the excessive footage given Harry Stubbs as the loudmouthed sheriff whom Ellery allows to take credit for solving the mystery. Also in the cast were Berton Churchill, Betty Blythe and Huntley Gordon.

Next year Republic came out with a sequel, *The Mandarin Mystery* (1936), wretchedly adapted from *The Chinese Orange Mystery* by John Francis Larkin, Rex Taylor, Gertrude Orr and Cortland Fitzsimmons, who together scuttled the entire *raison d'être* of Queen's novel. Ellery was played by Eddie Quillan, a wiry little vaudeville-hoofer type hopelessly miscast as the master detective, and Inspector Queen by the somewhat more adequate Wade Boteler. The cast was rounded out by Charlotte Henry, Franklin Pangborn, Rita LeRoy and George Irving. The whole mess was directed by Ralph Staub.

There followed a four-year hiatus in Queen films except for Paramount's *The Crime Nobody Saw* (1937), directed by Charles Barton from a script by Bertram Millhauser based on "Danger, Men Working," a minor stage play by Queen and Lowell Brentano. Lew Ayres played the lead, assisted by Ruth Coleman, Benny Baker and Eugene Pallette. It was an awful movie. Ellery was not in it, nor in the play.

During these intervening years Dannay and Lee themselves were working off-and-on as Hollywood screenwriters, first for Columbia, later for Paramount and M-G-M. Their highly argumentative methods of composition did little to soothe the nerves of the people in neighboring offices, and at one point the Paramount mimeograph department, which gave forth a constant clatter from dozens of machines, complained about the noise the cousins were making. Queen's contributions to the Hollywood product of the late Thirties were many but unfortunately never earned Queen a single screen credit. And as we have seen, the Hollywood experience was one of the prime factors that shaped the novels and stories of Period Two.

In 1940 Columbia inaugurated a new series of Ellery Queen movies, with a permanent cast consisting of Ralph Bellamy as Ellery, Charley Grapewin as the Inspector, James Burke as Sergeant Velie, and Margaret Lindsay as Nikki Porter, the character created by Queen to provide romantic interest for the EQ radio series that debuted in 1939 and will be discussed in Chapter Five. The first and almost certainly the best of this rather mediocre series was *Ellery Queen, Master Detective* (1940), directed by Kurt Neumann from a screenplay by Eric Taylor loosely and without acknowledgment based on Queen's 1937 novel *The Door Between.* The old silent film director Fred Niblo made a cameo appearance as the murder victim, and among the supporting players were Michael Whalen, Marsha Hunt, Ann Shoemaker, Douglas Fowley, Byron Foulger and Katherine DeMille.

Under its contract with Queen, Columbia had the right to adapt and exploit any element of Queen's published fiction, and in this and subsequent films exercised its right with a vengeance. As a tie-in with this first Queen movie, the studio commissioned a "novelization" of the script, also entitled *Ellery Queen, Master Detective* (Grosset & Dunlap, 1941; Pyramid pb #R-1799, 1968, as *The Vanishing Corpse*). Queen can no more be held responsible for this "novelization" than he can for the parent film, but it does provide us with a reasonably accurate prose rendition of the movie. Shortly after being informed by his doctor that he is dying of cancer, John Braun, wealthy physical culture tycoon and domestic tyrant, is found in his locked study with his throat slit. The weapon, a jewel-studded paper-knife, has vanished. The only other person in the room is a frightened young woman named Nikki Porter. Ellery happens on the scene, looks into her dark limpid eyes, reads therein that she is innocent, and at once undertakes to hide her from his father and to clear her by solving the impossible crime himself.

How did the logical successor to Sherlock Holmes wind up behaving like the idiot hero in a Had-I-But-Known romance? A quick review of *The Door Between* provides the answer. The core of *Ellery Queen, Master Detective* has been yanked bodily from Queen's novel, with the character of John Braun standing in for Karen Leith, Nikki Porter for Eva MacClure, Dr. Jim Rogers for Dr. John MacClure, the jeweled paperknife for the jeweled half-scissors, Joseph's raven for the Loo-Choo jay—and Ellery Queen for Terry Ring, the self-styled tough private eye whom Queen in a stroke of satiric genius had cast in his novel in the role of Rinehartian nitwit hero. Screenwriter Taylor and his novelizer further decided that they could improve Queen's book by placing the cancer motif at the beginning rather than the end, thus requiring their murderer to steal John Braun's body, while the police are on guard, not once but twice (he gets away with the corpse both times thanks to the officials going conveniently blind at all the proper moments). Finally, the film and novelization add to the plot several red-herring suspects, unrelated to any people in *The Door Between*, and unconvincing from start to finish.

As a specimen of film-making, writing, plotting or characterization, *Ellery Queen, Master Detective* is beneath notice. But it has some historic significance in that it provides a second version of Ellery's initial encounter with Nikki—a version completely at odds with the explanation Queen inserted in his first radio play. (A third and a fourth account were to come in Queen's later novels, *There Was an Old Woman* and *The Scarlet Letters*.) And, as I discovered at about age nine, the novelization is at least an acceptable vehicle for initiating child readers into the wonders of the genuine Queen canon.

The second film in Columbia's series was *Ellery Queen's Penthouse Mystery* (1941), with the same permanent cast as the first film, and featuring Anna May Wong, Eduardo Cianelli, Noel Madison, Russell Hicks, Theodor von Eltz and Mantan Moreland. James Hogan directed from another screenplay by Eric Taylor which according to the credits was based on a story by Queen although the plot resembles nothing Queen ever published. The movie is uniformly abysmal in every respect.

Once again Columbia commissioned a novelization, titled *The Penthouse Mystery* (Grosset & Dunlap, 1941; Pyramid pb #R-1810, 1968), which differs significantly from the movie in that it contains a few genuine Queenian overtones here and there, most noticeably in the "negative clue" gimmick which Queen would later perfect in *The Origin of Evil* and *The King Is Dead*. But even though it's possible that both film and novelization were remotely based on genuine Queen material—most likely a radio play—this novelization is as dreadful as its predecessor. A friend of Nikki's named Sheila Cobb asks Ellery to locate her ventriloquist father, who has vanished just after returning from a trip to war-torn China (the time is August 1940). Before long Ellery has found Gordon Cobb, strangled and stuffed into a trunk in the Cobb penthouse. Three other people in the same hotel turn out to have come over from China on the same ship with Cobb, and it soon develops that Cobb secretly brought with him a fortune in Oriental heirlooms, intended to be sold to aid the victims of Japan's war against China. The treasure is being sought by its rightful owners, Japanese spies, and free-lance American crooks. When all the red herrings have been cleared off the plate, Ellery exposes the murderer through a rather neat piece of deduction which doesn't figure at all in the movie. The novelization is a bearable way of killing an idle hour, but prose, people and most of the plot are as wooden as Gordon Cobb's dummy.

If the third movie, *Ellery Queen and the Perfect Crime* (1941), is one of the better entries in Columbia's series, it's only because of its more or less direct derivation from a Queen novel. The Bellamy-Lindsay-Grapewin-Burke team again starred, and Hogan again directed from a Taylor screenplay. The supporting cast included John Beal, H. B. Warner, Spring Byington, Douglass Dumbrille, Sidney Blackmer and Walter Kingsford. For the third and last time a novelization was published in connection with the film, and *The Perfect Crime* (Grosset & Dunlap, 1942, Pyramid pb #R-1814, 1968) again gives away its own source and that of its parent movie, namely Queen's novel *The Devil to Pay*. Ellery's friend Walter Mathews (in the novel, Walter Spaeth) is in love with Marian Garten (Valerie Jardin), whose father Raymond (Rhys Jardin) has been ruined in the Chickawassi petroleum debacle (the Ohippi dam swindle) by Walter's uncle, John Mathews (Solly Spaeth). Raymond must sell his priceless and beloved library to pay off his creditors, and Walter, who is wealthy in his own right, asks Ellery to purchase the library as a whole with Walter's money, so that Walter can restore it to his future father-in-law. That evening John Mathews is murdered under circumstances which point to either Walter Mathews or Raymond Garten, each of whom is trying to shield the other. Additional suspects include a lady of ridiculously affected speech named Carlotta Emerson (Winni Moon in the novel), the dead man's attorney, Arthur Rhodes (Anatole Ruhig), and the Garten librarian, Henry Griswold (Pink). The novelization adds to Queen's plot a meticulous diagram of the premises and a noble reconstruction scene at the denouement, complete with timetables, but somehow Ellery forgets to explain how he deduced the murderer's identity, although everything else in the case is elucidated neatly. *The Perfect Crime* is not in the same league even with Queen's weakest genuine novels, but it's by far the best of the three Columbia novelizations.

The film series continued to grind on, but without any more renditions of the scripts into prose. Fourth in the cycle, *Ellery Queen and the Murder Ring* (1941), was directed by Hogan from a screenplay by Taylor and Gertrude Purcell very freely derived from Queen's 1931 novel *The Dutch Shoe Mystery*. Bellamy, Lindsay, Grapewin and Burke again played the leads, assisted by George Zucco, Mona Barrie, Blanche Yurka, Tom Dugan, Paul Hurst and Leon Ames. The homicide-in-a-hospital plot was, to say the least, uninspired.

The final three films in the series were released in 1942 and starred William Gargan as Ellery—hardly an improvement over Bellamy who was himself no prize in the role. Although Queen was credited with the original story for all three movies, none of them had even the thinnest connection with published Queen material. Hogan continued as director, Taylor as scriptwriter, and Lindsay, Grapewin and Burke as Nikki, Richard and Velie. In *A Close Call for Ellery Queen* (1942) Ellery becomes involved in a blackmail plot and a man's hunt for his two long-lost daughters. If this brief synopsis reminds you of *The Dragon's Teeth*, it's the only reminder you'll find in the movie. Ralph Morgan, Edward Norris and Addison Richards were featured. *A Desperate Chance for Ellery Queen* (1942) brought the four leading players to San Francisco in an incomprehensible plot dealing with a missing man and a missing $100,000. John Litel, Jack LaRue, Noel Madison and Morgan Conway had supporting roles. The central elements in *Enemy Agents Meet Ellery Queen* (1942) are Nazi spies and a mummy-case mystery, with a cast including Gale Sondergaard, Gilbert Roland and Sig Rumann. With this seventh and last film the series came to an end, unmourned by any Queenian or any discriminating moviegoer.

Although the far better Queen radio series stayed on the air until 1948, there were no further visual representations of Queen until the end of the decade, and then only on the home screen. Those who bought their first television set early may recall the Queen TV series which was broadcast live in the very early Fifties, with first Richard Hart and later Lee Bowman in the lead, and which won the *TV Guide* award for the best television mystery series of 1950. A second Queen series was filmed and syndicated in 1955, consisting of 32 half-hour episodes starring Hugh Marlowe as Ellery and Florenz Ames as his father. Marlowe had earlier played the great man on radio, and both actors came quite close to the images of the Queens one derived from the novels, but the scripts were mostly wretched and the visual values nil.

The third and last Queen teleseries to date was conceived and produced by Albert McCleery, a top name in live TV drama during the Fifties, and broadcast on NBC during the 1958-59 season. McCleery's attitude towards his source material is illustrated by a statement he made to *TV Guide*: "That I had never read any of the Queen stories was unimportant. (Oh?) Of all the Queen material, we can use only four of the novels. (In fact, he used six.) Most of Ellery has been done before (false); the rest isn't suitable (oh)." *The Further Adventures of Ellery Queen* began live and in color on September 26, 1958, with George Nader in the lead. Just before the debut McCleery told *TV Guide*: "We're going to spend money for scripts and actors, not costly props and sets." But the acting turned out barely adequate at best, and the less said about the scripts the better. Six of the first eight weeks' shows were adapted from Queen novels—*The Glass Village, The King Is Dead, Ten Days' Wonder, The Door Between, Cat of Many Tails*, and *Double, Double*—and all but the first were outrageously bad. (The adaptation of *The Glass Village* stripped all the deeper meaning from Queen's novel and substituted Ellery Queen for Johnny Shinn but somehow preserved much of the novel's plot structure.) The remainder of the Nader cycle consisted of adaptations of other mystery writers' books, including two of Harold Q. Masur's Scott Jordan novels, a Bart Hardin story by David Alexander, and mysteries by William P. McGivern, Edgar Box (Gore Vidal), John Roeburt and Hillary Waugh. Needless to add that giving the name Ellery Queen to the central character of all these scripts did nothing to improve the show's quality. After twenty weeks Lee Philips took over the role of Ellery and the series switched to tape and to original scripts rather than adaptations. Philips played Ellery as a man of awareness and compassion, and the first episode of his cycle, "Shadow of the Past" by Sam Dann (2/27/59), struck me as so much the finest adaptation of Queen to any visual medium that until he denied it in person I was convinced "Dann" was a pseudonym of Frederic Dannay. But no subsequent script came even close to the premiere in quality, and long before the last show ("This Murder Comes to You Live" by Ben Hecht and featuring Hecht in a key role), the series had been given up as a lost cause by all reasonable Queenians.

After the summer of 1959 the only Queen on TV or in movies was an hour-long 1963 telefilm based on a Queen story without Ellery. Then at the turn of the decade from the Sixties to the Seventies came two ambitious and almost simultaneous attempts to put Queen on film. One was a purely American product: Universal Pictures prepared a two-hour-long pilot film for a proposed new Ellery Queen TV series. The series almost made it to prime time but was replaced at the last minute by *McMillan and Wife* with Rock Hudson and Susan Saint James. Finally the pilot film was aired in its entirety on NBC's *World Premiere* on November 19, 1971. *Ellery Queen: Don't Look Behind You* (originally announced as *Catch Me If You Can*) was directed by Barry Shear from a script by Ted Leighton based on what may well be Queen's finest novel, *Cat of Many Tails*. Peter Lawford played Ellery as a mod Londonesque swinger, complete with veddy accent and silver-streaked hair down to the eyebrows, while Harry Morgan with his Brooklyn twang played Richard Queen, Ellery's beloved—uncle. (I presume someone at Universal decreed this change on the ground that the two stars' accents were ludicrously incompatible for a father and son.)   The cast included E. G. Marshall as Dr. Cazalis, Coleen Gray as Mrs. Cazalis, and Stefanie Powers as Celeste Phillips. Screenwriter Leighton futilely attempted to update to 1970 a novel that is so deeply rooted in the late Forties that it can't be transplanted without killing it, and reduced Queen's rich characterizations to cardboard, and added several senseless "suspense" sequences with no equivalents in the novel, but at least preserved the bare bones of the original plot.   The direction was reasonably competent and the budget much higher than had ever been allocated to a Queen film before. Dannay told me that on the whole he liked the film and that it could have been much worse.

The second Queen project was *Ten Days' Wonder*, a film version of the Queen novel directed in English by the celebrated French film-maker Claude Chabrol in the fall of 1970 but not released in New York until April 1972. Paul Gardner's and Eugene Archer's screenplay was based on an adaptation of the novel by Chabrol's frequent collaborator Paul Gegauff. The role corresponding to Diedrich in the novel is played by Orson Welles, with Anthony Perkins and Marlene Jobert portraying the characters based on Howard and Sally. Ellery's functions are performed by Michel Piccoli in the role of Paul Régis, a philosophy professor in whose classes Perkins lost his faith in God and to whom Perkins comes for help in learning the cause of his strange blackouts as Howard came to Ellery in the novel. The setting is switched from Wrightsville, U.S.A. to an 80-room baronial estate in Alsace, but almost the entire plot structure of Queen's novel is preserved intact. And yet the film is an absolute disaster: slow, boring, unbearably pretentious in its symbolism, almost completely dehumanized except for the figure of Piccoli, whose evocation of somber and humane rationality is probably the closest cinematic rendering of the "real" Ellery there is. The trouble is that in Queen's novel the symbolic meanings become apparent only near the end and grow out of a wealth of thousands of realistic social and psychological details, whereas Chabrol sets the film in an abstract universe like the chessboard world of *The Player on the Other Side* and forces us to live with the heavy-handed symbolism and nothing else for a full 100 minutes, with never a breath of humanity except for Piccoli's performance. I found the film unbearable and cannot recommend it to any Queenians except those who might wish to suffer through it as Carlyle said he read the Koran, out of a sense of duty.

We must conclude, in short, that to date there has been no satisfactory visual evocation of Queen's abundant universe, although there have been a few worthwhile elements in the better Queen films and teleseries so far. Is there something about the Queen canon that defies translation into cinematic terms? I prefer to hope that the future will serve Queen better in this respect than the past.

CHAPTER FIVE

PERHAPS THE MOST STRIKING THING ABOUT QUEEN'S ACTIVITIES during the late 1930's is their staggering diversity. In addition to a novel a year, an occasional short story, scholarly and bibliophilic work, three screenwriting stints in Hollywood and an unfortunate attempt at a stage play,[1] Dannay and Lee somehow found time to branch out into a new medium that was about to enter its Golden Age: dramatic radio.

The cousins' radio work began in obscurity with a number of uncredited scripts for programs like *Alias Jimmy Valentine* and *The Shadow*, which paid them next to nothing but did permit them to develop some proficiency in the medium. Then they became involved in what Dannay still considers one of the most fascinating experiments in radio history. For about six months early in 1939 the cousins served as permanent panelists on a show they themselves created called *Author! Author!*, with Ogden Nash and later S. J. Perelman moderating. Each program would open with a brief dramatization of some inexplicable event: for example, a man walks into a jeweler's shop, offers one dollar for a clearly priced $500 watch, and the manager instantly accepts. At such a climax the curtain would fall, and the moderator would challenge each of the four panelists— Dannay, Lee, and two guests who varied from week to week—to devise on the spot a set of circumstances that would make sense of the scene. After the ad lib creation, each panelist would proceed to attack the others' constructions and defend his own. The whole concept of the show presupposed an absurdly mechanical approach to storytelling, but everyone seemed to have a good time, and the guest panelists included such distinguished names as Moss Hart, George S. Kaufman, Mark Van Doren and Dorothy Parker. *Author! Author!* was broadcast coast-to-coast for six months before being canceled for lack of a sponsor. But the memory of those weekly fun-and-games sessions led Dannay to reminisce about the show with loving nostalgia in several *EQMM* editorial prefaces, and in the late Sixties even inspired a new series of Ellery Queen short stories in which, as we'll see in Chapter 12, the framework of the show was reconstructed fictionally.

If *Author! Author!* was a pleasant by-way in the Queenian radio career, the main road was Queen's translation of his own universe into the form of radio drama. *The Adventures of Ellery Queen* debuted over the CBS network on June 18, 1939 with a one-hour script by Queen entitled "The Adventure of the Gum-Chewing Millionaire," directed by George Zachary. This was the first hour-long dramatic show in the history of radio. Hugh Marlowe (who later repeated the role on TV) played Ellery, Santos Ortega was the Inspector, and Sergeant Velie was portrayed by Ted de Corsia. There was also a new permanent resident in the Queen "family," a pert secretary named Nikki Porter (originally played by Marian Shockley) whom the cousins created in order to attract the female audience to the show. Nikki remained with the radio series throughout its duration, entered the Queen movies in 1940, and appears in two Queen novels, *There Was an Old Woman* and *The Scarlet Letters*, as well as in the short story collection *Calendar of Crime.*

The amazing thing about Nikki is that each time we meet her she has a different physical appearance and a different personal history. On radio she seems to have been a blonde, and according to the "Gum-Chewing Millionaire" play she was a professional typist to whom Ellery had been taking his near-illegible manuscripts until she decided to do both herself and Ellery a favor by asking for a job as his full-time secretary so that he could dictate to her instead. In the Columbia movies she was portrayed by brunette Margaret Lindsay, and in the novelizations of those movies there is mention of her "brown wavy hair," and according to the first of the Columbia films, *Ellery Queen, Master Detective* (1940), she and Ellery met not over a manuscript but over John Braun's body. *There Was an Old Woman* (1943) tells us that Ellery did not meet Nikki until the Potts murder case, and describes her as "a small slim miss with nice red hair." She is still a redhead in *The Scarlet Letters* (1953) but according to that novel she spent her girlhood in Kansas City and differs in several other respects from the three earlier Nikkis. We will pass over in silence the question whether these are mere oversights or Queen's way of paying tribute to the "infinite variety" of woman.

For about four months the hour-long Queen show remained on the air without sponsorship, presenting such adventures as "Napoleon's Razor," "George Spelvin's

Murderer" and "The Three R's." Each episode was interrupted at a point corresponding to that at which the Challenge to the Reader appeared in the early Queen novels, so that a distinguished guest could play detective in the studio and attempt to deduce the culprit before Ellery expounded his solution. Among the early guests were photographer Margaret Bourke-White and playwright Lillian Hellman, who according to a newsmagazine report (*Time*, 10/23/39) solved the mystery of Napoleon's razor in a nick. Late in October, at a time when the show was threatened with cancellation for lack of a sponsor, a water hose burst in the transmitter cooling system of Chicago station WBBM, forcing the Queen program off the air nine minutes before the end of "The Mother Goose Murders." The station received literally thousands of calls from listeners demanding to be told the identity of the murderer, which proved more conclusively than any poll could do that the program was pulling in a large and enthusiastic audience.

The demonstration attracted a sponsor for the show in due course, and on April 28, 1940 the series, now reduced to a half-hour format, began its commercial career for Gulf Oil with "The Adventure of the Double Triangle." Ellery and Nikki were played by a variety of performers over the next several years, but Ortega and de Corsia kept their respective roles of Richard Queen and Sergeant Velie until September 1947, when the show moved to Hollywood. During its nine years of radio life the program migrated from CBS to NBC and its sponsorship shifted from Gulf Oil to Bromo Seltzer and Anacin. The last new script, "The Adventure of Misery Mike," was broadcast on May 20, 1948, and on May 27 the very last Queen show, a repeat of an earlier script, was aired.

Throughout most of the program's nine-year life, every script was written by Dannay and Lee. But near the end, Dannay's workload as editor of *EQMM* and his desire to return to prose fiction led him to withdraw from the radio show, and the final scripts were co-authored by Lee and several uncredited collaborators, including Anthony Boucher. Out of these hundreds of radio plays sixteen survive in printed dramatic form and three others in form fairly close to the original. In addition, at least six more plays are available on tape from the collections of various radio buffs. For those who were too young to appreciate the original radio series or whose fathers preferred a rival program at the same time, these printed scripts and tape transcriptions are the only approach there is to Queen as a radio writer.

Frankly, few of the surviving radio plays are as good as even the mediocre Queen novels and stories. But we can't restrict an artist to two or three colors and expect him to equal the best paintings he did with a full palette, and neither can we fairly compare Queen's radio work with his prose fiction. The proper standard of comparison is with other writers' radio mysteries, and judged beside such others as I have read or heard, Queen's are far better than many, as good as most of the best, and surpassed only by some of John Dickson Carr's and Cornell Woolrich's scripts for *Suspense*. And, all questions of merit aside, Queen's radio work shows us vividly how a prolific creative mind under high pressure reshapes motifs from earlier writings into new forms.

The best place to begin is with the first two plays from the one-hour series, which exist today only as novelets. "The Adventure of the Last Man Club" and "The Adventure of the Murdered Millionaire" were published, in 1940 and 1942 respectively, as Whitman

Better Little Books, with the story on the left-hand pages and line-drawing illustrations on the right. (The two were reprinted in one volume without illustrations as *The Last Man Club,* Pyramid pb #R-1835, 1968.) The prose versions were not written by Queen and were couched in a painfully infantile style. "Reaching the door, Ellery tried the handle. It gave! Opened! The door Peter Jordan always kept locked was—UNLOCK-ED!" But buried beneath such unappetizing narrative are the authentic Queen radio originals, and we will judge them purely as radio plays.

"The Adventure of the Last Man Club," the second Queen radio play to go on the air, is one of the very best of the dramas that survive. Ellery and Nikki witness a hit-and-run death and are caught up by the dying man's last words into the affairs of a survivor-take-all club the victim belonged to. Ellery's solution is perfectly fair to the reader/listener and the clues are neat and subtle. The play's historical importance is that it's the earliest surviving example in Queen's radio work of the mislead-ing dying message, and the first appearance in any form of Queen's dwindling tontine motif. Certain elements of the solution are derived from *The Greek Coffin Mys-tery* and "The House of Darkness" but Queen reworks them superbly into the new context.

"The Adventure of the Murdered Millionaire," the first to be broadcast of all the Queen radio plays, is no-where near as good, though it starts out intriguingly as Ellery receives a friendly letter from a man he has never met, asking him to recommend a nurse, and is thereby entangled in the fatal bludgeoning of a crippled, gum-chewing, will-changing old tyrant. The central puzzle, here as in *The Four of Hearts,* is that no one seems to have had motive for the crime. But here the problem is handled rather poorly. Ellery never even considers the possibility that someone might have *erroneously believed* he would benefit from the old man's will, and the killer's actual motive is transposed from *The Dragon's Teeth* into a new framework where it fails to function convincingly. As for the solution, since Queen neglected to close his circle (i.e. to establish that the killer must be one of the people we have met in the story), Ellery's deduction that only one person within the circle possesses the characteristic he has determined the murderer must possess proves less than nothing. However, the play is historically interesting for its casual reference to how Nikki first entered the Queen household.

Between 1942 and 1944 ten Queen radio plays were reprinted in *Ellery Queen's Mystery Magazine,* beginning with "The Adventure of the Frightened Star" (Spring 1942), which deals with the locked-room death of a mysteriously "retired" Hollywood actress. The central plot device comes straight out of *The American Gun Mystery,* with the same massive defect it possessed in that novel; and Ellery's principal deduction, which presupposes the listener's knowledge of the workings of the World War II Postal Savings System, has been deprived of what fairness it originally had by dint of the passage of time.

"The Adventure of the Meanest Man in the World" (July 1942) opens with the staggering coincidence that both Ellery and Nikki are impaneled as jurors in the same murder trial. Impoverished defendant Will Keeler seems to have been the only one who could have plunged the paperknife into the back of skinflint Sylvester Gaul's neck, but Ellery, interpreting the evidence more rigorously, jumps out of the jury box, cross-examines witnesses himself, and extracts a confession in open court out of the real murderer. Queen's outrageous notions of courtroom procedure wound but do not kill an interesting plot, akin to but creatively different from the second murder in *The Dutch Shoe Mystery*.

In "The Adventure of the Mouse's Blood" (September 1942) Ellery happens to be outside the house where a blackmailer is stabbed to death by one of the four athletes who were to have made payoffs to him that night. As in "The Meanest Man in the World," Ellery's solution is based on deductions as to the left- and right-handedness of the suspects.

"The Adventure of the Good Samaritan" (November 1942) poses an unusual problem as Ellery tries to find the anonymous benefactor who has been sending stolen hundred-dollar bills to the needy tenants in a certain tenement building. Ellery works out the Samaritan's identity by original and cogent reasoning but never satisfactorily explains how the fellow engineered the elaborate cover-up for himself that he did.

In "The Adventure of the Fire-Bug" (March 1943) Ellery investigates a series of suspicious fires in his neighborhood, each of which destroyed a building owned by the same man. The fairness of his solution depends on how much high-school physics one remembers.

"The Adventure of the Man Who Could Double the Size of Diamonds" (May 1943) is the most unwieldy title but also one of the best radio plays in the entire series. The "impossible" theft from a locked vault is a brilliant adaptation of a device in Chesterton's "The Wrong Shape" that Queen transforms into a highly personal piece of misdirection. Ellery's comment about his adversary, "He devised a theft of such colossal simplicity that I was nearly taken in by the complicated props," is equally applicable to Queen himself.

"The Adventure of the Murdered Ship" (July 1943) is, at least from the perspective of thirty years later, a silly and frightening piece of war propaganda against "loose talk," i.e. saying anything to anyone that has not been released or approved by Big Brother. Ellery is asked by a nameless high official to find out how the slimy subs of the filthy Japs were able to ambush an American convoy on the high seas, and why the captured enemy commander was carrying the words "Ellery Q" on his person. After traveling all over the country and interviewing literally thousands of people, he arbitrarily pieces together three little scraps of "loose talk" out of the millions of words he has heard, assumes that the countless Axis agents assumed to be in our midst could do and had done the same, and thereby caps a little morality play about how the slip of a lip can literally sink a ship. The last few lines of the play deserve quotation in full.

> OFFICIAL: Yes, if people would only remember not to talk about anything, but what they hear over the radio or read in their newspapers!
> INSPECTOR (Quietly): We're all prone to be offenders once in a while, Sir. But we mustn't be—ever.
> NIKKI: I'll make the resolution to keep my mouth shut—right now!
> VELIE: That goes double.
> ELLERY: Amen.
> (The music comes up.)

When "Murdered Ship" was reprinted in Leslie Charteris' anthology *The Saint's Choice, Volume 7:*

Radio Thrillers (Hollywood: Saint Enterprises, 1946),
it was prefaced by a letter to Charteris which explained
the genesis of this and several other similar Queen plays.

> This was a 'command performance,' so to
> speak, by the OWI, with whom we co-operated
> in the 'loose talk' campaign. As a special as-
> signment from Washington, it represents—we
> think—something superior in radio propagan-
> da, inasmuch as it doesn't bat its audience
> over the head, but approaches the lesson
> through entertainment.
>
> This sort of program, serving a higher pur-
> pose than mere commercial entertainment,
> surely deserves being anthologized.

An entry in the war diary of George Orwell, who was
writing similar material in England at the same time,
provides the best comment on these lines. "All propaganda is lies, even when one is telling the truth."

In "The Adventure of the Blind Bullet" (September 1943) the war is forgotten and Ellery's job is to
protect a ruthless tycoon from an anonymous enemy
who has threatened to kill the magnate at a precise
minute of a precise day. The play is thus historically
important as a rough sketch for certain aspects of *The
King Is Dead*. But the threat is carried out in a pitch-
black railroad tunnel under the Queens' noses, and Ellery's main problem is determining how the killer could
see his victim in the dark, so that in essence the play is
little more than a rewrite of "The House of Darkness"
with the same gimmick.

"The Adventure of the One-Legged Man" (November 1943) is another morality play against "loose talk"

and in favor of war. (VELIE: "See those cannon?"
NIKKI: "Makes you feel all proud inside.") Fortunately, amid the OWI propaganda there is a neat little problem about one-legged tracks in the snow within a sealed
courtyard, one of the better puzzles in the Queen radio
canon.

The final play to be published in *EQMM*, "The
Adventure of the Wounded Lieutenant" (July 1944), is
another diatribe on the subject of loose talk. This time
the military catastrophe takes place in the China-Burma-
India theatre, and once again Ellery demonstrates that
enemy ears are ever waiting to connect scraps of casual
chat into the plans for the Normandy invasion.

Eight more Queen plays were published during the
Forties in various anthologies, collections and magazines.
The first of these to appear in print was "The Adventure
of the Mark of Cain" in *The Pocket Mystery Reader,*
edited by Lee Wright (Pocket Books pb #172, 1942),
in which Ellery, Nikki, the Inspector and Sergeant Velie
masquerade as servants in an attempt to prevent murder
among the heirs of eccentric millionaire John Cain.
After a full complement of clichés such as the gloomy
mansion with the lights not working and the enigmatic
servant who prowls in the night, a murder is indeed committed. It turns out the killer knew four detectives were
in the house, had no assurance that they would not
observe or interfere, yet proceeded to commit a murder
for grossly inadequate motives. Ellery's solution rests on
an interesting creative variant of the ticket-book clue in
The Tragedy of X.

"The Disappearance of Mr. James Phillimore,"
printed in Queen's suppressed 1944 anthology *The Misadventures of Sherlock Holmes,* I would rank as Queen's
finest radio play known to me. It's a superbly mounted

specimen of the impossible problem, based on Dr. Watson's famous cryptic reference to the man who returned to his house for an umbrella and was never seen again. Ellery, confined to bed, functions as armchair detective, devising wonderful suggestions as to how Phillimore could have vanished from a house surrounded by police, and finally topping even the best of them with his magnificent analysis of how the trick was actually worked.

In the disappointing "Ellery Queen, Swindler," which appears in Queen's 1945 anthology *Rogues' Gallery*, a respectable jeweler named Humperdinck bamboozles one of his employees out of $4000, the only hint of motivation being that the time is 1942 and Humperdinck's first name is Adolf. Ellery, with the equally unmotivated help of a certain Monsieur Jallet (in 1942 a good Frenchman needed no motive for entering the lists against an Adolf), works out a jewel-switching maneuver to get the young man's money back.

In 1945 there also appeared the most difficult to come by of all Queen collections, *The Case Book of Ellery Queen* (Bestseller pb #B59). Five of the eight items in this paperback collection are reprints from the two earlier collections, the *Adventures* and *New Adventures*, but the last three are radio plays never published in any other printed form, not even in *EQMM*. The first of these happens to be the first half-hour Queen play broadcast on radio, "The Double Triangle," which is by no means a great play but which ties together so many strands from so many earlier Queen works that to the student of Queen's development it's a source of endless fascination. Ellery tries to locate the anonymous lover who is romancing the wife of a volatile young bookkeeper; for his efforts to keep the lover from being murdered by the husband he winds up almost an eye-witness to the murder of the wife. The clue is based on the ways in which a man puts away clothes differently from a woman—a situation handled here so as to form the exact reverse of the pattern in *The French Powder Mystery*. The female who impersonates a male she wants to incriminate is derived from *The Dutch Shoe Mystery* and its reversal in *Halfway House*. The triangular burn in Tyler Monroe's camel's hair coat will remind readers of the similar rip in Rhys Jardin's coat in *The Devil to Pay*.

In "The Invisible Clock" Ellery and Nikki attend a society ball in order to keep watch on the hostess' price-less ruby, which to no reader's surprise disappears during the evening. The clue is a clock that is heard ticking where no clock exists, and the solution depends on a device called a "radio nurse" which Queen assumes is well known to the audience. And in the third *Case Book* radio play, "Honeymoon House," love rivalries among the offspring of munitions manufacturers lead to a bride's murder on her wedding night. Ellery admits that his solution is largely conjectural, and the problem is weak compared to those in Queen's best radio plays.

The last two of those plays to be published are also perhaps the hardest to come by. "The Invisible Clue," printed in Margaret Cuthbert's anthology *Adventures in Radio* (Howell Soskin, 1945) starts out beautifully with a terrified letter asking Ellery to wake the writer up at seven o'clock the next morning. Thus the great man walks into the case of the invisible persecutor, reminiscent of Chesterton's famous story "The Invisible Man" but without GKC's philosophic overtones, and solves it appropriately enough by means of the titular invisible (that is, negative) clue, although I find it incredible that the victim wouldn't have thought of the answer himself while he was being exhaustively questioned. Finally, in "The Adventure of the Curious Thefts" (condensed in *Story Digest,* September 1946), a well-known novelist whose marriage is at the crack-up point goes to Ellery when a rash of bizarre pilferings breaks out in his household, culminating in murder. The solution presupposes a fairly intimate knowledge of the Bible but has great historical importance as a rough sketch for certain elements in *Ten Days' Wonder.*

If the nineteen printed Queen radio plays are a mixed bag, running the gamut from excellent to indifferent, so too are the miscellaneous episodes that circulate in tape-recorded form among radio buffs. "The Mischief Maker," originally broadcast on January 15, 1944, is a routine little exercise giving Ellery the task of finding out who is writing a sequence of poison-pen letters to the residents of a single apartment building—in effect, the exact obverse of the problem in "The Good Samaritan." The motivation for the letter-writing binge turns out to be ridiculous, and I think Queen's reputation will survive without having this trifle preserved in print. Nor can I mourn the unavailability of "The Three Frogs," from about the same period. This one deals with Nikki Porter's miraculous reformation of a totally implausible juvenile delinquent whom she finds hiding in her new apartment, and with Ellery's quest for the identity of a modern Fagin known as The Frog who has organized a youth gang for criminal purposes. The crucial deductions are clever enough but rather easily anticipated by the listener. But I wish some publisher would let Queen's millions of fans share "The Adventure of Dead Man's Cavern" from 1944 or '45. Ellery is invited up to an Adirondack lodge near where a multiple strangler had operated a hundred years before, observes the tensions among his fellow guests and hostess, and neatly resolves the "locked-cave" strangulation of a psychic investigator by reasoning that creatively varies the climactic deductions in *The Egyptian Cross Mystery*. And in the equally excellent play "The Armchair Detective" from 1947 or '48, Ellery solves a poisoning on the Queen radio show itself. Queen hints at but never follows up the parallel with Orson Welles' famous version of *The War of the Worlds* which convinced panicked thousands that the Martians had invaded Earth. But the dying-message situation in this play is a neat spinoff from first-period Queen, with Ellery first interpreting the message in the obvious way, then getting fancy and working out a much more involved interpretation, whose possibility the killer has also seen and planted evidence to support.

"The Armchair Detective" is the latest script from *The Adventures of Ellery Queen* which I've been able to hear, but we aren't through yet with Ellery as airwaves investigator. In 1948, the last year of the show's radio run, two of the medium's many dramatic anthology series broadcast Queen radio plays which had never been heard on the *Adventures* show. One of these, "Nick the Knife," heard on *Mystery Playhouse* January 4, 1948, ranks among Queen's best radio dramas in its own right and is historically crucial as a forerunner of his masterpiece, *Cat of Many Tails*. The serial criminal in this version has slashed the wrists and faces of over thirty beautiful women on the night streets of the city. Finally a woman is attacked inside an ornamental maze with only one exit, watched by Ellery and several policemen. Subsequent events seem to prove conclusively that not one of the handful of suspects found in the maze can possibly be the slasher. Ellery resolves the dilemma beautifully, although most listeners would probably, as I did, fall into the trap for the too clever that Queen cunningly built into the story. Later in 1948 the original Queen radio director, George Zachary, reassembled the initial cast of Hugh Marlowe, Santos Ortega and Ted de Corsia for a final hour-long adventure, broadcast on the Sunday afternoon *Ford Theater.* "The Adventure of the Bad Boy" is constructed out of a large number of elements from very early Queen stories. The old brownstone overlooking Washington Square complete with secret room and vicious old matriarch and precocious little boy are derived from *The Tragedy of Y,* while the topper found on the murder scene recalls *The Roman Hat Mystery* and the vaudeville magician reminds us of "The Hanging Acrobat." Ellery's problem is to solve the murder of the hateful Sarah Brink who was poisoned by arsenic in a serving of rabbit stew and found dead in her bed with several dozen live bunnies loose in the room. I still can't understand how under the circumstances the one portion of rabbit stew could be safe to eat and the other deadly, and a simple phone call to the police prior to the first scene would have stopped the plot in its tracks. But the whole enterprise is diverting, and Brad Barker is quite good as the eight-year-old boy whose fantasies of intrigue and death suddenly become real.

So much for the visible and audible remains of Queen's work as a radio writer, comprising almost a play a week for nine years on top of all the other work Queen was doing in the Forties—not least of which is his work as editor, anthologist, bibliographer and scholar of his chosen genre, which we shall next consider.

CHAPTER SIX

QUEEN THE EDITOR, ANTHOLOGIST, SCHOLAR AND BIBLIOGRA-
pher has been even more prolific than Queen the author,
turning out more books of other people's fiction over
the years than volumes of his own. Although his contributions to these fields range from 1933 to the present,
they can best be taken into account in a single chapter.

After almost five years of writing novels about Ellery Queen and Drury Lane, Queen in 1933 undertook
his first venture as an editor, a magazine called *Mystery
League* that folded after four issues. In the words of
Manfred B. Lee: "*Mystery League* Magazine was the
child of the Queen imagination and early ambition. It
was published on the proverbial shoelace . . . and [Fred
Dannay and myself] were its entire staff. . . ; we did
not even have a secretary. We selected the stories, prepared copy, read proofs, dummied, sweated, . . . and
almost literally swept out the office as well." The four
issues are dated October 1933 through January 1934, a
fifth number having been assembled but never printed.
Those four legendary issues are today virtually unobtainable, even from rare-book dealers who specialize in

crime fiction, so for the convenience of Queenians I will list their contents in an Appendix. "All this was some thirty-five years or so ago, and the pain is only just beginning to ebb," Lee wrote in 1969. But in the process of sweating over *Mystery League* Queen picked up a liberal education in editorial arts which would be put to excellent use a few years later with the founding of *EQMM*.

Midway between *Mystery League* and *EQMM* came the first of Queen's dozens of anthologies, *Challenge to the Reader* (1938), in which he laid down his editorial credo that an anthology should not be simply a miscellaneous grab-bag of short stories but should "possess a unique central idea to hold it together, to differentiate it from any other anthology ever published." In *Challenge* Queen's structural principle was to change the name of each of the twenty-five detectives who appear therein and leave it to the reader to identify both the detective and the author of each story. The unfortunate and unforeseen result was that the book was cut off from any conceivable audience: those who had never before read any detective stories could not play Queen's identification game, and for those who had read even a few the game was too simple to play, especially since the names of supporting characters like Lestrade, Flambeau and Sergeant Velie remained unchanged. It took the publisher several years to sell out the original edition of *Challenge to the Reader*.

For the next few years Queen continued to build up his library of books of short crime fiction until it became the finest in the world. Then during 1940 and 1941 he literally stopped publishing new prose fiction, devoting all of his energies (except, of course, for chores like a weekly radio play) to the twin cornerstones of his editorial career, the finest mystery magazine and the finest mystery anthology ever published.

Ellery Queen's Mystery Magazine exploded onto the scene in the fall of 1941, its premiere issue featuring such luminaries as Hammett, Allingham, T. S. Stribling, Anthony Abbot, Woolrich, and an unrepentant rascal going by the name of Queen. The second issue boasted the bylines of Christie, Household, Stuart Palmer, Starrett, Sayers and Steve Fisher, and the third included stories by Freeman, Ben Hecht, Edgar Wallace, Futrelle and Michael Arlen. The pattern was clear: Queen was going to publish the widest diversity of stories and writers available. Old and new, pulp and slick, originals and reprints, hardboiled and ultra-intellectual, locked rooms and gang wars and damsels-in-distress; stories by professionals and debutants, stories set in every corner of the globe and at every time including the remote past and the remote future; stories written by North and South Americans, Britons, continental Europeans, Africans—the only constant that Queen demanded was quality.

Although he had published original stories before, in mid-1945 Queen took a giant step in encouraging the creation and submission to *EQMM* of first-rate new stories by announcing an annual prize contest for the best new work published in the magazine and a new series of annual hardcover anthologies for the preservation of those best beyond the short life of a magazine issue. With both the prestige of publication in *EQMM* and the generous cash prizes as incentives, it is unsurprising that the roster of authors appearing in just the first few volumes of *The Queen's Awards* is a virtual catalogue of greats of the genre: Carr, Charteris, Innes, Rice, Kenneth Millar (Ross Macdonald), Helen McCloy, Edmund

Crispin, Clayton Rawson and Ngaio Marsh, to name only a few. That the same three or four contents pages also boast the names of William Faulkner and Jorge Luis Borges[1] will surprise only those who put crime fiction and literature in separate watertight compartments. Thus *EQMM* passed majestically through the years, each issue a superbly diverse treat, rich in fine fiction and (until about 1955) in Queen's extensive editorial commentary. Note that I said fiction, not crime fiction; for in a deliberate effort to stretch the bounds of the genre, Queen included in *EQMM* an abundance of excellent stories—often by front-rank literary figures—that had only the vaguest relation to the mystery field as such. At the same time he attracted, encouraged and virtually collaborated with dozens of fledgling writers and eventually adopted a policy, still in effect, of printing one "first story" in every issue of *EQMM*. And at the same time he continued to unearth long-buried gems by the likes of Hammett, Christie and Woolrich; to promote the work of unclassifiable mavericks like L. J. Beeston and Vincent Cornier; to keep the old reliables, the Hugh Pentecosts and Q. Patricks and so many others, sending him tales both old and new; and even to reprint chapters from an autobiographical novel called *The Golden Summer* by a rascal signing himself Daniel Nathan.

Anthony Boucher in "There Was No Mystery in What the Crime Editor Was After" (*New York Times Book Review*, 2/26/61; *EQMM* 6/61) pointed out that each issue is edited to satisfy Queen's own taste. Indeed not only has Queen worked "almost collaboratively" with his authors to bring out their stories' full potential, but themes and motifs from Queen's own universe recur with awesome frequency in *EQMM* stories signed by others. Thus we find writers as far apart as Dashiell

Hammett and A. H. Z. Carr doing stories that emphasize
the Queenian theme of the affinity between the poetic
and the ratiocinative mind. Thus we find subtle echoes
of *Ten Days' Wonder* in a recent story by Hugh Pentecost, and subtle echoes of Dannay and Lee themselves
in a recent tale by Isaac Asimov. Thus we find literally
dozens of stories reflecting in one form or another
Queen's theme of "the lovely past": historical detective
stories, parodies or pastiches or variations on the Old
Masters, tales set in a quaint old club. I won't speculate
on how much of all this we should attribute to sheer
coincidence, to the conscious design of Queen, or to the
minds of shrewd authors out to sell to *EQMM*, but the
fact remains that the Queenian universe has overflowed
considerably into the writings of others.

In recent years the magazine has been printing far
more new stories and far fewer unsung high-quality reprints than in the past. This would seem to be attribut-
able to Queen's twin convictions that the well of undis-
covered old treasures has run near dry, and that in a
time when economic factors have come close to extin-
guishing the mystery short story he must preserve a
market for currently active writers and a sort of literary
sanctuary for an endangered species. Thanks to Queen's
encouragement and persistence, there is still a home for
the superb parodies of Jon L. Breen, the photographical-
ly realistic stories of Joe Gores, the cockeyed-wondrous
fantasies of James Powell, and such intensely personal
crime tales as Cornell Woolrich's "New York Blues" and
Stanley Ellin's "The Payoff." I can't conceive that any
serious student of the genre would deny that *EQMM*
over its more than thirty years of life has been the best
and most influential periodical of its kind in the world.

A few months after the first issue of *EQMM* saw

the light of print, Queen published his second and by all
standards greatest hardcover anthology, *101 Years' Entertainment: The Great Detective Stories 1841-1941,*
which is still in print as a Modern Library Giant. In this
book Queen intended to "paint a whole picture of what
the First Hundred Years have brought forth," for which
purpose he included stories by Poe and Doyle, Chesterton and Freeman and Post and Leblanc, and such
masters and mistresses of the Golden Age as Allingham,
Sayers, Berkeley, Carr, Christie (three stories!), and
Queen himself. Of the American pulp tradition only
Hammett appears, and he with a story from the *American Magazine* rather than from the pulps;[2] but aside
from this under-representation of the *Black Mask* school
101 Years' is a virtually perfect summation of short
crime fiction from Poe down to its own time, and
Queen's introduction and prefatory notes, at once
scholarly and charming, are as rewarding in their own
way as the stories. Aside from the title's fleeting allusion
to the *Arabian Nights,* also known as the *1001 Nights'
Entertainment,* the only principle of organization in *101
Years'* is the intrinsic quality of the stories—which suggests, I think, that a proper anthology does not require
the kind of central motif that Queen in *Challenge to the
Reader* and elsewhere has held to be necessary. Indeed
the majority of Queen's subsequent anthologies lack
such a structural device.

The resounding success of *101 Years'* insured that
Queen would do more anthologies, and so he did, at the
rate of one a year for the next several years. In *Sporting
Blood* (1942) he assembled twenty sports detective
stories, briefly prefaced by Grantland Rice. Doyle,
Chesterton, Sayers, Bentley, Christie, Charteris and
Queen himself (three stories!) are well represented and

the entire package is attractive, scholarly and meaty. Its successor, *The Female of the Species* (1943), was even more generous in size, with 420 pages devoted to (Women's Lib take note) the great female detectives and criminals. Although the authors are by and large more contemporary than the contributors to *Sporting Blood*— including Christie, Rinehart, Eberhart, Vickers, Palmer and Boucher—such old-timers as Fergus Hume and John Kendrick Bangs are also in evidence, for the pleasuring of more antiquarian palates.

The following year's masterpiece, *The Misadventures of Sherlock Holmes* (1944), consisted of 33 parodies, pastiches or variations of the Master by a host of distinguished figures from many literary fields, from Mark Twain, O. Henry and Bret Harte to Christie, Starrett and again Queen himself who is represented by that extraordinary radio play "The Disappearance of Mr. James Phillimore." This anthology was suppressed through the machinations of Adrian Conan Doyle, Sir Arthur's son and executor, and the few copies still available are among the most hotly sought of collectors' items.[3] In the first section of Queen's Introduction (pp. v-ix) Frederic Dannay evoked a poignant picture of his boyhood in Elmira beside "the gentle Chemung" and of his introduction to Sherlock Holmes at the feverish age of twelve. Queen later included this memoir in his book of shoptalk *In the Queens' Parlor* under the title "Who Shall Ever Forget?" and it has recently been reprinted in my anthology *The Mystery Writer's Art* and in Queen's own anthology *Ellery Queen's Mystery Bag*. For, being the first intimation of the "lovely past" theme that dominates so much of Queen's later novels, the reminiscence tells far more about Queen than about Holmes.

In his next anthology, *Rogues' Gallery* (1945), Queen added one more laurel to his editorial crown. His selection of 32 stories dealing with the great criminals of modern fiction is second only to *101 Years'* among all his anthologies. Sinclair Lewis, O. Henry and Arnold Bennett are only three of the distinguished of general letters who contribute, and among the greats of crime fiction we find Hammett, Bailey, Christie, Sayers, Edgar Wallace, Charteris and (each with a rare radio script) Carr and Queen.

This was the last of Queen's annual *patterned* anthologies. The same year, 1945, saw the first of his many unpatterned anthologies derived from *EQMM*, but these we shall consider separately a few paragraphs from now. His next patterned anthology was done as a favor for his colleagues in a newly-formed, obscure little club calling itself the Mystery Writers of America. Many lazy editors in the past had constructed books simply by asking each of two dozen or so well-known authors to select his own best story of a certain type: detection, horror, espionage, etc. In *Murder by Experts* (1947) Queen varied the formula—and made infinitely more work for himself—by canvassing the entire membership of MWA (much smaller then than now, of course) and soliciting each member's choice of five or six favorite short mysteries *by others*. The tasks of collation, elimination of the over-familiar, and cajoling each of the twenty members finally chosen to write an introduction to the story he selected, fell upon Queen, like a ton of bricks to judge from his exhausted comments on the project. But the end result was worth the nine months of Queenian labor.[4]   Among the riches of this outsize volume it's instructive to note that Helen McCloy chose a tale by her then-husband, Brett Halliday; that the atheistic Leslie Charteris selected one of Chesterton's Father Brown stories; that locked-room enthusiast Clayton Rawson opted for a sealed chamber exercise by John Dickson Carr, and Baynard Kendrick, creator of the blind detective Duncan MacLain, for an adventure of the first blind sleuth, Max Carrados, by Ernest Bramah.

Queen's final pair of patterned anthologies appeared almost two decades apart, and together form a fitting capstone to this aspect of his editorial career. *The Literature of Crime* (1950) brings together 26 short detective, mystery or crime stories by luminaries of general literature, including Hemingway and Faulkner, Lewis and Steinbeck, Lardner and Thurber, Stevenson, Dickens, Maugham and a host of others. Seventeen years later Queen matched the 1950 volume with *Poetic Justice* (1967) which contains 23 crime tales by distinguished poets, from Chaucer through Byron and Poe and Whitman to such contemporaries as Robert Graves and Dylan Thomas. There is an odd tone to these two anthologies, as if Queen were trying to refute the cultivated snobs of the Edmund Wilson variety, who proclaim themselves too intelligent to waste their time on mystery fiction, by the absurd argument that one mystery apiece (mystery in the broadest sense) by a few dozen poets and literary men guarantees the genre's respectability. But if these books are polemical they are also highly personal, especially *Poetic Justice* with its insistence on the affinity between the poetic and the deductive mind. Frederic Dannay, remember, is himself a poet.

Ever since the fall of 1941 and throughout the years of annual patterned anthologies Queen was also editing dozens of superb issues of *EQMM*. At times during the Forties he must have been sorely tempted to take the easy way out, throwing *EQMM* stories whole-

sale into his hardcover anthologies and reprinting the
contents of his anthologies in the pages of *EQMM*. He
did not succumb, and the overlap between *EQMM* 1941-
1945 and the patterned anthologies is minimal. As a
result Queen had an abundance of stories to choose
from when in 1944-1945 he edited his first non-thematic
anthologies since *101 Years'*. *Best Stories from Ellery
Queen's Mystery Magazine* (1944) and *To the Queen's
Taste* (1945) have no central motif but consist respectively of 23 and 36 tales from the magazine's first four
years. Of the 23 *Best Stories*, 12 are also reprinted in
To the Queen's Taste, 6 are replaced in *Taste* by other
tales from the same authors, and the remaining five and
their creators (Allingham, Boucher and Woolrich among
them) are completely unrepresented in *Taste*. Of the 36
stories in *Taste,* 12 come straight out of *Best Stories,* 6
are replacements for tales in *Best Stories,* and the remaining 18 are direct from *EQMM* and unrepresented in the
former anthology. Among the gems in *Taste* are excellent "lost" stories by Chesterton and Bentley, first-rate
contributions by Ambler and Cain and Stribling and
Twain, and the definitive parody of Raymond Chandler
by S. J. Perelman. More than a quarter century later
these two volumes still stand as worthy successors to
101 Years'.

In 1946 there appeared the first of the many volumes of *The Queen's Awards*, each containing the best
new *EQMM* stories of the year. Although both the
magazine and the hardcover annuals continue down to
the present, Queen in 1962 dropped the running title of
the anthology series and substituted individualized metaphorical titles such as Ellery Queen's *Crime Carousel,
Grand Slam,* and *Headliners*. But despite changes in
title, publisher, format and content over the years, the

quarter-century of *Awards* remains a unified and unsurpassable corpus of the best short crime fiction of its time.

Yet with a magazine of such high quality as *EQMM* it would have been unthinkable to preserve only a dozen or so stories a year in the relative permanence of an anthology. Therefore Queen worked out three strategies to bestow longer life on the stories he gathered together. First and historically most important was his series of original paperback collections of stories by individual authors, published by Mercury between 1944 and 1952. Within this series the most priceless from the literary standpoint was the Dashiell Hammett Octet—virtually the complete short stories of this giant of the genre, in eight slim and today almost unobtainable paperbacks. (A belated ninth collection, *A Man Named Thin,* appeared in 1962, bringing the last stragglers between covers.) Equally treasured by collectors of criminalia are the books of stories by Allingham, Carr, Palmer, Vickers and O. Henry which Queen edited under the Mercury imprint. In recent years Queen has added four new titles to this aspect of his work, a volume apiece of shorts by Erle Stanley Gardner, Lawrence Treat, Edward D. Hoch and Michael Gilbert; and one can only hope that he'll continue this noble endeavor.[5]

The second strategy was that of editing special out-of-sequence anthologies culled from *EQMM*. This was a less fruitful line of approach than the first, for it led only to two or three volumes, depending on how you count; but both (or all three) are of singularly high quality. In the "Living Library" volume *20th Century Detective Stories* (1948) Queen included obscure stories by Chesterton, Hammett, Christie, Stribling, Bentley, Carr, Boucher and others, capping the book with the first version of *Queen's Quorum,* a magnificent sixty-page bibliographic/critical guide to short detective fiction.   A revised version of the anthology (Popular Library pb #SP333, 1964) omits the *Quorum* and replaces eight of the fourteen stories from the original version with an equal number of more recent tales, most of them familiar from the annual *Awards* volumes. Finally and most recently has come *Ellery Queen's Mini-mysteries* (1969), a royally generous selection of the best short-short stories from *EQMM.*

The third and final strategy, to which I must confess some reservations, is that of reshuffling old and almost-new stories from *EQMM* into first annual and then semi-annual paperback anthologies issued by Davis Publications, and even into a short-lived series of volumes published by Dell and Pyramid. These items are thrown together by Pyramid so hastily and haphazardly that often when an introduction to a story is used at all, it is lifted verbatim from the *EQMM* issue or the earlier anthology in which the story appeared, without even the semblance of updating. Thus in *Ellery Queen's Mystery Jackpot* (Pyramid pb #T2207, 1970) one introduction states that a story by John Dickson Carr is included to celebrate his receiving the MWA Grand Master Award (an event that took place in 1963); another embodies a plea from Queen to Anthony Boucher, who died in 1968, to write more Nick Noble stories for *EQMM*; and a third refers four times in one paragraph to its own origin in one of the Davis semi-annual reshufflings. The stories in these reshufflings are almost always good if sometimes overfamiliar, and the present restriction of these volumes to the Davis series is at least a step in the right direction.

Finally we must pay brief tribute to Queen's contributions as scholar, bibliographer and raconteur. In 1942 he published *The Detective Short Story,* the ground-breaking bibliographic study of books of short detective fiction in the century after Poe. Then in 1951 he issued *Queen's Quorum* (expanded from the long essay in the 1948 version of *20th Century Detective Stories*), which is the unsurpassable evaluative work on the subject of short crime fiction. Finally, in *In the Queens' Parlor* (1957) he collected some of his fugitive writings and *EQMM* editorial shoptalk on matters bibliographic and criminous. All three of these volumes were reprinted in 1969 by Biblo & Tannen, the first and third being verbatim reprints but the new *Queen's Quorum* incorporating two new supplements (from *EQMM*, November and December 1968) which complete the coverage of books of short crime fiction through 1967. Queen's most recent scholarly endeavor is his long introduction to *The Celebrated Cases of Dick Tracy* (1970), in which he "proves," with what I think and hope is only mock-serious erudition, that Chester Gould's comic-strip cop was the first procedural detective in the genre.

Much of Queen's criminous commentary remains uncollected, buried in the issues of *EQMM* roughly from 1946 to 1955; if *In the Queens' Parlor* had sold decently, Dannay told me, there would have been a sequel in which this material would have been brought together. But an even greater abundance of Queenian creativity lies in his thousands of letters to authors and readers, in the writers' workshops in which he has taken part, in the courses he taught during his brief stint at the University of Texas, and in the innumerable conversations on his craft to which he has contributed. Those who have been privileged to talk with Queen, to see and hear him at work, have truly "been to the mountain" and can verify his inexhaustible creative energies. If Queen had done nothing his whole life long but what has been too briefly summarized in this chapter (and in this chapter, as I stated in the Introduction, "Queen" almost always refers to Frederic Dannay), his greatness would still have been assured. As surely as *EQMM* is The Magazine, Queen is The Editor.

CHAPTER SEVEN

CALAMITY TOWN *(1942) IS SUBTITLED "A NOVEL," NOT "A* Problem in Deduction." Ellery Queen is the central character, but he is not the same Ellery who solved the mysteries of the earlier Queen stories. He has dropped his pince-nez and polysyllables and is no longer a detached intellect resolving terrible events but a human being involved in and torn by them. This novel opens Queen's third period, in which the formal deductive problem merges with rounded characterization, superb writing, and intellectual and imaginative patterns of a depth long believed both impossible and inappropriate to crime fiction.

On the afternoon of August 6, 1940, Ellery steps off the train and into Wrightsville, a small tight-knit American community that with the outbreak of war in Europe has become a boomtown. He needs a place to stay where he can write a novel, but neither hotel rooms nor furnished houses are available—except for Calamity House. Old John F. and Hermione Wright, heads of Wrightsville's first family, had had the house built next door to their own home, planning to give the house as a

111

wedding present to their daughter Nora and her fiance, Jim Haight. But Jim had vanished from town the day before the wedding, and later a potential purchaser had dropped dead of a heart attack in the house itself, and the house developed a reputation as a jinx. Ellery rents it nevertheless, and is quickly lionized by the Wright family, and comes close to falling in love with the family's youngest daughter, Pat, who is herself on-again-off-again in love with county prosecutor Carter Bradford. And then Jim Haight comes back to town, and he and Nora are reconciled and married and move into the house built for them three years before, and little by little the marriage goes bad—threats, arguments, and the shadows of hints, slowly rising to near-certainty, that Jim Haight is planning to kill his wife.

Murder comes with the new year. At the traditional family party, one of the drinks with which the Wrights toast the beginning of 1941 is poisoned. Wrightsville's first homicide in twenty years tears apart both the Wright family and the town; indeed this is one of the very few novels which makes the reader feel what it would be like to have murder strike among loved ones. The investigation, the town's reaction, the sensational trial and the events thereafter are evoked not as pieces of a puzzle (although a fine plot is hidden among them) but as nightmare events happening to real people, and Ellery is simply one among these people, powerless to affect the events and making no contribution until the last chapter.

Several commentators on mystery fiction have written of *Calamity Town* as if it were a simple-minded tribute to the goodness of an unspoiled American community. Actually, however, Queen's Wrightsville is a fairly realistic microcosm of the United States, with plenty of rot and inhumanity and strife alongside all the grace and bucolic peace. And the bad qualities are not confined to selected citizens in black hats, like the bitterly jealous Frank Lloyd, and the kids who stone Jim Haight on the street, and Aunt Tabitha who runs out on the Wright family in its crisis. Such qualities are also evident in the "good" people, like Hermione Wright when she made her divorced daughter Lola an outcast. No one in this novel is overwhelmingly good, and almost no one is overwhelmingly bad, but some are clearly better than others, and the very few like Pat, who give fully of themsleves and expect nothing in return, are better than most.

However, *Calamity Town* is not only a novel of society but also and perhaps even primarily a novel of nature, and the rhythms of nature are at the heart of the book. The central imaginative pattern of the novel is a dialectic. *One: In the midst of life, death.* Nora Haight's illnesses come on Thanksgiving and Christmas, death strikes with the toast to the new year, Jim is arrested on St. Valentine's Day, Nora dies on Easter Sunday. *Two: In the midst of death, life.* The child born of Nora's dead body lives. The old trees in the cemetery sprout every spring "with sly fertility," as if nourished by the dead in their graves, "as if death were a great joke." Out of the horror of the full truth, revealed by Ellery on Mother's Day, comes the possibility of happiness for two young people and a baby. Ellery's explanation is itself counterpointed by quotations from Walt Whitman, the poet of nature's rhythms. The action of the novel covers nine months, the cycle of gestation.

One of the clearest evocations of this dialectic occurs at the very beginning of Chapter 28.

He was looking at the old elms before the new Courthouse. The old was being reborn in multitudes of little green teeth on brown gums of branches; and the new already showed weather streaks in its granite, like varicose veins.

There is sadness, too, in spring, thought Mr. Ellery Queen.

And so, even though the book ends on notes of hope, Queen gives us no cause to believe that this is anything more than another moment in the eternal alternation of nature's rhythms. Among all the giants of the genre Queen is the most somber in world-view, except for Cornell Woolrich.

In view of its central imaginative pattern, it's especially fitting that *Calamity Town* is itself the out-growth and flowering of Queen's far less successful experiments of 1936-1939. The long trial sequences are a considerable improvement over those in *Halfway House*, and the intuitiveness of much of Ellery's reasoning recalls *The Door Between*. The superb evocation of Wrightsville marks a tremendous advance over the picture of Hollywood in *The Four of Hearts,* which didn't work because its different facets canceled each other out. In *Calamity Town* Queen employs even more divergent facets than in the *Four* but remains in full control, playing them creatively upon each other so that they mutually reflect and illuminate.

Some mention should be made of a few of the influences on *Calamity Town* and of a few later works which the novel itself influenced. The volume which Dannay in conversation with me has stressed as most influential is Edgar Lee Masters' *Spoon River Anthology*

(1914-1916), that sardonic free-verse classic in which the dead of a "typical American town" speak their own stories from their graves. Both books do in fact share a similar bleak tone and outlook and a sense that everything changes, everything passes. But I believe that a deeper influence on *Calamity Town* was exerted by Thornton Wilder's famous play *Our Town* (1938), to which Queen obliquely refers on page 137 of his very next novel, *There Was an Old Woman*. Although *Our Town* takes place at the beginning of the century and has no criminous elements, it has much in common with *Calamity Town*. The physical description of Wrightsville contains many echoes of the tour through Grover's Corners at the beginning of Wilder's Act One, and in both works the graveyard is central to the author's vision and there is a similar intuition of the flux of life and a similar sense that beneath the superficially happy small-town existence of Middle America are bottomless "ignorance and blindness."

On the criminous level, the central influence on *Calamity Town* seems to have been Alfred Hitchcock's 1941 film *Suspicion,* to which Queen refers directly in his next novel but one, *The Murderer Is a Fox.* In both *Suspicion* and *Calamity Town,* a charming but mysterious male outsider marries a superficially unattractive girl whose family is at the top of the pecking order of a closed small-town society, and much of both stories deals with the corrosion of the marriage relationship and the fear that the husband is, for financial reasons, in process of murdering his wife.

Of course *Calamity Town*'s milieu, people, plot details, overall framework, and everything else about it are fully organic to Queen's own vision, not yanked bodily from any prior source but shaped in part by earlier work just as everything we say and do is shaped at least in part by what others have said and done before us. And just as our own words and actions shape the subsequent work of others, so *Calamity Town* seems to have been quite influential on later work in the mystery genre, and especially on another extraordinary film of Alfred Hitchcock, *Shadow of a Doubt* (1943), whose primary scenarist was—and this is not coincidence—Thornton Wilder. The town in *Shadow of a Doubt* bears some resemblance to Grover's Corners in *Our Town* but even more resemblance to Queen's Wrightsville. The girl Charlie in the film (played by Teresa Wright) is not like any character in *Our Town* but is a near-perfect cinematic image of Pat Wright in *Calamity Town,* even to the point that both girls' fathers are bankers. The theme of "ignorance and blindness" beneath small-town placidity takes several forms in the film, such as the idiot neighbor who keeps blatting about the corking good murder mystery he's just read, while a mass murderer is only a few feet away. Another example is in the last scene of the film, the town's glowing eulogy at the death of Uncle Charlie. A few years later came another magnificent suspense film that showed Queen's influence, Orson Welles' *The Stranger* (1946), in which again we find the insular New England town, the newcomer who marries the daughter of the local aristocracy, the corrosion of the marriage, the fear that husband will kill wife, the gallery of shrewd-seeming Yankee types blissfully ignorant of the horrific drama taking place around them.

So *Calamity Town* is not just an autonomous unit but an integral part of a great tradition. Queen took some things from predecessors, used them in ways suited to his own needs, added to them and shaped them into a work uniquely his own which then took its place in the

stream of tradition and itself served as source and influence for others' work and others' visions. This is what
it means to be a part of a cultural tradition, and it is fitting that the Queen work which has most influenced
others is also the choice of many as the greatest of
Queen's own works.

Dannay and Lee were uncertain that *Calamity
Town* with its radical departures from earlier Queen
books would be a success, so the next adventure of Ellery was deliberately planned as a return to the old
manner, rich in convoluted counterplotting and deductive masterstrokes. But despite this and other links to
the past, *There Was an Old Woman* (1943) is clearly unlike almost everything Queen had done in the Thirties,
and in some ways is even more radical than *Calamity
Town.* Previous Queen novels had integrated the formal
deductive problem into the woman's mystery (*The Door
Between*), the Hollywood novel (*The Four of Hearts*),
and regional Americana (*Calamity Town*). This time
Queen decided to merge the complex puzzle with a
relatively new development in crime fiction, the way-out
wacky mystery, which had been practiced by Alice Tilton and Craig Rice and Richard Shattuck and others in
the late Thirties and early Forties. Queen took this approach, molded it into highly personal form, and wound
up with the first sustained specimen of his private brand
of black humor.

In a recent interview in *Look*, Frederic Dannay
described this aspect of the Queen canon as "Ellery in
Wonderland." The technique rests on plunging the
quintessential man of reason into a milieu as mad as the
underside of Carroll's rabbit-hole and requiring him to
forge some sort of order out of the chaos. The Wonderland theme first appeared in Queen's 1934 short story

"The Mad Tea-Party," which is still Dannay's favorite among Ellery's short adventures, probably because of this very Wonderland aspect. The theme recurs every so often in Queen's two Hollywood novels of the Thirties and in the drinking-bout sequence of *The Dragon's Teeth*. But *There Was an Old Woman* is the first Queen novel to which the theme is central.

Through a chance meeting in a courtroom corridor, Ellery becomes caught in the tentacles of the crackpot Potts dynasty, proprietors of the largest shoe empire in the world. At the head of the clan is Cornelia Potts, seventy years old and with a heart that should have given out long ago, but still a matriarchal gargoyle *par excellence*. Squashed beneath the Potts shoes are Cornelia's six children, three by each of her two husbands. The older trio, fathered by the long vanished Bacchus Potts, wear their nuttiness, so to speak, on their sleeves. Horatio Potts lives in a gingerbread cottage full of children's toys, writes juvenile adventure stories, has completely dropped out from the adult world, and, in Ellery's words, is either the looniest or the sanest man alive. Louella Potts is a wild-haired crackbrain scientist living in a turreted tower and working feverishly on a formula for a plastic shoe that will put the Potts company out of business. Thurlow Potts is a tubby, foul-tempered troglodyte whose hobby is the filing of endless defamation suits against everyone who makes the slightest crack about the family. The three offspring by Cornelia's second marriage are also surnamed Potts— Cornelia forced her second husband to change his name to hers as a condition of the marriage—but they are normal, as normality goes in this world. The twin brothers Robert and Maclyn manage most of the Potts shoe empire. Their sister Sheila is in love with Charley Paxton, the family lawyer, but for a variety of reasons (fear of madness in the family, unwillingness to be disinherited by her mother) she refuses to marry him until Cornelia's heart shall have given out.

The case begins when little Thurlow, miffed at the court's dismissal of one of his daily defamation suits, announces that in the future he will wreak personal vengeance on whoever dares sully the glorious Potts name. Attorney Paxton enlists Ellery in a conspiracy to keep Thurlow from killing anyone, but that very evening the tubby terror climaxes a business argument with his half-brother Robert by challenging him to a pistol duel at dawn beneath the huge sculptured shoe on the grounds of the family's Riverside Drive estate. Ellery substitutes blanks for the live ammunition in the dueling weapons, but death strikes nevertheless, the first of a series of deaths within the potty family. Among the clues that pile up as the deadly farce proceeds are two pairs of twin pistols (one hidden in a bird's nest), a plate of cold soup beside a corpse, and a misplaced reverse pencil impression of a signature. Ellery disrupts the climactic wedding ceremony with an impromptu solution which throws off fireworks of virtuoso reasoning but demands perhaps too much technical knowledge of the reader. (Which reminds me that in the recent *Look* interview Dannay comments that Queen is "completely fair to the reader" and Lee qualified: "We are fair to the reader only if he is a genius.")

Certain motifs in the complex plot of *There Was an Old Woman* are intimately related to earlier and later elements we find in the Queen canon. The killer's use of another person as literally his living murder weapon, and the long-missing family member who never appears in his own person but just might be posing as someone else, will recur (far more satisfyingly) twenty years later in *The Player on the Other Side.* The family of grotesques cursed with a sort of metaphysical syphilis leading to madness goes back to *The Tragedy of Y* and reappears in various forms even into the Sixties. The account of Ellery's first meeting with Nikki Porter completely contradicts the two earlier accounts, in the first Queen radio play and Columbia's first Queen movie, and the fourth and final rendition of the meeting ten years later in *The Scarlet Letters.*

The idea of mixing Mother Goose and multiple murder goes back as least as far as S. S. Van Dine's masterpiece *The Bishop Murder Case* (1929) and was employed by writers as far apart as Agatha Christie and Richard Sale before Queen began to play his own variations on the theme. But Queen's novel is the only one of this sort I have read that can qualify in its own right as a novel of the Absurd. Joseph Heller himself might envy the stock-market maneuver scene in which the grieving Cornelia connives at making a tidy profit out of her son's death, or the "board of directors" sequence where the incompetent twerp Thurlow elects himself president of the Potts empire. At several points in the book the possibility of committing one or more of the family to an asylum is discussed, but the recurring objection is: They are not insane. Which is absurd in the light of what we've seen them doing, but that is exactly the point, mad is sane, sane is mad, and we've all tumbled into the rabbit-hole without knowing it.

Unhappily Queen's vision of the Absurd occupies only part of the book. The balance consists of a convoluted formal deductive problem, for purposes of which the absurd gargoyles of the Wonderland scenes simply shed their grotesque qualities and take their places as

figures in a typically solid Queen plot. (It's impossible
to believe that the dotty Thurlow could be the consum-
mate actor he needs to be when the book goes "serious.") As a result, *There Was an Old Woman* must ulti-
mately be judged a fascinating two-books-in-one, at odds
with itself at every step, with some fine individual sequences in both the novel-of-the-Absurd and the detective-story sections, but never adding up to an integrated
whole. To cite an apt phrase in the novel itself, it's "too
rich a mixture of sense and nonsense, a mixture too
thoroughly mixed."

By the time Dannay and Lee prepared to write
their next novel, *Calamity Town* had proved itself, and
so another Wrightsville case seemed called for. But in
order to provide that case they had to rewrite the town's
history slightly. In Chapter 14 of *Calamity Town* Chief
of Police Dakin had remarked to Ellery: "Ain't never
had a homicide in Wrightsville before, and I been Chief
here for pretty near twenty years." However, in *The
Murderer Is a Fox* (1945) Ellery probes a twelve-year-old
Wrightsville murder.

The time is the summer of '44, and the problem
grows out of the return of Captain Davy Fox to his home
town. Twelve years before, Davy's mother had died of
a dose of digitalis administered in a glass of grape juice,
and his father, who alone had opportunity, had been
convicted of her murder and sentenced to life imprison-
ment. Ten-year-old Davy had thereafter been raised by
his Uncle Talbot and Aunt Emily, and their adopted
daughter Linda became first a sister to Davy and later his
wife. Davy's adolescence had been a nightmare of failed
attempts to escape the stigma of his father's crime and
the fear of his own "tainted blood" and "killer instinct."
Then came the War, and two days after marrying Linda,

Davy had been sent as a fighter pilot to the China-Burma-India theater, where the blood of many men stained him. A series of unsigned letters arrive from home, intimating that Linda has been unfaithful, and upon his return to the States, nerve-shattered Davy finds himself wrestling with an uncontrollable compulsion to kill his wife. Linda, remembering the trouble in the Wright family, asks help of the man who had helped then—Ellery Queen. And Ellery concludes that the only way to release Davy from the trap in which the past holds him is to reopen the twelve-year-old murder case, to try to prove that Davy's father did not kill his mother and that he is not the son of a murderer.

Parts Two and Four of *The Murderer Is a Fox* deal with the investigation of Jessica Fox's death and might well have been subtitled The Detective As Historian. Ellery's loving and meticulous reconstruction of the exact events of June 14, 1932 in the house of Bayard and Jessica Fox is carried out with the historian's intellectual tools and generates the same sense of excitement that spurs the conscientious historian in his search for truth. To merge the detective story and historical reconstruction is a diabolically difficult feat (the classic work in this vein is Josephine Tey's 1951 *The Daughter of Time*), and a lesser artist than Queen would probably have fallen into the trap of gifting all or most of the parties to the ancient crime with implausibly photographic memories. But Queen skirts all the pitfalls, permits the witnesses to forget a great deal, and lets not a moment pass when someone's recollection of events seems after twelve years too precise. The book culminates, as do a large number of Queen novels since, in a false or partial solution which is followed by the true, final and stunning solution, although here as in *The Door Between*

Ellery's ultimate solution rests not on reasoning but on intuition in the Maigret manner.

The Murderer Is a Fox does not have the thematic unity or imaginative design of a Calamity Town, but in no other novel does Queen communicate so well the excitement of the quest for truth. I suspect this is why Ellery's ultimate solution is left completely unverifiable, for the truth historians seek is also unverifiable and in the search for historical truth there is no analogue to the device of the murderer's confession in detective fiction. Even if its characters were far less well drawn, its prose much flatter and its plot a great deal clumsier, The Murderer Is a Fox would still be noteworthy for its depiction of historical thinking in action, for its images of the intellectual exhilaration which Aristotle hinted at when he said: "The activity of mind is life."

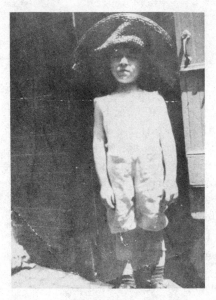

Frederic Dannay at the age of three. Elmira, N.Y., 1909. Photo courtesy Frederic Dannay.

Manfred Lee as a small child, probably around 1910. Photo courtesy Frederic Dannay.

Manny (left), age 7, and Danny (right), age 6, during the summer of 1912, while Manny was visiting his cousin in Elmira. Photo courtesy Frederic Dannay.

The Nathan family's Elmira home in 1915. Photo courtesy Frederic Dannay.

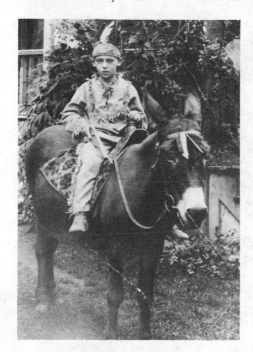

Both pictures of Danny Nathan in 1915. Photos courtesy Frederic Dannay.

Both pictures Manfred Lee in the 1930's, without and with his EQ mask.
Photos courtesy Frederic Dannay.

Lee (left) and Dannay (right) in their EQ office, around 1942. Dannay is reading an EQ radio script. Photo courtesy Graphic House, Inc.

Ellery Queen

a double profile

BY ANTHONY BOUCHER

Artist's conception of Lee (left) and Dannay (right) in the early 1950's.

Manfred Lee in his study in Roxbury, Conn., around 1960. Photo Courtesy Frederic Dannay.

Dannay and Lee in Dannay's study, Larchmont, N.Y., 1967. Photo courtesy Marc and Evelyne Bernheim.

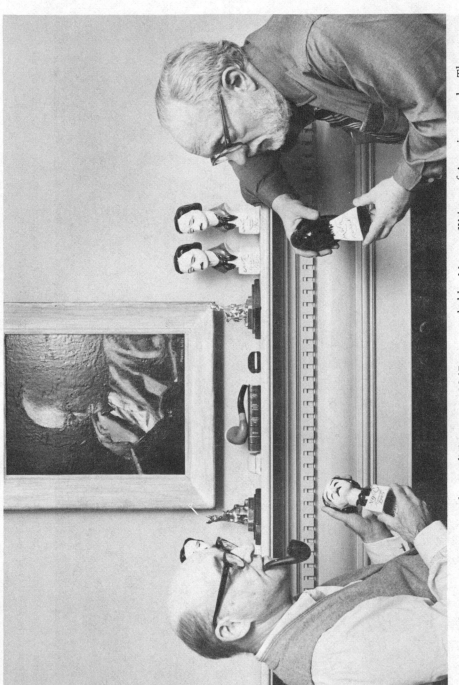

Dannay and Lee in Dannay's Larchmont living room, 1967, surrounded by Mystery Writers of America awards. The portrait of Dannay above the mantel is by Maurice Libby. Photo courtesy Marc and Evelyne Bernheim.

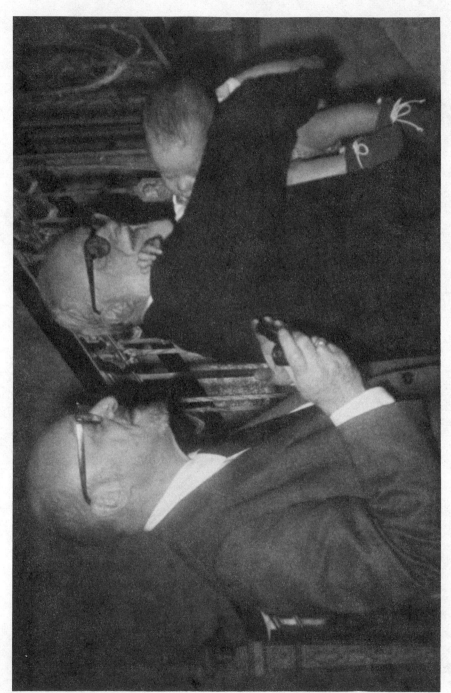

Dannay, Lee, and one of the next generation of Ellery Queen fans. The last known photograph of the cousins together, taken at the Mystery Writers of America annual dinner, May 1, 1970, in New York City. Photo courtesy Robert E. Washer.

Dannay in 1973. Photo courtesy Santi Visalli.

CHAPTER EIGHT

"*IN THE BEGINNING IT WAS WITHOUT FORM, A DARKNESS THAT* kept shifting like dancers." A reader sensitive to atmosphere and allusion may perceive even in that first line, with its echo of Genesis I:2, the direction of Queen's next book. *Ten Days' Wonder* (1948) marks another radical departure for Queen, probably the most radical of his whole career up to that time, although its full audacity does not become apparent until the novel's final phases.

Throughout mystery fiction and films of the last years of World War II and the immediate postwar era—Hitchcock's *Spellbound,* for instance, and Queen's own *The Murderer Is a Fox*—there is the recurring figure of the mentally disturbed young veteran with fears of past or future blood on his hands. In the opening chapters of *Ten Days' Wonder* Queen again takes up this theme, but this time he retains the psychiatric approach throughout the book. Howard Van Horn, sculptor son of the multimillionaire Diedrich Van Horn, comes desperately to Ellery for help after a series of amnesic blackouts that began on the night of his father's mar-

riage to the beautiful girl Diedrich had raised from childhood.   Howard believes that he has done or will do
something dreadful during one of these blackouts.
Psychiatrists having proved unable to help him, Howard
invites Ellery to visit the Van Horn estate and watch
over him. The location of the Van Horn estate is a town
called Wrightsville.

And so Ellery returns for the third time to the
town where twice before he seemed to have failed, and
being the kind of man he is, he is drawn into the hopeless
trap in which Howard and Sally Van Horn are caught.
Against his better judgment he agrees to act as their go-
between with an anonymous blackmailer, and comes
very close to being jailed for grand theft. A midnight
chase through a stormtossed graveyard, an old religious
fanatic woman who prowls in the night, and a missing
necklace combine with other less obviously sinister elements to create constant undercurrents of familial intrigue among a cast of (excluding Ellery) only four
central characters. In the final quarter of the novel there
is a murder, followed by one of the most dazzling re-
constructions of a crime in the history of the genre,
which is itself followed by an even more stunning solution, revealed by Ellery to no one but the murderer.

Psychologically, *Ten Days' Wonder* is an in-depth
study of the Van Horn family, and especially of Diedrich,
Howard and Sally, all three evoked and observed so
vividly they all but step off the page. And likewise
Queen brings the Wrightsville setting to life with the
same photographic clarity. His prose has rarely been so
rich nor his plotting so involuted. But the book's heart
and soul is not prose or plot or characterization or social
observation, but theology. And since I can't discuss the
theology of the book without revealing much of its

solution, I suggest that anyone who hasn't yet read the novel should skip the next three paragraphs.

The central event of *Ten Days' Wonder* is the breaking of the Ten Commandments. Diedrich Van Horn, learning that his young wife has committed adultery with his adopted son, manipulates events so that Howard will be made to break or seem to break the other commandments, culminating in the violation of "Thou shalt not kill." Diedrich plans, after the other commandments have been broken, to murder Sally in such a way that (1) Howard will believe he killed her during one of his blackouts and (2) Ellery will uncover the Ten Commandments element but will conclude that the violator in each and every case has been Howard. Throughout the novel Diedrich Van Horn is clothed in the attributes of deity: tremendous power, apparently limitless goodness, awesome knowledge. However, the solution reveals him as a being of monstrously evil nature and with an unerring ability to manipulate weak mortals to his own designs. At the end of the final, thunderous interview, Ellery forces Diedrich to kill himself. The god has been found out to be not the good and loving being he seemed but a moral monster, manipulating the trapped creatures under his sway, coldly determined to degrade and destroy the puny human beings who have usurped his divine prerogative. Therefore the forces of reason and humaneness demand the death of God.

Diedrich Van Horn was not the first puppet-master god that Queen created. As far back as 1932 he had created another figure of deep humanity who became obsessed with the desire to manipulate and who wound up killing others and finally himself—Drury Lane. Nor is *Ten Days' Wonder* Queen's first attempt to create a theomachy, a war between more-than-human powers, within the framework of the detective story; for there were some stirrings in that direction in the 1935 novelet "The Lamp of God." But *Ten Days' Wonder* is far more ambitious than its forerunners. Queen beautifully integrates his symbolic allegory with psychology, showing how the influence of Diedrich's sadistic hell-preaching father, combined with his childhood immersion in the vengeful God his father worshipped, led Diedrich to become himself a god of the same kind, as if in simultaneous mockery of the proverb "Like father like son" and of the teaching that man was made in God's image.

Once Queen decided to frame his allegory in detective-story terms, he was almost forced to use the device of the satanic manipulator, the Iago-like villain who knows how his pawns will respond to every stimulus. However, it's almost impossible to make this kind of figure naturalistically credible. From Iago himself down to Gavin in Hitchcock's *Vertigo* and Yost in John Boorman's film *Point Blank,* the manipulator is charged with an air of the more-than-human simply because we can't believe that any mere man could see the moves of his pawns that far ahead. And likewise in *Ten Days' Wonder,* despite all of Queen's skill at explaining, we simply can't accept Diedrich as just a phenomenally perceptive psycho-strategist. But Queen knows we can't accept it and has built the whole structure of this book and all its religious imagery on the basis that we will not accept it, so that we are thrown back willy-nilly into theology and theomachy.

Very few mystery writers have ever dared to mingle crime fiction with cosmic drama. *Ten Days' Wonder* is Queen's most sustained and successful attempt up to that time to do so, a dazzlingly rich work embracing dimensions that seemed utterly incompatible with the genre until Queen showed that it could be done. It is a nearly inexhaustible book, and certainly ranks among his half-dozen finest novels. And in the following year Queen produced another and perhaps even greater masterpiece.

At the beginning of *Cat of Many Tails* (1949) Ellery has renounced his habit of intervening in the lives of others, and has returned to the ivory tower of the novelist. "Just let me be. . . . I've given all that up. I'm not interested any longer." He holds himself responsible for "causing a death or two by the way" in the Van Horn case, and as a burnt child dreads fire, Ellery dreads being again responsible for others' lives. Deeper down seems to be a residue of sullen resentment at being bested (except for a purely intellectual victory that came too late) by his adversary in *Ten Days' Wonder*. And at the deepest level of Ellery's mind we may sense something of the guilt and despair at the death of God of which Nietzsche spoke so eloquently.

So Ellery has dropped out, detached himself from the mess and horror of the real world, performed an "inner emigration." The theme of detachment has recurred time and time again in the Queen canon. In *Calamity Town* it was exemplified in Aunt Tabitha, who ran out on the Wright family in its crisis, and in *There Was an Old Woman* it was embodied in the escapist Horatio Potts. But in *Cat of Many Tails* the theme is directly connected with Ellery himself.

The novel opens in New York City during the wilting heat of summer a few years after the end of World War II. The atmosphere is full of impending holocaust, with references to Hiroshima, the Nazi death camps, the Cold War, the quadripartite division of Vienna, the first Arab-Israeli conflict, the anti-Communist witch hunts,

and the threat of nuclear destruction. At one point
Ellery wakes up in the midst of a crisis and asks: "What
is it? War?" But the international headlines that daily
remind each man of his own mortality have been
dwarfed by local headlines conveying the same message.
A mass murderer is at large in the city. He has strangled
six victims in less than three months, and each victim is
utterly without connections to any of the others, each
is completely different from all the others ethnically,
economically, socially, geographically, and in every other
way.   The faceless bachelor from the Gramercy Park
area, the aging prostitute living above Times Square, the
struggling shoe salesman from Chelsea, the madcap heiress who loved the subways, the bitter paralytic of East
102nd Street, the black girl from Harlem, and the later
victims of the Cat share only the cord of Indian tussah
silk found knotted about the neck of each. The bait of
involvement is dangled before Ellery again, with all its
pain and risk, and once again Ellery snaps at it, im-
mersing himself in the city-wide Cat hunt until like his
father and the police commissioner and the mayor and
everyone else involved he is ready to drop in his tracks
from the exhaustion and frustration of strategy confer-
ences, statements to the press, radio addresses, co-ordina-
tion among official agencies, liaison with a team of
psychiatrists, attempts to avert violent confrontations
with the neighborhood self-defense committees that
spring up in the wake of the Cat murders, endless review-
ing of endless files and unceasing plodding up blind
alleys until, suddenly and beyond human expectation,
the link (so obvious and yet so subtle) connecting all the
victims and making sense of the entire bloodbath leaps
into sight.   As usual in third-period Queen, the full
explanation is finally topped by an even fuller and more

stunning solution. And, as in *Ten Days' Wonder,* Ellery is shattered by that solution.

There are other similarities between the two contiguous novels. The murder method in both is strangulation, the "player on the other side" in both is several times compared to a god, and in both Ellery's failure to comprehend has cost others their lives. The difference, however, is that in *Cat of Many Tails* Ellery learns wisdom. In key scenes at the beginning and middle and end of the book he receives instruction from a father-figure: first from his physical father, who is instrumental in making Ellery involve himself again; then from the titan Prometheus, founder of civilization according to Greek mythology, who appears to Ellery in a dream after the carnage of the Cat riots; finally from Dr. Bela Seligmann, the great Viennese psychiatrist, the "grandfather of the tribe," who has seen all the terrors in the world and in the heart of man.

The last line of the book, the "great and true lesson" which Seligmann asks Ellery to remember, is a quotation from the gospel of Mark: "There is one God; and there is none other but he." In view of the apparent irrelevance of the lesson, the reader may conclude that Queen has fallen victim to the old Hollywood custom of dragging God in by the heels at the last moment to whitewash the horrific events. Careful reading will show, I believe, that such is not the case. Neither Seligmann nor Queen is saying that there is a literal divine being whose existence somehow makes the pain go away. In context, Seligmann's wisdom can be paraphrased: If you take part in the world you will be hurt yourself and you will hurt others. This is man's experience, this is man's fate. No human can escape tragedy; only a being with the attributes traditionally ascribed to God could do so.

Knowing this terrible knowledge, go back into the world and struggle to change it for the better. Or, in Seligmann's own words: "You have failed before, you will fail again. This is the nature and the role of man." At the point of decision between detachment and involvement, between ice and fire, Ellery is told to be committed, to care.

And yet the point is made so paradoxically, so ambivalently, that it's impossible to be sure a commitment has been made at all. Part of the paradox is simply that Seligmann himself has performed the "inner emigration" that he talks Ellery out of. "I do not read newspapers since the war begins. That is for people who like to suffer. I, I do not like to suffer. I have surrendered myself to eternity. For me there is today this room, tomorrow cremation, unless the authorities cannot agree to allow it, in which case they may stuff me and place me in the clock tower of the *Rathaus* and I shall keep reminding them of the time." And Queen's evocation of New York City and its people—clinically detached, without affection and with a deep repugnance, as in the riot scenes and the acid little Christmas-shopping sequence and in every other presentation of people in sizable groups—hints that Queen does not completely disagree with Seligmann.

But although Queen in *Cat of Many Tails* shows a fastidious contempt for humanity, the abstract mass, the mob, he also shows how much he loves the individuals he has created by the fullness of life which he has infused into almost all of them (the single exception being Jimmy McKell, the millionaire reporter, who is so glaringly artificial it hurts). Even the Cat's victims, none of them ever seen alive but only talked about by others, become as real as the living people, each one carefully delineated and distinguished, a person rather than a statistic. And from the interweaving of the lives of the victims and their survivors and the scores of officials and the thousands of bystanders—from the portrayal of how each of these persons lives and what he thinks and hopes and fears, of the place where each lives and the things each does with her time—from all these emerges the portrait of the city as a fully rounded character in its own right. Queen evokes countless aspects of life in the city from the racial turmoil (a short but prophetic encounter with an outraged black father in a Harlem stationhouse) to the struggle against the stifling heat, from the chaos of a full-scale riot to the delights of popular radio programs like *The Shadow* and *Stella Dallas*. And besides portraying the city in vivid detail and penetrating deeply into the hearts of his major characters, Queen also integrates thousands of tiny fictional elements into a unified mosaic embodying a very personal vision of existence. *Cat of Many Tails* is the most abundant novel Queen ever wrote, stands with *Calamity Town* at the pinnacle of his work, can be read and re-read with unceasing satisfaction, and offers permanent testimony to what can be accomplished within the framework of the mystery story.

After two masterpieces Queen was entitled to relax a bit, and his next novel, *Double, Double* (1950), is less intense than its predecessors though no less distinctively Queenian. Like *There Was an Old Woman*, it centers around a children's rhyme, and the relations between Ellery and the female lead and the murderer are quite similar in both books. But whereas *Woman* had a Theater of the Absurd milieu tied to a "straight" puzzle, in *Double* the setting is unremarkable middle-American Wrightsville while the weight of the Absurd is borne by the plot.

Ellery is sent a series of clippings from the Wrightsville *Record*, detailing the "natural" death of an old
miser who was discovered to have died rich and the
"suicide" of a local manufacturer who was discovered
to have died broke. Three days later another clipping
arrives, describing the disappearance and presumed death
of old Tom Anderson, the intellectual alcoholic who had
quoted Whitman in counterpoint to Ellery's solution in
Calamity Town. The very next day Anderson's daughter
Rima visits 87th Street and asks Ellery to find out why
and by whom her father was killed. And so Ellery—who
falls instantly in love with his beautiful flower-child
client—returns to Wrightsville once more, and becomes
involved in the lives of a crotchety and terrified old
doctor, a *nouveau riche* attorney, a bitchy female news-
paper publisher, a philosophical gardener whose em-
ployers have a habit of dying in droves, and other
Wrightsvillians fair and foul. The bodies continue to
accumulate after Ellery's arrival, and the facts are so
equivocal that Ellery cannot even satisfy himself that all
the deaths are connected, let alone that they are murders. (The title comes from the witches' incantation in
Macbeth but refers specifically to Ellery's observation
that reality is Janus-faced, that each set of events can be
interpreted in two ways.) Eventually Ellery stumbles
across the connecting link between the dead men and
the apparent harbinger of additional deaths as well: an
old children's counting jingle.

The key to Ellery's final exposure of the person
who killed so as to make a rhyme come alive is, as in
The Four of Hearts, an analysis of motive, and the
linchpin of Ellery's reasoning is precisely the point he
failed to consider in "The Adventure of the Murdered

Millionaire," thereby leaving a sizable logical hole in that first of Queen's radio plays. The pattern which Ellery uncovers stands as a noble specimen of Queenian black humor: the murderer, in the best tradition of the sorcerer's apprentice, follows the words of the child's jingle up to a certain predetermined point, then to his horror finds the jingle forcing him to conform more and more killings to it. "Think of it in terms of lunacy," Ellery advises, "and it at once becomes reasonable." Unfortunately the formal deductive problem is a poor vehicle for Queen's key concept, since it prevents us from ever seeing and sharing the murderer's horror as the pattern he created runs away with him. There are glimpses, but no more than glimpses, of this missing dimension at certain points, most notably in Dr. Dodd's words: "With all our sulfas and atomic bombs and electronic microscopes and two hundred inch telescope lenses, we don't begin to know the powers that fill the universe. All we can do is wait and try not to be too afraid." It's our loss that Queen did not find a more suitable form in which to clothe the heart of his darkness.

But though not a major work *Double, Double* does at least have the warm and wonderful Rima, the Thoreauvian hippie girl who in the early chapters confounds Ellery at every turn, shows up his "wisdom" with her "foolishness," and leaves him no choice but to fall in love with her. Unhappily, as the book progresses she becomes more and more like the silent majority around her, dull and girdled and conventional, so that despite the hint at the end that Ellery may come back for her, we can be thankful that he didn't bother. Wrightsville itself is superbly evoked—how superbly can be measured by the almost personal sense of loss we feel

at the casually dropped news that John F. Wright and
Doc Willoughby have died since Ellery's last visit—but
the sense of place is spoiled by a great deal of overdone
satire on the theme of the noble natives vs. the slimy
arrivistes, and by a closely analogous little literary attack
on Mickey Spillane and his imitators, who in Queen's
eyes are related to the classic tradition of mystery fiction exactly as Malvina Prentiss and the other Snopesian
interlopers are related to the indigenous solid-American
Wrightsvillians. *Double, Double* is certainly among the
lesser products of Queen's third period, but it followed
masterpieces next to which almost anything would be a
letdown. And the book that followed it turned out to
be almost as good as the two that preceded it.

CHAPTER NINE

BETWEEN THE TIME QUEEN FINISHED DOUBLE, DOUBLE AND THE completion of his next novel, civil war broke out in divided Korea, the United States intervened in the conflict almost at once, and the likelihood that the "police action" would escalate into universal nuclear war seemed to increase daily. Although the war was still in its early stages while Queen was working on *The Origin of Evil* (1951), the grim reflections on human nature that inform the novel must seem prophetic considering how many hundreds of thousands were senselessly killed and maimed on that obscure peninsula over the next few years.

The book opens in mid-June of 1950, shortly before the outbreak of the war, and Ellery has returned to gay gaudy goofy Hollywood to work on a novel but finds that the place has changed. The movie industry on which its economy had rested has been virtually wiped out by that new toy of the middle class, the TV set, and endless munitions factories and retirement communities are filling up the economic vacuum. Ellery's work on the novel is interrupted by lovely nineteen-year-old

Laurel Hill, who claims that her foster father, a wealthy jeweler, was literally frightened to death two weeks earlier upon finding a dead dog lying on his doorstep. Although the police have laughed off her theory, Laurel contends that Leander Hill's partner, a foul-tempered invalid named Roger Priam, has also been receiving strange warnings but is keeping his mouth shut about them. At this point (though not by coincidence) Roger's lush and exotic wife, Delia Priam, arrives on the scene to ask Ellery's help, confirming that something strange is indeed happening to her husband. So Ellery becomes entangled in the bizarre Priam household—which includes an enigmatic secretary, a wandering philatelist, and a young man who lives in a treehouse—but still the sense-less warnings keep arriving on the Priam doorstep. Part-way through Ellery's investigation the war begins, and the novel then proceeds on three fronts: the intensifica-tion of the mass slaughter, the deepening of Ellery's knowledge of and involvement with the Hill and Priam households, and the continued arrival of such unrelated objects as a mess of dead frogs, an empty wallet and a portfolio of worthless stock certificates. Eventually El-lery discovers the pattern, and his solution, capped by a second and even more breathtaking solution, superbly ties plot and theme into an organic whole.

Not only is *The Origin of Evil* by far the best of Queen's Hollywood novels, it's one of his best books of the Fifties also. The plot is full of distinctively Queenian elements—murder by psychological shock as in *The Door Between*, a killer who uses another person as his living weapon as in *Ten Days' Wonder,* the solution within a solution, the "negative clue" device, and the series of seemingly absurd events connected by a hidden logic as in *Ten Days' Wonder, Cat of Many Tails* and *Double,*

Double.   The religious motifs of *Ten Days' Wonder*
return in low-key with the appearance of not one but
two Diedrich-like manipulators, each playing upon the
other, one referred to as "the invisible god" and the
other as "the god of events."   As in *Ten Days' Wonder*
the truth turns out to be devilishly complex; in fact my
only serious objection to the story is that the murderer's
plot *requires* the presence of a master detective to unravel certain complexities the killer wants to be discovered, although Ellery's entrance into the case is totally unexpected and accidental.

But, as usual since *Calamity Town,* Queen is up to
more than just a good detective novel.   The subject of
The Origin of Evil is clearly stated in the title, and the
answer to the title's implicit question is, quite simply,
human nature.   As in *Cat of Many Tails,* Queen's meaning is most accessible in a scene wherein Ellery receives
instruction.   Near the end of Chapter VII he approaches
Collier, the old retired naturalist-adventurer, and asks
him bluntly: "Have you any idea what this is all about?"
Collier replies: "I'll tell you what this is all about, Mr.
Queen. . . . It's about corruption and wickedness. It's
about greed and selfishness and guilt and violence and
hatred and lack of self-control. It's about black secrets
and black hearts, cruelty, confusion, fear. It's about not
making the best of things, not being satisfied with what
you have, and always wanting what you haven't. It's
about envy and suspicion and malice and lust and nosi-
ness and drunkenness and unholy excitement and a
thirst for hot running blood.   It's about man, Mr.
Queen."

Of course this speech is not the only indication of
Queen's intent. It's no accident that every major character in the novel except Ellery and his nemesis is com-

pared over and over again to various animals, nor that
the imagery of the jungle recurs every few pages. Both
the killer's adopted name and his plot are grounded in
Darwinian biology with its themes of the endless struggle
for survival and of "nature red in tooth and claw." The
player on the other side turns out to be quite literally
"the old Adam," and at the end of the novel the old
Adam is not only unbeaten but has become the intimate
and familiar of Ellery himself. This union of apparent
opposites seems especially apt when we recall Ellery's
all-too-human reaction of moralistic outrage and contempt when he learned of Delia's sexual habits, despite
his very clear desire to have her himself. No man can
call another animal, for the same nature stains us all.
Or, in the words of old Collier, "People mean trouble. . . . There's too much trouble in this world."

But the major trouble with this book is that Queen's
treatment of the Korean war and of impending nuclear
holocaust is completely at odds with his grim view of
man. The conflict in Korea is portrayed not as one more
monument to man's power-hunger and blood-lust but
in the standard propaganda terms of the filthy Commies
from the North attacking their peaceful democratic
neighbors in the South. And the threat of World War
III is presented literally as a hoax, a publicity gimmick
dreamed up by a young would-be actor to get himself
into the movies (the actor quite fittingly winds up
volunteering for the crusade against evil in Korea). We
must remember, of course, that in those days when Joe
McCarthy ruled the land, thousands of Americans had
their careers ruined for raising doubts about matters
such as these; and it seems clear that in 1951 Queen was
not yet ready to put his body on the line. So if *The
Origin of Evil* fails to cohere thematically, the reign of

terror in which it was written is more to blame than Queen.

No such weighty issues are dealt with in Queen's next book. As an editor Queen had long held that a mystery anthology should be not merely a gathering of miscellaneous stories but an organic unity informed by a central concept or theme. But the early volumes of his own short stories—*The Adventures, The New Adventures,* and *The Case Book*—were merely collections of shorts, lacking any such theme. Then in the late 1940's Queen conceived the idea of a book of shorts that would be bound by a unifying concept. The stories were published intermittently in *EQMM* over the next few years and were collected in 1952 under the title *Calendar of Crime*: one story for each month of the year and revolving around an event associated with that month. A few of the associations are distinctively American but most are of broader scope, and the stories range in quality from the magnificent to the indifferent.

"The Inner Circle" (*EQMM* 1/47) opens the proceedings splendidly. One of the last survivors of the Januarians, the 1913 graduating class of Eastern University, visits Ellery shortly before the annual New Year's Day class meeting and tells him of a survivor-take-all tontine among an "inner circle" of Januarians, and of the sudden and recent deaths of three members. The murder puzzle is mounted beautifully, the solution neatly deduced from a word-association clue, and Queen's skill at evoking the Old Grad ethos and giving life to a huge cast of alumni is as awesome as his later feat of vivifying New York City in *Cat of Many Tails*.

There is no crime in "The President's Half Disme" (*EQMM* 2/47) but there is nonetheless an intellectual adversary worthy of Ellery's mettle, one George Washing-

ton by name. The problem is to find a rare coin believed
to have been buried by the first president on a remote
Pennsylvania farm in 1791. The answer is sublimely
simple (perhaps a little too easy to work out), and
although the whole story is built on multiple coincidence, the effect in this particular case is delightful.

The calendar reference in "The Ides of Michael
Magoon" (*EQMM* 3/47) is to the income tax, which at
that time fell due on March 15. Queen's client in this
case is himself a detective, or eye or op if you will, but
emphatically not in the Spade or Marlowe mold, being
middle-aged, overweight, asthmatic, near-sighted, and
not too bright. Michael Magoon reports that someone
stole all his income tax records from his briefcase 48
hours or so before the filing deadline, but the oddball
theft quickly balloons into a case of blackmail and murder, which Ellery resolves deftly, surprisingly and with
full fairness to the reader.

In 1955 the income tax deadline was shifted to the
fifteenth of April. Had Queen waited a few years, he
could have pushed "Michael Magoon" a month ahead
and spared us one of his weakest stories. The characters
and atmosphere of "The Emperor's Dice" (*EQMM* 4/51)
are standard old-dark-house, and the problem revolves
around the apparent ten-year-old murder of a millionaire
collector of gambling devices. Ellery's elucidation of
the "dying message" is so absurd as to sound like a Jon
L. Breen parody, and the final surprise infuriates more
than it surprises.

Queen returned to his stride with "The Gettysburg
Bugle" (*EQMM* 5/51, as "As Simple As ABC"), in
which Ellery stumbles upon the tiny hamlet of Jacks-
burg, Pennsylvania, and into a case involving another
dwindling tontine, with the survivor slated to enjoy a

fabled Civil War treasure. The solution to the series of Memorial Day deaths among the town's Union Army veterans is neat and satisfying but takes a back seat to Queen's loving depiction of patriotic solidarity in small-town America.

June is the traditional month of happy weddings, but in "The Medical Finger" (*EQMM* 6/51) the lovely and very wealthy young bride drops dead seven minutes after the ceremony, chief but by no means sole suspect being a violent-tempered old flame who had threatened to kill the girl rather than see her married to another. Unfortunately Ellery has almost nothing to do in the case, and the deductions he does make are both illogical (neither eliminating the other suspects nor pinning the guilt on the culprit conclusively) and too late.

Ellery enters the July adventure of "The Fallen Angel" (*EQMM* 7/51) through the auspices of Nikki Porter, whose girl friend, recently married to an aging laxatives tycoon and installed in his monstrous family mansion, seems to be involved in a triangle with her husband's young artist brother. But when murder enters the picture, the plot drops its echo of the Diedrich-Sally-Howard intrigue in *Ten Days' Wonder,* picks up a few elements from "The Hollow Dragon," and culminates in an alibi gimmick that is incredibly chancy (if Ellery were even a few minutes late for his appointment the scheme would literally go up in smoke), but at least integrates the story deftly with its month.

This is more than can be said of "The Needle's Eye" (*EQMM* 8/51), which takes place in August but has no other connection with the month. A retired explorer, on whose private island Captain Kidd is rumored to have buried part of his treasure, asks Ellery to investigate his niece's new husband, but Ellery's digging becomes literal rather than metaphorical when he arrives on the island and becomes involved in a treasure hunt and in the murder of his host. The crucial clue is very neatly handled, the use of the treasure motif reminds us of its similar utilization by Queen that same year in *The Origin of Evil*, and the nostalgic treatment of pirate lore is comparable to the romance-of-childhood evocations in Frederic Dannay's autobiographical novel *The Golden Summer*.

In September the world's young people and their teachers return to the classroom, but in "The Three R's" (*EQMM* 9/46) the administration of Barlowe College has to retain Ellery to locate one of its faculty, a Poe scholar who vanished in the Ozarks over the summer. Ellery's investigation along the Missouri-Arkansas border turns up some intriguing clues—a detective-story manuscript, a skeleton with two missing fingers—but the way he assembles the pieces sounds once more like Breen rather than Queen, and the Birlstonean final surprise turns the whole show into a farce.

"The Dead Cat" (*EQMM* 10/46) is, however, a horse of another color—a tightly plotted fair-play puzzle in which Ellery and Nikki attend a Hallowe'en party in cat costume and stay to find out who cut the throat of one of the guests in total darkness during a game of Murder. The main intellectual problem confronting Ellery—that is, figuring out how the murderer overcame the main obstacle confronting *him*—is similar to that in "The House of Darkness" (and its later radio rewrite "The Blind Bullet") but is resolved in a much different way. I'm still wondering how the killer could have anticipated that someone would suggest the Murder game, but otherwise the results are fully satisfactory.

I'm nowhere near so satisfied with Queen's Thanksgiving story, "The Telltale Bottle" (*EQMM* 11/46), in which Ellery and Nikki go out delivering holiday food baskets to the poor, blunder into a cocaine-pushing operation and murder, and resolve the mess through means both unworthy and incomprehensible (I challenge anyone to make sense out of the story's last six paragraphs).

But Queen saved the best for last. In "The Dauphin's Doll" (*EQMM* 12/48) Ellery, his father and dozens of the Inspector's men combine to protect the titular doll and its 49-carat diamond crown from a modern Lupin known as Comus who has boasted that he will steal the figure while it is on exhibition at a major department store on the day before Christmas. Despite a gauntlet of security arrangements the thief lives up to his boast, and brilliantly; but Ellery's even more brilliant deductions as to how the impossible crime was done net both the thief and the doll as Christmas dawn floods the city. By far the best story in the book, spiced with countless learned digressions in the Sayers/Innes manner and with a sardonic evocation of the Christmas rush that presages the more sustained treatment of the same subject in *Cat of Many Tails,* "The Dauphin's Doll" is indisputably Queen's finest effort in the short form between the two great sports tales of 1939 and today. No collection of anyone's stories could end more satisfyingly.

In Queen's novel for 1952, *The King Is Dead,* the international politics that formed a small part of the background of *The Origin of Evil* dominates the stage. Ellery and his father are suddenly spirited away from New York City and escorted by armed guards to the secret island empire of weapons tycoon Kane (King) Bendigo, perhaps the most powerful living human, whose lust for and abuse of power have been responsible for literally billions of deaths and maimings. The King has been receiving anonymous death threats from someone in his entourage, and his Prime Minister and brother, Abel Bendigo, has conscripted the Queens for the task of finding the culprit. Ellery and Richard thereby gain the opportunity to see fascism close-up and to meet the rest of the royal family. In addition to the King and his brother Abel, there are the King's wife, Karla, an international beauty of royal blood, and his second brother, Judah, a saintly ineffectual lush whose caches of Segonzac VSOP cognac are strewn all over the island. Despite the Queens' presence the messages continue to reach the King, each one narrowing down a little further the exact moment when he will die. And as the hour approaches, even after the potential assassin's identity has become known, the tension mounts higher and higher, until finally a man points an empty gun at a solid wall and pulls the trigger, while in a sealed room on the other side of a guard-filled corridor, the King falls. Ellery eventually unravels this superb locked-room problem, but his knowledge of the truth avails him nothing and he is completely unable to influence the course of events—a paradigm of the man of good will's helplessness in the nightmare of international politics.

The elements of *The King Is Dead* can apparently be traced back to a variety of sources. Queen may have derived the idea of doing a political thriller with the whole of international relations as its stage from Upton Sinclair's novels about presidential agent Lanny Budd, but Queen's use of this approach, in which the world-historical ramifications are discovered by research, is quite different from that favored by Sinclair, who had his protagonist directly observe them. The character of

King Bendigo clearly seems to be modeled on the central figure of Orson Welles' first and greatest film, *Citizen Kane* (1941). Kane Bendigo and Charles Foster Kane share the same name and a similar ruthlessness and lust for power; both appear with a full head of hair at one point and bald at another; both live on isolated baroque estates (the Italian marble fireplace in the Bendigo reception room suggests the huge one before which Kane's wife in the film did her jigsaw puzzles); and the investigation into the childhood and young manhood of the dying giant is a key motif in both works. Turning to plot details, Queen's evocation of mounting suspense as the hour of a predicted but seemingly impossible death comes nearer owes much to Cornell Woolrich's great (perhaps greatest) novel, *Night Has a Thousand Eyes* (1945), whose earliest form, the 1937 novelet "Speak to Me of Death," Queen had reprinted in *EQMM* for March 1949. In effect Queen took Woolrich's root idea, purged it of all preternatural elements, added a beautiful locked-room puzzle, and met the rigorous technical challenge of explaining the whole affair in fully naturalistic terms and with complete fairness to the reader, while at the same time maintaining the suspense at Woolrich's own level. The solution to the puzzle is childishly simple but obscured by titanic misdirection, as in "The Lamp of God," and the device of the negative clue, the object whose absence is the linchpin of the case, has been used more brilliantly only by Queen him-self.

Unhappily several other aspects of *The King Is Dead* are nowhere near so well handled. On the plot level, it's simply inconceivable that anyone in his right mind would devise such a bizarre way of getting rid of an enemy as the conspirators employ, especially since they could accomplish the same end so much more easily just by doing what is actually done before the beginning of Chapter XVII. And even if some rational mind might have hatched such a plot, it's impossible to believe that any of the people in this book could have done so. On the psychological level, we just can't accept the "reformation" of Abel Bendigo. As the Inspector comments: "Do you think I can believe that? . . . That the leopard can change his spots? You were in it up to your neck for twenty-seven years." Equally implausible are the fact and the explanation of King Bendigo's fear of water which is central to the story. Politically, I have trouble swallowing the notion of a total revolution being accomplished merely by the assassination of the one man at the top, and no less trouble imagining how the successful revolutionaries can possibly use a multi-billion-dollar armaments empire as a force for good. Finally, when Ellery at the end bleakly comments: "The King is dead, long live the King. . . . Now who keeps an eye on the incumbent?" and Judah very calmly replies "I do," it's hard to resist the temptation to add one cynical last line to the book: " 'And who will keep an eye on you?' asked Ellery." For, appealing though Judah is as an ineffectual Dostoevskian saint, his values are too unreliable to bear the weight Queen places on him. "In the world we live in," Judah tells King, "munitions are unfortunately necessary, and someone has to manufacture them. But to you the implements of war are not a necessary evil, made for the protection of a decent society trying to survive in a wolves' world. They're a means of getting astronomical profits and the power that goes with them." In other words, Judah's conscience would seem to be satisfied if his brother would only *believe* his own propaganda about the free world and godless totalitarianism while carrying on business as usual. Since *The King Is Dead* was written, the consciences of the committed have come to demand quite a bit more of the powerful, with the result that Judah doesn't seem fully trustworthy to readers today.

But indefensible in naturalistic terms though the novel is, it's both defensible and intelligible as an allegory or fable or, to be more precise, as another Ellery-in-Wonderland novel. Like the Potts estate in *There Was an Old Woman,* Bendigo Island is a separate little universe with its own paradoxical laws and ways of behaving. Thus, Cain first seems to save the life of Abel and then is killed by Abel; thus, the treason of Judas is a holy act. Nor is it accidental that virtually everything that happens in the book, even the central confrontation between the King and Judah in Chapter IX, is an intricately staged act played for the Queens' benefit—an unsettling anticipation of the more recent idea that theatre and revolution are interchangeable. Unfortunately the same structural defect that plagued *There Was an Old Woman* also pops up in *The King Is Dead.* In the earlier novel Queen couldn't integrate a serious deductive plot into the topsy-turvy milieu, and in the later he can't make an organic whole out of a locked-room puzzle, a serious psychological study, and a fable about fascism and revolution. Nevertheless the suspense and the misdirection and the central clue and many other aspects of the book are all of the highest order. Even when a Queen novel fails as a whole, it never lacks wondrous parts.

The following year Queen again tried something completely different and again ran into technical snags he couldn't lick. The challenge he set himself in *The*

Scarlet Letters (1953) was to create a complex milieu and breathe life into a very small cast of characters and generate an atmosphere of intense urgency, but without employing any strictly criminous elements until the last two chapters of the book. However, he fell into the trap of letting the book's novelistic and deductive aspects collide and smash each other up, and the net result is another fascinating failure.

The story revolves around two of Ellery's and Nikki's acquaintances: Dirk Lawrence, a morbid, childhood-haunted, insanely jealous novelist, and his wife Martha, older, a millionairess, amateur Broadway producer, and a born martyr to Dirk's rages. In its fourth year the marriage falls apart, with Dirk constantly accusing Martha of sleeping around and taking drunken swings at her suspected lovers. Martha goes for help to her childhood friend Nikki Porter, and Nikki drafts Ellery into trying to reach the roots of Dirk's phobia. Soon, however, evidence accumulates that it's not all phobia: Martha has been and is making alphabetically coded assignations, in hotel rooms and elsewhere, with an aging but still virile ex-Broadway matinee idol. Ellery's threefold task now is to find out why Martha is acting as she is, to keep Dirk from learning of the affair, and to pull the fangs of the sexual blackmailer. These non-violent non-deductive events occupy roughly 75% of *The Scarlet Letters*, but then come a bloody double shooting, a splendid dying message, a murder trial, and Ellery's exposure of some stupendous double-dealing.

Perceptive readers will find many links between this and earlier Period Three novels. The concept of the war veteran whose father apparently murdered his mother and who himself becomes murderously jealous of his wife goes back to *The Murderer Is a Fox,* where it was never fully developed. The tiny cast of characters, the influence of the killer's father, the murder plot based on convoluted manipulation of other people, all these spring from *Ten Days' Wonder*. But, as usual when Queen reworks elements, he does not mechanically borrow from himself but stresses in the new work what was subdued or latent in the old, and integrates all his elements into the new context.

The most unexpected aspect of *The Scarlet Letters* is not the plot but the milieu. The world of theatre people and Broadway columnists and swank night spots is evoked economically and convincingly, and the feel of the early 1950's is superbly communicated through a wealth of tiny details, such as the references to the *Stork Club* TV show, Canasta, and Sid Caesar's Saturday night variety hour. There's no mention of the impact of McCarthyism and the blacklist on the entertainment world, but Queen would more than make up for that in his next novel. Each member of the small cast is not only well-drawn but an integral part of the milieu: Ellery and Dirk *are* novelists, Martha *is* a producer, Van Harrison *is* an actor, Leon Fields *is* a gossip columnist, and we aren't just told their occupations, we see them at work. Even Nikki Porter, who on radio and in some of the short stories was often no more than a stereotyped Sleuth's Gal Friday, here becomes a full-blooded person in her own right,[1] and so real that we wish this had not been her final appearance.

With all these excellences of story and character and setting, the first three-quarters of *The Scarlet Letters* is superb reading. But once we come to the murder and the traditional apparatus of mystery fiction, the novel suddenly becomes incredibly weak (though the weaknesses are apparent only in retrospect). Ellery's solution is based on reasoning so gossamer and speculative as to suggest Maigret or a character in Woolrich rather than the logical successor to Sherlock Holmes. That Queen has subtly evaded almost all the legal problems raised by the solution should be obvious even to nonlawyers (as both attorney and reader I would love to know what happened back in the courtroom when Judge Levy returned to the bench after Ellery's lecture). But worst of all is that once we learn the answers, we see that Queen has misled us monstrously in the body of the book. Although we have seen and been told, over and over, how much like clandestine lovers Martha and Van Harrison were acting, the revelation of their true relationship makes utter nonsense of all her observed and reported behavior.[2]   Equally infelicitous is Queen's treatment of the satanic manipulator theme, which simply can't work where the villain is a fully fleshed naturalistic figure with no intimations of the more-than-human such as Queen properly added to the corresponding figures in *Ten Days' Wonder* and *The Origin of Evil.* Finally, even though the murderer's entire plan depends on Ellery and Nikki learning certain facts prior to the murder, he does absolutely nothing to point them towards those facts, which Ellery uncovers by sheer good luck. Indeed the killer's appalling stupidity at certain points (as when he deliberately blocks Martha from her most public meeting yet with Harrison) makes one wonder how he ever graduated from Iago's Academy of Fiendish Manipulators in the first place.

But for all its flaws, there are enough good things in *The Scarlet Letters*—prose, social observation, depiction of character and time and place—to require a reading and repay a re-reading. Nowhere near the best of Queen, it's still distinctly and unmistakably Queenian.

CHAPTER TEN

BY THE TIME QUEEN HAD COMPLETED THE SCARLET LETTERS,
the reign of terror spurred by Joe McCarthy and HUAC
and their ilk had been raging for several years. Tens of
thousands of Americans were labeled pinkoes or Com-
mie sympathizers and fired from their jobs, blacklisted,
jailed or deported. Vicious and absurd categories like
"guilt by association" and "Fifth Amendment Communist" became common currency, and trials or hear-
ings to determine whether one was "subversive" were
held on a grand scale, without even the semblance of
Due Process safeguards.[1] The theatre, film and literature were extremely hard hit, and even mystery fiction
which is generally considered an apolitical genre was
hurt when Dannay's friend Dashiell Hammett was jailed
for 6 months. It was in this atmosphere of terror that
Queen wrote his next novel, *The Glass Village* (1954),
which two decades later still stands out as a breathtakingly readable book and which has "dated" not one
iota.

The setting is the back-country hamlet of Shinn
Corners,[2] once a thriving New England factory town but

presently a withering village of thirty-six people, all but
a few of them embittered puritanical bigots. The single
part-time resident, who keeps one foot in Shinn Corners
and the other in the more enlightened world outside, is
Superior Court Judge Lewis Shinn. The judge is spend-
ing a week in the village of his birth, playing host to his
nephew, Johnny Shinn, an ex-major in military intelligence who has just returned from Korea. There are
hints that Johnny was sexually mutilated in the war:
he dreams of North Koreans jamming lighted cigarettes
against his nipples "and other places," and later remarks:
"I'm not a man, I'm a vegetable." The net result of his
experiences in World War II (where he witnessed
Hiroshima), postwar America, and in Korea is that he
has lost all belief and all hope and all ability to love, and
has become "the missing link between the fauna and
the flora," with a strong preference for the flora.[3] Judge
Shinn still recites, and claims to believe in, the patriotic
formulas of grammar-school civics class—"Communism,
hydrogen bombs, nerve gas, McCarthyism, and ex-majors
of Army Intelligence to the contrary notwithstanding"—
but admits that his faith is being shaken. "As we get
poorer, we get more frightened; the more frightened we
get, the narrower and meaner and bitterer and less secure
we are." He knows the monstrous evils that America
has committed against other peoples, and goes out of his
way to point them out to Johnny in their conversations,
but insists that those who act on their beliefs, "rightly
or wrongly," are better than those who believe in nothing. This outrageous judgment was a commonplace of
the 1950's (for properly contemptuous commentary see
Walter Kaufmann's *The Faith of a Heretic*, Doubleday
1960, Chapter IV), but I doubt that it's a live option
today, and in any case Queen isn't asking us to agree

with the Judge. The book focuses not on the Judge but on Johnny and his slow journey back to the human race.

What precipitates his return is a brutal murder. Aunt Fanny Adams, the famous 91-year-old primitive painter who made her home in Shinn Corners, is bludgeoned to death in her studio one rainy afternoon. A foreign-looking tramp had been through the village begging shortly before the murder, and the outraged citizens of Shinn Corners hunt this man down, beat him, come near to lynching him, refuse to turn him over to the state police, and insist on trying him for murder themselves. (Today this might be called Community Control, and one of the grimmest aspects of this book is that the common purpose of lynching another human being does indeed forge a true sense of community in the town, with neighbor helping neighbor, shared chores and meals.) To avert a gun battle between his neighbors and the police, Judge Shinn gets permission from the governor to hold a mock murder trial in Shinn Corners— a trial deliberately packed with ridiculous legal errors and designed to placate the townspeople for now and be reversed by an appellate court later. Among the jurors is Johnny Shinn.

The trial itself is a farrago of procedural obscenities. Ten of the twelve jurors admit under oath that they are already certain the defendant is guilty, the bailiff and the court reporter and most of the jurors and even the judge himself testify for the prosecution, the judge takes over as prosecutor while the prosecutor testifies against the defendant, the defense counsel fails to object to gross violations of his client's rights but fights loudly over the admissibility of trivia, and the judge solemnly bangs the darning egg that serves as a gavel and hands down rulings of law he knows to be dead wrong. As a passing newspaperman points out, a new branch of the law is being born in Shinn Corners—the musical comedy murder trial. Or, to relate *The Glass Village* to a central Queen motif, we might call it a study in due process on the other side of the rabbit hole. Queen had dealt with legal themes many times before but had seldom gotten his law straight; this time, by creating a context in which the legal procedure *has* to be ridiculously wrong, he turned out the finest law novel of his whole career.

It's also one of his best detective stories of the Fifties, complete with bizarre clues, the functional e-quivalent of a dying message, and a full measure of inspired misdirection. It may seem slightly incredible that every single one of the 37 Shinn Corners residents is able to produce an alibi for the time of the murder, but Queen handles each little detail leading to this con-clusion so neatly and naturalistically, and then flabber-gasts us so beautifully with what the sequence is *really* driving at, that objections simply vanish in a gasp of wonder.

Although Queen originally intended and 1954 readers would interpret the trial as a commentary on the McCarthyite and HUAC perversions of due process (analogous to those of the Salem witch-hunters and Stalin's judges), what strikes a reader of the Seventies with maximum force, I think, is Queen's acid contempt for that great superhero of our times, the "silent majority." The gallery of vicious boobs Queen creates, like Hube Hemus and his sons, Merton Isbel, Peter Berry, Prue Plummer and virtually every other patriotic citizen of Shinn Corners, makes it impossible to think of "middle America" without a shudder. And when Johnny Shinn literally vomits at their display of sadism,

bigotry and business-as-usual during the capture of
Kowalczyk, we tend to doubt that he's as dehumanized
as he thinks he is. When Merton Isbel in the jury room
keeps snarling "Take a vote! . . . Ye think to balk
the will of the majority? Vote guilty!", and Rebecca
Hemus, cheated of a victim, cries "It's a conspiracy,
that's what it is!", and her son Tommy screams "You
a Commie-lover?" at whoever disagrees with him (Com-
mie being the functional equivalent of nigger in a community whose harsh climate killed off all the slaves long
ago)—what then are we to think of "the system"?
Queen's answer comes out, I believe, in a reflection of
Johnny Shinn near the end of the book, that "man was
a chaos without rhyme or reason; that he blundered
about like a maddened animal in the delicate balance of
the world, smashing and disrupting, eager only for his
own destruction." Thus the root of all evil is not any
political or economic system (Johnny says he never became a Communist because Marxism was too optimistic
a philosophy for him to accept); the root, as Collier told
Ellery in *The Origin of Evil,* is man himself. At the end
of the novel, Johnny breathes in the peace of the new
day, and to the Judge's remark that it's a "fine, fine
day in the making," Johnny replies: "I've seen worse."
That is the last line of the book. What the events have
taught Johnny is simply that he never really lost his
humanity as he claimed to have done, and that to be human does not require him to believe in or hope for anything, but only to care—which is very close to the wisdom of Dr. Seligmann (another man of detached compassion) at the end of *Cat of Many Tails.*

The major flaw in *The Glass Village* is that the
crucial scene in which Johnny convinces his fellow
jurors not to lynch Kowalczyk yet, and argues that he

can prove someone else committed the murder, is literally non-existent. After what he showed us of those jurors, Queen must have realized that they'd be unlikely to listen to anybody or anything that would cheat them of their blood; but he evaded the problems of the scene simply by stopping the action at a crucial point and shifting forward to the swamp, thus presenting the startled reader with a *fait accompli*. Aside from this lapse, however, it's a magnificent novel, rich in plot and character and atmosphere and commentary on the reign of terror of the Fifties that has lost none of its relevance.

Instead of publishing a new novel the following year, Queen put together most of the short-short stories he had been writing for *This Week* since 1949 into a collection he called *Q.B.I.: Queen's Bureau of Investigation* (1955),[4] which proved him a master of this as of all other lengths of crime fiction.

The collection opens with two competent but unspectacular cases, "Money Talks" (*This Week*, 4/2/50, as "The Sound of Blackmail"; *EQMM* 8/52), in which Ellery determines which of Mrs. Alfredo's boarders is trying to blackmail her, and "A Matter of Seconds" (*TW*, 8/9/53; *EQMM* 1/57), wherein he is named as pay-off man in the kidnapping of a big-name boxer from his Colorado training camp just before the big fight, makes a neat but esoteric deduction (esoteric at least to me, whose knowledge of pugilism is nil), and saves $100,000 in ransom money before the bell goes off for the first round. But the next pair of stories are gems of the first water. "The Three Widows" (*TW*, 1/29/50, as "Murder Without Clues"; *EQMM* 1/52) is a beautiful little impossible-crime story dealing with how wealthy Sarah Hood could have been poisoned under locked-room conditions, and the much reprinted "My Queer Dean!" (*TW*, 3/8/53; *EQMM* 11/56) concerns a priceless copy of the essays of Francis Bacon, the theft of $10,000 from a university administration building, and the outrageous spoonerisms of Dean Matthew Arnold Hope, which enable Ellery to make sense of the case.

In "Driver's Seat" (*TW*, 3/25/51, as "Lady, You're Dead!"; *EQMM* 11/55) Ellery neatly solves a problem in elimination, deducing which of the three surviving Brothers brothers stabbed the fourth Brothers brother's widow to death in the middle of a teeming rainstorm. "A Lump of Sugar" (*TW*, 7/9/50, as "The Mystery of the 3 Dawn Riders"; *EQMM* 2/53) is Queen's earliest dying message short-short, much earlier in fact than its 1950 magazine publication would suggest, since it's a reworking of the Vienna adventure related by Drury Lane in Act III Scene 3 of *The Tragedy of X*. The reason why the victim's last act was to clutch some sugar from a nearby table is different in each of the two versions but more ingenious in the 1950 than in the 1932 account.

If Barnaby Ross influenced "A Lump of Sugar," the major influence on "Cold Money" (*TW*, 3/20/52; *EQMM* 1/56) was Cornell Woolrich, a bitter recluse given at times to secreting large sums of cash in his hotel room, whose brilliant novelet "Mystery in Room 913" Queen had reprinted in *EQMM* for December 1949. Queen's own story deals with a vanishing $62,000 payroll and the murder of an ex-convict who had holed up in another hotel room numbered 913—both matters resolved by Ellery with fiendish neatness. On the other hand "The Myna Birds" (*TW*, 12/28/52, as "The Myna Bird Mystery"; *EQMM* 9/56, as "Cut, Cut, Cut!") is influenced by none but Queen himself; who else would have his detective solve the murder of a bird-loving millionairess by an analysis of what her myna said upon her death? But with "A Question of Honor" (*TW*, 9/13/53; *EQMM* 5/58), in which Ellery proves that the "suicide" of a visiting Scotland Yard man and Shakespeare scholar is murder, we see again the gaunt shadow of Cornell Woolrich, whose "Murder with a U," collected in book form in 1952, was based on a similar gimmick.

The only tale of true short-story length in the collection, "The Robber of Wrightsville" (*Today's Family*, 2/53; *EQMM* 12/54, as "The Accused"), brings back one major and two minor characters from *Ten Days' Wonder*: Wolfert Van Horn, Delbert Hood (the bellhop whom Ellery had paid to watch the door of Room 1010 in the Hollis Hotel) and Jeep Jorking (the policeman who was guarding Howard Van Horn just before his death). Ellery returns to Wrightsville on a skiing trip but gets sidetracked into clearing Delbert on an armed robbery charge and reconciling him with his stepfather who was the robber's victim.

Ellery's problem in "Double Your Money" (*TW*, 9/30/51, as "The Vanishing Wizard"; *EQMM* 9/55) is to find out how a clever confidence man disappeared from a locked and guarded office seven floors above the street —and the answer is both simple and satisfying. Less rewarding, at least to my taste, is "Miser's Gold" (*TW*, 6/18/50, as "Love Hunts a Hidden Treasure"; *EQMM* 4/54), where the problem involves interpreting the last words of a miserly bibliophilic pawnbroker and determining where in his crammed-full shop he hid four million dollars in cash.

If I had to pick a single favorite Queen short-short it would be "Snowball in July" (*TW*, 8/31/52, as "The Phantom Train"; *EQMM* 7/56), in which, one sizzling summer morning, an entire train apparently vanishes on a straight stretch of track between two upstate New York whistlestops six minutes apart. As in all of Queen's best miracle problems, the answer is blindingly obvious but concealed by masterful misdirection. On the other hand, the answer to the problem in "The Witch of Times Square" (*TW*, 11/5/50; *EQMM* 5/53)—which of two claimants to a fortune is the real John Gaard—is forthcoming only after an uninspired and lucky bluff. Readers of Agatha Christie's "The House at Shiraz" (in *Mr. Parker Pyne, Detective*), which contradicts Queen's story on a key point in genetics, are assured by my science-intoxicated wife that Queen is right on this issue.

"The Gamblers' Club" (*TW*, 1/7/51; *EQMM* 3/55) is a con-game tale involving an anonymous dispenser of accurate stock-market tips, not inordinately difficult for Ellery to unravel but neatly mounted and satisfying. "GI Story" (*EQMM* 8/54), the only short-short in *QBI* that was not originally published in *This Week*, is another Wrightsville story and another dying message story. Once again Ellery gets sidetracked from a skiing trip and propelled into a crime problem, this time a murder case. One of wealthy merchant Clint Fosdick's stepsons—Wash, Linc or Woody—poisoned him for the inheritance; the murdered man's last act was to write the letters GI; two of the suspects had been in the military and the third still is. This is a superb little story, one of Queen's all-time best at this length.

The perpetrator of the impossible in "The Black Ledger" (*TW*, 1/26/52, as "The Mysterious Black Ledger"; *EQMM* 12/55) is not a criminal but Ellery, and the narcotics ganglord whose empire will collapse if Ellery gets the ledger safely to Washington is relegated to the position of detective. Ellery is captured on the Capitol Limited, stripped and searched over and over, but his adversary has not been keeping up on his Carr and Rawson, and Ellery pulls off the miracle with the aplomb of a Houdini, even providing the reader with a subtle pointer to the document's location.

The final story, "Child Missing!" (*TW*, 7/8/51, as "Kidnaped!"; *EQMM* 6/58) deals with the disappearance of seven-year-old Billy Harper five weeks after the separation of his wealthy parents, and the subsequent delivery of a ransom note demanding payment under physically impossible conditions.   The solution to this riddle is breathtakingly simple and brings *QBI* to an end on a note of gentle humor.

Queen's next book, *Inspector Queen's Own Case* (1956), was his second novel in a row without Ellery; and, as with *The Glass Village,* the result was a superb book that would have been impossible had Ellery been in it. As Dannay himself and such critics as J. R. Christopher have pointed out, the leitmotif of the novel is gerontology, the process of growing old—a theme possibly related to the fact that both Dannay and Lee had passed the half-century mark between *The Glass Village* and this novel.

As the book opens Richard Queen has been involuntarily separated from the police department, having reached the compulsory retirement age of 63. Ellery is traveling in Europe for the summer, and Richard is visiting an old NYPD teammate, Abe Pearl, now chief of police in the sleepy hamlet of Taugus, Connecticut. Richard's mood is glum, he feels himself useless, decaying, tumbling downhill into senescence. Then by chance he meets Jessie Sherwood, still attractive at 49, a trained nurse employed by the millionaires Alton and Sarah Humffrey to care for their newly adopted baby; and the rest of the book is devoted largely to the ripening of

Richard's and Jessie's relationship, which is evoked in
all its ups and downs with delicate and subtle witchery.
But the event most responsible for bringing them together is a peculiarly hideous one: the suffocation of two-
month-old Michael Stiles Humffrey one summer night.
Although Chief Pearl and the coroner's jury and the
Humffreys themselves agree that the death was accidental, Jessie is certain that the baby was murdered. Richard Queen—partly because he has nothing else to do,
partly because he wants to see more of Jessie, hoping
against hope that he is not making himself look
ridiculous to her, and perhaps in part simply because he
believes her—takes up the quest with her, and tries to
prove that the dirty handprint she is convinced she saw
on the pillow that smothered the baby (although it was
not there when the police arrived) is more than a figment
of her overwrought imagination. The trail leads to a
shady lawyer, a fading nightclub singer, a walled sanitar-
ium, a plush Park Avenue apartment, and to more
deaths, these indubitably murder. And the solution, although completely fair and deducible by the reader, is
not in fact deduced by any character in the book, but is
merely discovered.

The gerontology theme is embodied in several other
aspects of the book besides the Richard/Jessie relationship. Thus every significant character with two exceptions is well past his or her prime, and even one of the
exceptions, Connie Coy, is described as beginning to age.
(The other exception is the baby, who provides deliberate contrast.) Nor is it chance that when Richard needs
help on the case he goes to five retired police veterans,
all feeling as useless as he and all delighted as children
at the opportunity to see action again. (They call themselves the 87th Street Irregulars, after the Baker Street

Irregulars who were of course a group of young boys.) Even the structure of the plot serves Queen's theme in its own way, derived as it is from the traditional Gothic suspense-romance—the female outsider who comes to the lonely mansion to work for a gaunt and wealthy master, who claims that an apparent accidental death was murder but can get no one to believe her, who prowls about the mansion alone by night and is trapped by the killer and rescued at the last minute by her ardent swain—but with the unique switch that hero, heroine and all other participants are pushing fifty or higher.

As usual in third-period Queen, *Inspector Queen's Own Case* resounds with echoes from earlier works. The true/false confession goes back to 1933 and *The Siamese Twin Mystery,* in which the killer also has the same first name as here; the functions of the Humffreys closely resemble those of the Cazalises in *Cat of Many Tails;* the construction and fortuitous timing of the Connie Coy murder recall the death of Margo Cole in *The Dragon's Teeth.* But since Queen has fully reworked these elements and integrated them into the new framework, their effect is to make *Inspector Queen's Own Case* not just a superbly written story of people who come alive on the page,[5] but an excellent mystery as well, one of Queen's two finest novels of the Fifties.

Inspector Queen's Own Case had been subtitled: November Song by Ellery Queen. The obvious inference is that with December the Queen canon will end. And his next novel is not only set largely in December but is entitled *The Finishing Stroke* (1958). Most of it takes place in 1929, and the young Ellery has just published his first book, *The Roman Hat Mystery,* suggesting that Queen (or at least Dannay, the poet) knows T. S. Eliot's

"In my end is my beginning." The evidence is persuasive that he intended to lay down his pen for keeps after *The Finishing Stroke.*

The opening sequence takes us back to 1905—the year Ellery and his creators were born—and deals with the last days of publisher John Sebastian and with the birth of his son in the middle of an ice storm. The bulk of the book, however, unfolds between Christmas Eve of 1929 and Epiphany of 1930. Arthur B. Craig, Sebastian's ex-partner, has invited a number of guests to a twelve-day house party at his estate; at the end of the festivities his ward, John Sebastian Jr., is to come into his father's fortune and marry the fashion designer he is in love with. The guests include a composer, an actress, a doctor, a lawyer, a clergyman, a publisher, and a cock-sure young literatus named Ellery Queen. The festive mood begins to dissolve when a costumed Santa Claus distributes gifts, and vanishes. Then a series of bizarre objects starts to pop up, addressed to John Sebastian, and each accompanied by a piece of doggerel derived from the traditional English carol "The Twelve Days of Christmas." The first gift is a sandalwood ox, followed by a toy house, a tiny lead camel, and so on. An un-identified body is soon discovered in the Craig library, more weird gifts continue to turn up, John Sebastian begins to act like a schizophrenic, blackmail and a love quadrangle and a second murder enter the picture—and the young Ellery is unable to shed any light. Not until twenty-eight years later, when chance has again thrown the case in his path, does he see the truth.

The characters of *The Finishing Stroke* are little more than line drawings, the prose is direct and un-adorned, and the extremely simple plot abounds in all of the genre's hoariest clichés, including the snowbound house-party, the thirteenth guest, murder with an antique dagger in the lordly mansion's library, a séance, identical twins, mysterious clues dropped by an unseen hand. Of course Queen knows that these elements are deadeningly overfamiliar and he chose them quite deliberately so that his "last bow" would reduce the genre to which he had devoted his life to its barest fundamentals. Everything about *The Finishing Stroke* is stylized, reflexive, nostalgic, elegiac—in a word that ties together much of the book's matter and manner, abecedarian.

J. R. Christopher has pointed out that much of the structure of *Inspector Queen's Own Case* is derived from Shakespeare's Seven Ages of Man passage in *As You Like It,* but that the final stage of life, second childhood, was pointedly omitted from that novel. Now, in *The Finishing Stroke,* second childhood moves to center stage. For not only is the plot childishly simple, but at the end of the novel both Arthur Craig and Inspector Queen himself are quite literally in Shakespeare's last stage of "second childishness and mere oblivion,/Sans teeth, sans eyes, sans taste, sans everything." And after the seventh age of man, what can come but the end/ beginning? It's no accident that the letters "ABC" are repeated in the last line.

Once again the plot resounds with echoes from earlier stories. The intrusion of a host of seemingly unrelated objects into an isolated house-party setting goes back to "The Mad Tea-Party," and Ellery's irrelevant efforts to connect each suspect with the number 12 parallels the long and equally irrelevant game of Who Is Backward in *The Chinese Orange Mystery.* Queen also attempts to conjure up one more "player on the other side" with an uncanny ability to manipulate others' thinking, as in *The Greek Coffin Mystery* and *Ten Days'*

Wonder, but the whole ambience of *The Finishing Stroke*
—stylized, elegiac, tranquil, *eine kleine Nachtkriminal-
roman*—makes the attempt singularly feeble and unconvincing. Even more disturbing is the whopping implausi-
bility of a fair amount of the plot, which could not have
happened but for the drooling idiocy of John Sebastian's
keeping quiet about his brother, for no reason at all,
even after the murder. Yet John's behavior is a model
of lucidity next to that of his brother, who as far as I
can see had neither the motive nor the requisite knowledge to make the two blackmail attempts that the
book credits to him. And the pattern of the gifts
seems more like another Jon L. Breen parody than an
authentic Queen gambit.

Internal evidence suggests that Queen wanted to
end his career on a note of quiet mastery. Thus at the
beginning of Chapter VI there is a discussion about an
All-American halfback who is about to play his last college game, and who in the event acquits himself "with
valedictory brilliance." And in the discussion of popular
musicians in Chapter VIII, Ellen Craig remarks: "They
play standard works familiar to everybody, and they
play them beautifully." Clearly in both passages Queen
is thinking not just of halfbacks and pops orchestras but
of himself. It's unfortunate that not all of the substance
of *The Finishing Stroke* lives up to Queen's hopes. He
deserved a more perfect "December Song."

CHAPTER ELEVEN

AFTER THE FINISHING STROKE *QUEEN PUBLISHED ALMOST* nothing for five years. The millions of his readers who hungered for new stories of Ellery and his father had to be content with the abortive NBC television series of the 1958-59 season, which is discussed in the Cinematic Interlude. Finally in 1963 Queen returned to action, and the novel he published that year proved worth waiting for.

The setting of *The Player on the Other Side* is York Square, an isolated little pocket of the past in New York City but not of it. At each corner of the square is a castle, and in its center a diamond-shaped park. The cold, precise philatelist Robert York inhabits the castle at the southwest corner; the white-haired, determined social worker Emily York the northwest; the gentle, mentally unbalanced lush Myra York the southeast; the aging philanderer Percival York the northeast. The four cousins are required to live in York Square by the terms of Nathaniel York Senior's will, under which, after ten years of residence, they inherit his millions in equal shares, the share of any cousin who dies during the residence period to be divided among the survivors— yes, our old friend the tontine again. A weak-brained, robot-like handyman named Walt serves as caretaker for all four cousins, three of whom share the housekeeping services of a Mrs. Shriver as well. Robert York employs a young intellectual named Tom Archer to help him with his stamp collections and Myra engages the lovely Ann Drew as her nurse and companion. These eight people— along with a ninth, Nathaniel York Jr., the long-dead (or is he?) son of the founder of the York empire—are at the heart of the novel, where murder and madness strike.

From the very beginning of the book we know the identity of the murderer. The person who is sending a paper polygon stamped with a cryptic initial to each of the York cousins in turn and is then killing the cousins one by one is the caretaker, Walt. But the zombie-like Walt is merely carrying out the detailed written instructions of someone who is manipulating him, using him as a living murder weapon—someone who signs himself Y. Walt is a simple soldier, following orders. The mystery is who is giving him the orders.

When we first see Ellery, he is suffering from both writer's block and existential ennui. It soon dawns on him that his problems are caused by modern technology and police science, which have rendered implausible and obsolete both the rationalistic detective story and Ellery himself, the quintessential man of reason. Personally, I suspect his diagnosis is quite right, and that this is one of the reasons for the decline of the formal deductive problem. In fact when we look back at Queen's novels of the Fifties like *The King Is Dead, Inspector Queen's Own Case* and *The Finishing Stroke*, we may safely conclude that this problem had been gnawing at Queen for years, and that the isolated settings of those novels were, at least in part, designed so that the apparatus of modern technology would be plausibly unavailable in the milieu, thus allowing room for the exercise of the unaided reason.   But in *Player* Queen comes to full self-consciousness about the crisis of formal deductive fiction, and by creating York Square he devises a strategy to cope with the crisis which, with variations and with varying success, he will employ again and again during the Sixties.   He creates a world that is isolated not so much geographically as aesthetically, a milieu as remote from external reality as the inside of an egg and as stylized as a chessboard.   (The game of chess is the unifying image in *Player,* York Square being a chessboard and the four castles being placed in the exact positions of the rooks, or castles, at the beginning of the game.)   This type of milieu is what binds together Queen's output since 1963, and it expresses not only a response to a technical problem but an increasing alienation from the nightmare of living in the real America of our time.

In *Cat of Many Tails* Richard Queen prodded Ellery out of his guilt-haunted detachment by dangling before him the bait of involvement with the real world, but in *Player* the Inspector prods him out of the real world and into the chessboard of York Square.   And as the murders continue, and as Ellery several times comes achingly close to the part of the truth that we have seen from the beginning, and as possibilities multiply and secrets are bared, the complex patterns of Queen's web slowly become more and more intelligible until finally they coalesce in the encounter with Y, the player on the other side.

Those who have not read *Player* should skip this paragraph.   Those who have are aware that Y, or JHWH as he also signs himself, is revealed to be not only a flesh-and-blood human being but also, in a very real sense, God himself, Yahweh, Jehovah, the patriarch, the god of vengeance and stern justice. A morally irresponsible murderer whose acts are under the control of a Y, indeed of a father and a York, carries us all the way back to 1932 and *The Tragedy of Y*. But the revelation of Y's identity in *Player* parallels even more closely the conclusion of *Ten Days' Wonder,* and in both novels the climactic moment comes when Ellery witnesses the death of God. And just as the structure of *Ten Days' Wonder* inverts the traditional teaching that man was made in God's image, so that of *Player* inverts the maxim that God manifests himself in the meek and humble of heart. The difference between the two books is that the earlier deals with manipulation from the outside and the later with manipulation from within. But manipulation of one sort or another has been a dominant Queen theme since the first Drury Lane novel back in 1932, and we shall see it in one more guise in *And On the Eighth Day*. Reduced to over-simplicity, the point of *Player* is that we are not in control. "One is played upon, not player."

Within this framework Queen plays innumerable variations on his theme. Just to give two examples, Ellery himself becomes a species of manipulator-god when in chapters 18 and 19 he confronts the suspects with those cryptic words "I know all about it"; and the interview between Richard Queen and Miss Sullivan in Chapter 11 evokes an unmistakable sense that the woman is in her own way no less a dissociated personality than Walt-Nathaniel-Y. Perceptive readers will be able to add to this brief list with no difficulty.

One historical footnote seems in order here.

Queen's inspiration for *Player* apparently came not only
from his own *Ten Days' Wonder* and *The Tragedy of Y*
but also from Alfred Hitchcock's great 1960 film *Psycho*.
In a way then, Queen in borrowing from Hitchcock for
Player was being amply repaid for the influence *Calamity
Town* had exerted on Hitchcock's *Shadow of a Doubt*
exactly two decades earlier. That both *Psycho* and
Player remain unforgettable once encountered stems
perhaps from the intimation of each that the condition
it is concerned with—trappedness by the past for Hitchcock, manipulation and being manipulated for Queen—
is somehow a paradigm of the human condition. Such
is the extent and depth of meaning possible in a Queen
novel, and one that set out to be deliberately divorced
from the "real" world!

In Queen's next novel, perhaps the most contro-
versial of his career, he plumbed even further. *And On
the Eighth Day* (1964) is set in the spring of 1944, when
the world was ravaged by the worst war in its history.
Ellery has been in Hollywood four months, writing
scripts for Army training films, until finally, at the point
of collapse from sheer exhaustion, he is sent home.
Driving across the western desert, he loses his way and
comes upon what amounts to a lost race—a religious-
socialist community that has made its home in the desert
and has made the desert bloom. The Teacher of the
community, on hearing Ellery's name, prostrates himself in awe; for the Sacred Book had foretold that this
man would come, and that a time of great trouble would
visit the community with him, and that a second visitor,
greater than the first, would follow. Exhausted and un-
sure whether he is dreaming or awake, Ellery enters the
Valley of Quenan and learns the way of life of the community. All property is held in common, there has been

no crime or violence of any kind for fifty years, the word war is not in the people's vocabulary, no man is alienated from the labor he performs, there is a natural harmony between man and the earth. In short, the scene is Eden before the Fall.

But the fall seems imminent. On the second night of Ellery's stay, someone tampers with the Teacher's key to the sanquetum, the forbidden room in the Holy Congregation House which none but the Teacher may enter. The following night the tampering is repeated, and the next afternoon Storicai the storesman is found bludgeoned to death in the Holy Congregation House. Murder in Eden, and Ellery, the only person in the valley who knows anything about crime, must identify the murderer.

Such is the basic structure of *And On the Eighth Day*, a structure which Queen has deliberately kept very simple, since the first violent act in a civilization can hardly be made to happen under locked-room conditions. Besides being very simple, the plot as plot is rather uninteresting and even in some respects totally incredible, for instance the matter of those fingerprints on the hammer. But of course one can't legitimately expect a great deal of intellectual excitement from what amounts to the murder of Abel by Cain. And in any event, far from being an end in itself, the plot of *And On the Eighth Day* perhaps more than that of any other Queen novel is merely a pretext for Queen's deeper explorations.

The thrust of these explorations has been miscon-strued by several critics, apparently including Anthony Boucher, as a one-for-one allegory of the passion, death and resurrection of Jesus as related in the Gospels. Of course the Teacher can, up to a point, be identified with

Jesus—his last supper, his trial, his taking upon himself and suffering and dying for the sins of the community. But at the same time he is also Socrates, judging from the manner of his death, and a Buddhist or Hindu figure as well, judging from the fact that he is not physically resurrected but rather his spirit is reincarnated in another. And if Ellery is meant to stand for John the Baptist, the forerunner of the Greater who is to follow, he also represents both Moses (the encounter with the flaming bush, the trek through the desert to the promised land) and Pilate (the prosecutor of the Teacher). Likewise the Crownsil of Twelve is multi-functional, standing in part for the Apostles, in part for the Sanhedrin (the condemnation of the Teacher) and perhaps in part for organized Christianity (greed for temporal power and material wealth leading it to betray its Teacher's simple message of peace and love). The only figure that can be straightforwardly related to a single Biblical personage is Storicai, whose name is an anagram of Iscariot and whose acts are easily identifiable with those of the Biblical Judas. But Storicai is the exception that proves the rule. And Queen goes far out of his way to evoke all sorts of non-Biblical resonances—Cortez and Montezuma, Churchill, Bernard Shaw and Amy Lowell, to name only a few—in order to create a sense of "the recurrence of the great and the famous across the shifting planes of space-time."[1] Queen intends this sense of historical awe to supplement the sense of religious awe, the intuition of the presence of the numinous, which is the central thrust of *And On the Eighth Day*. "It is too much . . . —too much, too much, too much; it's more than reason can bear. . . . Too much, an infinite complexity beyond the grasp of man. Acknowledge. Acknowledge and depart."

In this sense the book can be considered a religious novel. In another sense it is a social novel, a protest against the world outside the holy community, the world with its war and greed, its acquisition and competition and pollution and hate. And we can also look at the novel simply as an integral part of the Queen canon, filled with characteristic Queen themes and devices—the isolated milieu; the false-solution-followed-by-the-true; the enchantment with "the lovely past"; the distrust of human nature, even in Eden, coupled with the hope of redemption implied by the book's final moments; and the pervasiveness of a condition which in any other atmosphere but the numinous one of this novel we would have to call manipulatedness. Finally we should not overlook the fact that *And On the Eighth Day* is a *tour de force* in which Queen uses the detective-story form, which presupposes the power of reason to order chaos and comprehend the truth of phenomena, in a manner calculated to undercut our idolatrous faith in reason. It is not an intellectually exciting detective story in its own right, but the wonder of it is that it is so much more than a detective story.

Queen's 1965 publications were far less intense, less meaningful, more relaxed than *The Player on the Other Side* or *And On the Eighth Day*. The early months of the year saw the appearance of *Queens Full*, a mixed bag of two novelets, one normal-length short story and two short-shorts, including specimens of Queen at his best, his worst and his most typical. The lead novelet, "The Death of Don Juan" (*Argosy*, 5/62; *EQMM* 8/64), is set in Wrightsville and deals with the attempt of the town's amateur theatrical company to stage a creaky old turn-of-the-century melodrama. When the once-famous alcoholic wreck slated for the leading role of

Don Juan breaks his wrist and ribs shortly before opening night and another has-been is rushed in as a replacement, the scene is set for offstage murder, complete with dying message. Fortunately Ellery is in the opening-night audience and actually hears the crucial last words himself, but it's only after he eliminates some red herrings through a dental test of his own design (shades of *The Dragon's Teeth*!) that he construes the message rightly and pins the guilt on a fairly obvious Least Likely Suspect. The plot is trim and competent, the people and prose pleasant, the satiric opportunities latent in the milieu are largely wasted, and Wrightsville's new and hostile police chief, Anse Newby, is a pale shadow of old retired Chief Dakin. Lacking anything one could either fault or get excited about, "The Death of Don Juan" is a dim reflection of the glory of the greatest Wrightsville tales.

In "E = Murder" (*This Week*, 8/14/60; *EQMM* 5/61), Ellery's lecture at Bethesda University is interrupted by the murder of a noted physicist working on a top secret project in a limited-access tower. Both Dr. Agon's dying message and Ellery's interpretation are consciously far-fetched in what was soon to become the standard fun-and-games manner of Queen's recent short-shorts, but so much is packed into the eight pages of this tale that we are too busy sorting out possibilities to object.

Probably Queen's worst story of the Fifties, "The Wrightsville Heirs" (*Better Living*, 1-2/56; *EQMM* 11/57) is concerned with the death of wealthy Bella Bluefield Livingston suspiciously soon after her announcement that she is about to disinherit her three dissolute step-children and leave her fortune to her paid companion. Chief Dakin, not yet retired, summons Ellery to help him find out which of the trio smothered the old lady to death. The answer is surprising, but only because it's based on reasoning unworthy of a cretin, a ridiculous trap that proves less than nothing, and a colossally misinformed notion of how estates are administered. Queen seems to have slanted this story directly for the women's slick market, whose demands for soft lights and sloppy thinking were totally alien to his talents, but he never, thank heaven, made that mistake again.

"Diamonds in Paradise" (*EQMM* 9/54) is a neat little vignette in which Ellery untangles the last words of a very unlucky gem snatcher and recovers a pair of emeralds for a Broadway sex goddess without ever leaving the Queen apartment. Both in its original form in *EQMM* and in the considerably revised *Queens Full* version, the story reads as if Queen had been dipping into Damon Runyon before putting pen to paper.

Last and by far the best work in the collection is "The Case Against Carroll" (*Argosy*, 9/58; *EQMM* 9/60), which has a thin formal plot and only a small role for Ellery but which is so rich in character interplay and moral ambiguity and leashed tension as to win it a place near the top of the Queen canon. Attorney John Carroll is charged with the murder of his brutal partner, Meredith Hunt, who was on the point of ruining him; he swears that he has a perfect alibi but can't prove it, and frantically he begs Ellery for help. The situation is vaguely reminiscent of Woolrich's *Phantom Lady*, but the death-house climax, in which Ellery deliberately seems to do an act of terrible evil in order that he may accomplish some small good, recalls most vividly Queen's own *The Tragedy of Z*, and gives almost as vivid form to Queen's detestation of capital punishment. I would rank this story as one of his finest tales of the Fifties (along

with *The Glass Village* and *Inspector Queen's Own Case*),
and among his novelets as second only to "The Lamp of
God," and among the contents of *Queens Full* as far
and away the finest mystery, the best study of character,
the fullest embodiment of Queen's world-view.

In the novel he published later that year, *The
Fourth Side of the Triangle* (1965), Queen attempted
the offtrail experiment of a novel set in the present but
filled with characters and attitudes more appropriate to
the crime fiction of the early 1920's, with Ellery the
nominal detective but incapacitated and offstage for
most of the book and unsuccessful when he finally does
some detecting. The experiment was not a howling
triumph but the fact that Queen was still experimenting,
still not content with a formula after more than 35 years
of mystery writing, is more significant than the specific
weaknesses of this book.

As in *Ten Days' Wonder* there are very few central
characters and most of them are concentrated in one
family. Head of the clan is graying, aggressive Ashton
McKell, the last merchant prince in a long line. His wife
Lutetia is a vague, submissive scatterbrain whose half-
century of patrician existence has been sheltered beyond
belief. Somehow she and Ashton managed to produce
one child, Dane McKell, a handsome and headstrong
young man with little real talent but great ambition to
be a novelist and a generous independent income to
support his ambition. The precipitating crisis arises
when Lutetia tells Dane that Ashton has admitted a
sexual affair with another woman. Dane decides to find
out who his father's mistress is, and then to take Ashton's place as her lover so that Dad will return to pas-
sionless fidelity. Dane's motives, which he understands
only in part, seem to be partly Oedipal and Freudian

and partly Drury Lanean. What is at work here is not only his desire as a son to supplant his father sexually (and symbolically to castrate him) but also his ambition as a creative person to intervene in a real-life drama and manipulate living persons rather than fictitious characters. He shadows his father to a rendezvous right in the McKell apartment building, takes steps to meet the lovely fashion designer who rents the penthouse, begins his own campaign of sexual conquest which is cut short by murder within the four-sided triangle. Ellery Queen, with both legs broken in a skiing accident, can do no more than sit on the sidelines and make suggestions as the investigation leads to a first, then a second, then a projected third murder trial. When his limbs heal and he is ready to name the murderer, surprise and humiliation are waiting for him.

Unfortunately *Fourth Side* leaves a great deal to be desired. The structure of the story, with one trial leading to another leading to a third, soon becomes mechanical and predictable, and what is worse, presupposes some staggeringly silly notions of police work. Thus, Richard Queen's staff turns up first all the evidence pointing to A, then all the pointers to B, then to C, conveniently missing every clue against B until the end of A's trial and all the clues pointing to C until the end of B's. That the book's structure also requires several whopping lapses of memory on the part of various characters does not make the machinery run any more smoothly. The whole milieu is impossibly upper-upper, and the incidental lower-class characters, like the Irishwoman and the bartender, are ethnic caricatures right down to the yes-sor-me-name-is-O'Rarke vaudeville dialect. In effect then, the book propels us back into the ambience of the mystery novels of the early Twenties without giving us any of the delights of a true period novel. The device of the false-solution-followed-by-the-true can be seen coming long before it arrives.

Thus neither the plot nor structure nor characterizations nor the treatment of legal matters displays Queen's talents at anywhere near their peak. Yet the book does have a few virtues, notably a convincing evocation of the world of high fashion, a beautifully hidden but fair key to the unraveling of the puzzle, and the spectacle of Ellery having to be rescued from intellectual error by his long-suffering father. And, of paramount importance, *Fourth Side* shows that Queen's zest for experiment had not diminished as he entered his seventh decade.

This zest gave rise in the following year, 1966, to another radical departure, but one that in a sense had been waiting twenty years for Queen. The supposition had long tantalized readers that Victorian London's greatest consulting detective and its most fiendish unpunished criminal *must* once have crossed swords. That the published papers of Dr. John H. Watson contain no account of a duel between Sherlock Holmes and Jack the Ripper has not dimmed the light of speculation on this subject among Holmesians. In his introduction to *The Misadventures of Sherlock Holmes* (1944), Queen had printed Anthony Boucher's description of a Spanish-language original entitled *Jack, El Destripador* in which Holmes runs the Ripper to earth.[2] Then in 1945 *The Woman in Green*, one of Universal's Holmes films directed by Roy William Neill and starring Basil Rathbone and Nigel Bruce, brought into the present not only Holmes and Watson but the Ripper too, though in subdued form: his victims are not prostitutes, he does not disembowel them after death but merely slices off a

finger from each, and he turns out to be a tool of
Professor Moriarty! Finally, twenty years later came the
British film *A Study in Terror,* directed by James Hill
from a screenplay by Donald and Derek Ford, starring
John Neville as Holmes and Donald Houston as Watson.
The film is set in a convincingly garish gas-lit London
and evokes the menage of Holmes and Watson lovingly,
but bogs down in an impossible-to-keep-straight plot
pitting Holmes against the Ripper. As part of its promo-
tional campaign Columbia Pictures commissioned a
"novelization" of the screenplay. After John Dickson
Carr turned down the assignment on grounds of poor
health, the author who wound up with the contract was
Ellery Queen.

A novelization of a film falls by definition into a
very low order of creativity, with the novelizer ordinarily
being a low-budget hack who takes about a week to put
the screenplay into prose. Insofar as he departs from
the script and uses it as a launching-pad for his own
concepts, he is not novelizing but writing his own
original—which is very close to what Queen did with *A
Study in Terror.* Not only did he sneak Ellery himself
into the book and give him a role equal in scope to that
of Holmes, but he gleefully scrapped most of the latter
half of the screenplay and rewrote it into something not
too remote from a Queen novel, complete with the
customary false-solution-followed-by-the-true. In other
words he broke every rule of the novelizer's game, and
turned out one of the few movie novelizations, perhaps
the only one, that is worth reading and discussing as a
novel in its own right.

As recast by Queen, the story opens with Ellery
receiving an anonymous package containing a manuscript
that purports to be by one John H. Watson, M.D. Rac-

ing to meet a manuscript deadline of his own, Ellery squeezes in time to read the material and attempt to trace its sender. The manuscript likewise opens with Holmes receiving an anonymous package, this one containing a complete set of surgeon's instruments except for one missing post-mortem scalpel. The ensuing scene in which Holmes reels off deduction after effortless deduction from the condition of the instrument-case is the highspot of the entire book. The case soon leads Holmes and Watson into the demesne of a demented duke, the chill shadows of a combination hostel and mortuary in the slums of Whitechapel, and into numerous pubs and abattoirs and brothels on the trail of Jack the Ripper.

Unhappily Queen leaves the plot with at least a dozen loose ends and unplugged holes, and allows Holmes far too much baseless lucky guesswork. The fast pacing and sex and gore are enough to remind one of a private eye novel, and even though Queen tries his best with these elements from the screenplay, and even though we know from Steven Marcus' *The Other Victorians* and similar works that Holmes' London *was* full of filth and sex and gore, still Queen's proper objective in this book is not to recreate the true London of 1888 but London as Conan Doyle perceived it, and except for the superb first chapter of the manuscript he does not succeed in maintaining this illusion. (Can you imagine the original Holmes and Watson entering a brothel and conversing casually with some half-clad ladies of the evening?) Even aside from the mid-20th-century elements there are too many weak spots, as when Lestrade (just like Dennis Hoey in the Rathbone films) addresses the Master as 'Olmes, or when Watson clairvoyantly informs us that Holmes *will* raise bees after his retirement.

Further, as Erik Routley points out in *The Puritan Pleasures of the Detective Story* (Gollancz, 1972), the entire Watsonian "manuscript" is full of Americanisms in both narrative and dialogue. So all in all the book falls considerably short of being a proper addition to the Adventures and Memoirs. The chapters set in the present and involving Ellery are somewhat more successful, and the great man's deductions from the end of the manuscript are more intriguing than anything in the manuscript itself after the first chapter. The two solutions device marks the book instantly as pure Queen, and the competition between Holmes and his logical successor recalls the famous tales in which Ellery matched wits with George Washington and Abraham Lincoln. In brief then, Queen exercised far more autonomy over the screenplay of *A Study in Terror* than any ordinary novelizer would either desire or dare, enough to transform it partially but not totally into a Queen novel; yet the work's many imperfections cannot diminish its fascination as another Queenly experiment.

With *Face to Face* (1967) Queen not only returned to the simon-pure detective novel but put Ellery squarely at center stage—a combination he had not employed since *The Player on the Other Side*. The result was a novel that in a curious way is *Player*'s mirror image. For in *Player* the physical murderer was known from the outset and the problem was to locate the manipulator who was using him as a weapon, while in *Face* the manipulator's identity is clear at once and the task is to deduce whom *he* used as his living weapon.

Ellery returns from England on New Year's morning, accompanied by a new acquaintance, Scottish private investigator Harry Burke, and the two detectives find an urgent call for help waiting at the Queen apart-

ment.   Actress Roberta West tells them that seven
months ago the notorious philanderer Count Carlos
Armando, with whom she had been romantically entangled, had asked her to murder his wealthy and much
older wife for him. Roberta had turned him down flat
and run out of Armando's life for good, she says; but
now, seven months later, Mrs. Armando—better known
as the once-famous radio singer Glory Guild—has just
been shot to death at a time when Armando has a perfect
alibi, namely that he was with Roberta in her own apartment at the time of the murder. Roberta is convinced
that Armando persuaded another of the countless women
in his life to do the dirty work, but there is no clue to
which one did it except for Glory Guild's cryptic dying
message, the single word FACE. The detectives' investigation unearths a host of the Count's female acquaintances and leads to such elements as a long-lost niece, a
will that says too much, and a panhandler who knows
too much, but the developing relationships among the
central characters are even more crucial to the plot,
which culminates in the finest piece of fair bamboozle-
ment of the reader that Queen perpetrated during the
Sixties.

Technically *Face* like *Player* is a superb specimen
of innovation within a framework of strict tradition,
much of it rooted in earlier Queen novels. The manipu-
lator-living weapon concept, as we have seen, has a long
and honorable lineage in Queen's writing. The murder
trial that hinges on the defendant's having forgotten the
single fact that will save his or her skin comes straight
out of *The Fourth Side of the Triangle* but this time is
handled somewhat more plausibly. The sexual blackmailer and the jaded gossip columnist echo the similar
characters in *The Scarlet Letters*. The climactic counter-

point between the Episcopal marriage ceremony and the exposure of the murderer will be recalled from *There Was an Old Woman.* And devotees of Queen's earliest novels need no reminder of where they first heard of the Roman Theater or Judge J. J. McCue. But, as usual when Queen borrows from himself, the effect is not of mechanical reshuffling but of integration into a new context. And the new context includes a May-December gambit that combines a masterfully concealed clue and a stunningly surprising murderer.

What is most memorable about *Face to Face,* however, is not the identity of the woman who pulled the trigger for Armando but Queen's treatment of her in human terms. After Ellery has explained everything in brilliant but bloodlessly mechanical words, she takes center stage, insists that she really had fallen in love and wanted to start a new life after being used by Armando and left with nothing; and now her new life too is rubble. Queen does not let us forget that at least to some extent she *allowed* Armando to use her, but he stresses with equal force that she was a tool in Armando's hands and that she was on the point of a lasting relationship with another man when Ellery discovered and smashed her. This mingled compassion and revulsion for her which Queen evokes at the climax, this sense of moral ambiguity reminiscent of Hitchcock (specifically of his treatment of Judy/Madeleine in *Vertigo*), seems to me the most fully human aspect of Queen's work in the Sixties; and the fusion of this ambiguity with splendid technical expertise raises *Face to Face* to high rank within the Canon.

CHAPTER TWELVE

IN 1968 JUST AS IN 1965, QUEEN PUBLISHED A MIXED BAG OF short fiction early in the year and later a novel that didn't work. *Q.E.D.: Queen's Experiments in Detection* brought together most of his uncollected shorter work of the Fifties and Sixties, including some good stories, some not so good, and at least one that must be called great. The title embodies not only a play on words but a characteristic Queen pattern of experiment within strict tradition, and every story in the book, good or bad, is at least distinctively Queenian.

"Mum Is the Word" (*EQMM* 4/66), the only novelet in the volume, stands dead center in the classic tradition, complete with Wrightsville setting, an isolated houseful of suspects, a missing million-dollar pendant, and a properly impenetrable Dying Message. Flower seed tycoon Godfrey Mumford, who in retirement has become a fanatic devotee of the chrysanthemum, announces some drastic financial retrenchments to his expectant heirs, suffers a severe stroke, and is stabbed to death in his bed with his own letter-opener, writing the three letters MUM on a bedside pad before breathing his last. Ellery once again happens to be in Wrightsville for the fatality and Chief Anse Newby enlists his aid. But his solution turns out to be uninspired and the murderer's motivation to be incredible, besides which certain plot elements are lifted bodily from other Queen stories (e.g. the Englishwoman and the sleeping pills in the hot milk from "Eve of the Wedding," also in *Q.E.D.*) and others are staggeringly implausible on their face (no hospital room nor even a private nurse available for a seriously ill millionaire!). But Ellery's analysis of the possible meanings of "Mum" and his explication of "doubleness" are outrageously fantastic in the best Wonderland vein.

Next come four "Contemporary Problems in Deduction," each story being intended to explore a characteristic urban problem, such as juvenile delinquency, the housing shortage and poverty. In "Object Lesson" (*This Week*, 9/11/55, as "The Blackboard Gangsters"; *EQMM* 4/58) Ellery visits the neighborhood high school to give a talk on crime and winds up having to solve one—petty theft from the teacher's desk—before the end of the period. This he does quite neatly, but the story is just too slight to bear the heavy sociological weight Queen tries to impose on it. In "No Parking" (*TW*, 3/18/56, as "Terror in a Penthouse"; *EQMM* 2/58) the crime is murder—a Broadway actress who disappointed several suitors is shot during a fierce rainstorm—but Ellery's solution is logically weak and unconvincing. "No Place to Live" (*TW*, 6/10/56, as "The Man They All Hated"; *EQMM* 3/58) concerns murder in an apartment full of unauthorized subtenants, the plot centering on a GI just back from Europe who (a) carries around $3,000 in cash amid a veritable nest of vipers, (b) doesn't bother to tell his bride that he has this money, and (c) forgets to tell the police where in his room he had kept the bills hidden before they were stolen. One sensible act on his part would have frozen the story in its tracks. In "Miracles Do Happen" (*EQMM* 7/57), by far the best of the quartet, Ellery and his father investigate the murder of a usurer who was calling in his loans—a case distinguished not only by a skillful and fair solution but by an evocation of urban lower-middle-class life more convincing than the portrayals of the other social problems dealt with in these stories. The structure of "Miracles" is reminiscent of but much better handled than the old EQ radio play "The Meanest Man in the World."

Now come eight stories headed "Q.B.I.: Queen's Bureau of Investigation," most of them deliberately stylized, abstract, artificial, embodying what Dannay likes to call "fun and games." Heading this subsection is the very first Queen short-short, "The Lonely Bride" (*TW*, 12/4/49, as "The Lady Couldn't Explain"; *EQMM* 12/51), which confronts Ellery with the problem of locating $20,000 hidden "in a book" in an apartment where there are no books—a problem which he solves adroitly, though he leaves unsolved the puzzler of how the story's rather dim-witted thief could have found the money at all. In "Mystery at the Library of Congress" (*Argosy*, 6/60, as "Enter Ellery Queen"; *EQMM* 2/63) the problem is to crack a book-title code being used by a ring of narcotics smugglers whose leisure reading would seem to have included Queen's *The French Powder Mystery*, and the solution may be anticipated by any reader who cares to glance at recent photographs of Dannay and Lee for inspiration. With "Dead Ringer" (*Diners' Club Magazine*, 3/65; *EQMM* 10/66) Queen returns to the dying message gambit. Why did the spy who was posing as a tobacconist use the last moments of his life to pull off the shelf an empty canister labeled MIX C? You won't believe the answer, but file it under Fun & Games, and right alongside it the solutions to "The Broken T" (*TW*, 7/27/63, as "Mystery in Neon Red"; *EQMM* 5/66), which concerns a vanishing neon sign, and to "Half a Clue" (*TW*, 8/25/63, as "Half a Clue to Murder"; *EQMM* 8/66), in which Ellery solves the poisoning of a druggist literally as the body hits the floor. "Eve of the Wedding" (*EQMM* 8/55, as "Bride in Danger") is set in Wrightsville, where Ellery is invited to a marriage ceremony which comes close to being canceled when the bride starts receiving anonymous threatening letters. Neither the denouement nor the reasoning makes too much sense, but the people are far more real than in most recent Queen shorts. The challenge in "Last Man to Die" (*TW*, 11/3/63; *EQMM* 1/67) is to figure out which of two ancient butlers, last survivors of a tontine, died first, and not only the neat solution but every word of this superbly fashioned little puzzle entitles it to classic status. On the other hand we can dismiss "Payoff" (*Cavalier*, 8/64, as "Crime Syndicate Payoff"; *EQMM* 7/66) as Fun & Games once more, a pale imitation of the name gimmick in "The Inner Circle."

The next two stories are headed "The Puzzle Club," which is a tiny coterie of enthusiasts who meet regularly to propound riddles to each other. In effect this series, which Queen has continued in several more recent stories, is a fictionization of his old *Author! Author!* radio show, with the switch that in the stories the object is to construct the ending, not a rational beginning, for the puzzle. In "The Little Spy" (*Cavalier*, 1/65; *EQMM* 9/66) the group invites Ellery to become a member, and by way of initiation rite poses for him a problem in elimination—by what means on or in his person was the titular agent attempting to get The Plans out of the country? It's a far better puzzle than the one propounded at a later meeting in "The President Regrets" (*Diners' Club Magazine,* 9/65; *EQMM* 7/67). When affairs of state prevent LBJ from attending, Ellery improvises a riddle of presidential caliber for the club, but it's just another name-game coupled with a replay of the multi-suitored actress problem in "No Parking."

"Historical Detective Story" is the heading of *Q.E.D.*'s final tale, which is the best not only in this volume but in the last two decades of Queen's career. In "Abraham Lincoln's Clue" (*MD,* 6/65; *EQMM* 3/67) Ellery tracks the quintessential Collector's Item, a lost first edition of *The Gift: 1845,* containing Poe's "The Purloined Letter" and autographed both by Poe and by Abraham Lincoln. Uniting such Queenian passions as bibliomania, philately, history, the art of the riddle, and Poe and Lincoln scholarship, this near-perfect story catches the pure essence of Queen and shows us that he is still a force to be reckoned with.

However, his next novel, *The House of Brass* (1968), turned out to be a great disappointment, with a variety of links to earlier Queen stories that prove much more fascinating than the book's own internal workings. Returning to West 87th Street from their honeymoon, ex-Inspector Queen and his bride discover a mysterious letter addressed to Jessie Sherwood. The letter invites her for an extended visit to The House of Brass, the ancestral seat of the millionaire Brass family of jewel merchants, and encloses a $100 bill for traveling expenses and half of a $1000 bill for bait. Hendrik Brass, signer of the letter and the last survivor of the line, is a complete stranger to both Richard and Jessie, but their curiosity draws them upstate to the village of Phillipskill and to the grotesque mansion. The house is filled with hundreds of pieces of brass-plated bric-a-brac and with about half a dozen miscellaneous guests who have received similar invitations. Waiting upon the guests is a manservant named Hugo, built along the general lines of Frankenstein's monster. In due time the blind old schemer, Hendrik Brass himself, reveals that his reason for bringing all these people together is simply to observe them, and eventually to choose from among them the heir or heirs to his six-million-dollar fortune. And, remembering the source of this plot in Ben Jonson's *Volpone,* not to mention *The Origin of Evil* and Queen's low opinion of human nature in general, we are not surprised when the specter of greed rears its head among the guests. An attempted murder is followed by a successful one, the publicity-hungry village police chief is clearly out of his depth, and Richard Queen takes up the case unofficially with the aid of Jessie and his old ex-police buddies in the 87th Street Irregulars. Eventually Ellery takes a hand in the proceedings, baits a trap just like Sidney Toler in the Grade Z Charlie Chan movies of the middle Forties, and snares the killer.

As we have seen, Richard Queen met and fell in love with Jessie Sherwood in *Inspector Queen's Own Case* (1956), in which Richard was exactly 63 years old and which remained consistent with the chronology of the Queen novels that preceded it. Then in *The Finishing Stroke* (1958), Richard's age soared to over eighty and Jessie of course was nowhere in evidence. In the novels of the early and middle 1960's Richard seems to hold fast at just under retirement age, and remains unwed. With *The House of Brass* he and Jessie are exactly

as old as they had been in *Inspector Queen's Own Case*
to which *Brass* is a sequel. (Jessie will again vanish into
nothingness in *The Last Woman in His Life* and *A Fine
and Private Place*.) In effect then, *Inspector Queen's
Own Case* and *The House of Brass* run on their own
separate and independent time-track, even though echoes
from the rest of the Queen canon resound throughout
The House of Brass. The isolated house-party ambience
takes us back to *The Finishing Stroke*. Ellery's last-
minute solution, rescuing his father from the ignominy
of intellectual error, is the mirror image of Richard's
rescue of Ellery in *The Fourth Side of the Triangle*. The
obsessive animal imagery and the concern with the
depravity of human nature go back of course to *The
Origin of Evil*. The figure of "Hard" Boyle, a/k/a
Vaughn J. Vaughn, reminds us of Queen's put-down of
Spillane in *Double, Double*. And, needless to say, the
false-solution-followed-by-the-true has been seen once
or twice before in Queen.

Queen wanted to write something like a modern
version of *Volpone*, and used such overfamiliar devices
as the isolated house-party, the will-manipulating old
tyrant, the enigmatic servant, the missing heir, and the
atmospheric storm in an attempt to attain the universal-
ity of the original play. But he wasn't able to make it
work. He allowed far too many of the characters to be
"good guys," immune from the disease of acquisition
that is supposedly his target, and he made the greed of
those who do not wear white hats so stylized and artificial that it neither convinces nor repels us. Which is to
say that for all his virtues Queen simply is not a Ben
Jonson. He handled similar themes far more successfully without the Jonsonian framework in *The Origin of
Evil*.

The House of Brass is even worse considered purely as a detective story. Both Richard's and Ellery's reasoning is fallacious, baseless and frequently witless. The deductions of the Inspector in Chapters 11 and 13, of Ellery in Chapter 15 and of Dr. Thornton in Chapter 8 are almost invariably wrong, and illogical even when right, the only exception being Richard's truly inspired hunch about the torn $1000 bills. If the rest of *The House of Brass* had been on the level of that segment, it would have been a first-rate book. As things stand, however, we must write it off as another less than satisfactory experiment of Queen's most recent period.

He tried an even more radical experiment the following year. The dust-jacket of *Cop Out* (1969) billed it as "Queen's 40th Anniversary Novel" and as "Different From Any Detective Story Ellery Queen Has Ever Written." And in fact the book is described by that latter phrase so accurately that many readers found it hard to believe Queen had written it. The scene is New Bradford, Taugus County, Connecticut, and the story-line is simplicity itself. We open on the nighttime theft of a $24,000 payroll from the Aztec Paper Products Company, staged by the most vicious trio of criminals in the Queen canon. Hinch who is a loutish and sadistic ape, and little Furia who thinks he is the brains of the trio, are both under the thumb of Goldie, a cheap New Bradford-born tramp who does all the real thinking for the three of them. Their theft is discovered unexpectedly soon and a State Police cordon on the major highways traps the trio inside the New Bradford area. At this point Goldie comes up with a brainstorm: leave the moneybag for safekeeping with a certain local cop named Wes Malone and take the Malones' little daughter as security for the money. And so Wes Malone comes home late that evening to find his wife and child held at gunpoint by the trio, all wearing bear masks. The rest of the book is devoted to several rounds of cat-and-mouse, with many sudden reversals of fortune and endless agonies of suspense and conflicts of loyalty and sex and violence.

Readers who find the adventures of Ellery Queen too artificial and intellectualized and remote from the real world should be overjoyed by *Cop Out,* which in essence is an average-grade swiftpaced hardnosed paperback original that just happens to be in hard covers. If it had been signed by Day Keene or Harry Whittington or Jim Thompson or any of the other well-known practitioners of this form, one might have balked a bit at the pretentious pseudo-cinematic prose but could otherwise have sat back and accepted *Cop Out* on its own terms. However, the name Ellery Queen on the cover arouses a whole complex spectrum of expectations, every single one of which the book frustrates. What is Queen's name doing on a novel containing naturalistic, credibly evil gangsters, knowledgeable details of police routine and suburban bourgeois living, voyeurism, fellatio, excremental allusions in abundance, and a finger-search up a suspect's vagina? Although none of these elements is objectionable in itself, their combined appearance in a Queen novel seems so out of place that one might almost believe the wrong byline got on the book through a printer's error. In fact, if Frederic Dannay had not told me unequivocally and to my face that he and Manfred Lee and no others conceived and executed *Cop Out,* I would not have believed it. The book does contain a few distinctly Queenian elements, such as the allegorical character-names, the theme of manipulation (in a minor key), and the county-name Taugus which harks back to

Inspector Queen's Own Case. Everything else in it could have been done by almost any competent journeyman mystery writer. Dannay told me several times that the objective in *Cop Out* was to do something utterly and completely different from anything Queen had ever done before. In this the authors succeeded beyond their wildest dreams.

The following year Queen again returned to Ellery and his father, and just as *The House of Brass* took up where *Inspector Queen's Own Case* left off, so this new book about Ellery opens where the last closed. At the end of *Face to Face* Ellery was at JFK Airport watching a BOAC jet take Harry Burke away, and he is still there on the first page of *The Last Woman in His Life* (1970). A few minutes later, in the airport restaurant, Ellery and his father happen upon two of Ellery's Harvard classmates: the much-married jet-setting millionaire John Levering Benedict III and his attorney and buddy Al Marsh. Johnny-B invites the worn-out Queens to rest up at his 200-acre sylvan retreat in a little New England town called Wrightsville. (Or, to be precise, between Wrightsville and the "glass village" of Shinn Corners.)

Ellery finds that Wrightsville has changed for the worse but it's still a "viable Shangri-La" for him, until Johnny-B and Al and all three of Johnny-B's rapacious ex-wives converge on the Benedict estate for a show-down financial conference. Under premonition of trouble Johnny executes a quick holographic will;[1] each wife suddenly and simultaneously loses an article of clothing; then Johnny is bludgeoned to death in his bedroom and all three articles—a wig, an evening gown, a pair of gloves—are found near the body. Also left behind (no surprise to any devout Queenian) is a Dying

Message. Chief Anse Newby enlists the Queens' aid in
locating not only the murderer but also the mysterious
"Laura," Johnny's true love, the one to secure whose
future he was about to reduce his bequests to his three
exes from a million to a piddling hundred thousand
dollars apiece—the last woman in his life.

The long middle section of the book is precisely
what *The House of Brass* should have been but wasn't,
a sardonic portrait of greed-driven power plays by
various potential heirs to a fortune. Audrey, the third-
rate actress; Marcia, the tough-talking showgirl; Alice,
the mousy nurse; Sanford Effing, the fittingly named
legal leech who sniffs a fat fee; Foxy Faulks, the cheap
gambler with large ideas; several hundred opportunists
trying to pass themselves off as the missing Laura—all
are consumed by money madness. The only exception
is the self-effacing little social worker Leslie Carpenter,
who lacks the tough-mindedness to fight for the fortune
on behalf of the poor on whom she would spend it.

The next two paragraphs will reveal the solution
to the murder and should be skipped by those who
haven't read the book. Aside from Leslie's commitment
to the poor, there are only two manifestations of human
decency in *The Last Woman*. One is the relationship
between Ellery and his father, the other is Al Marsh's
love for Johnny Benedict. That Al is a homosexual,
that he killed Johnny in a rage of fright after Johnny in
fury and contempt threatened to expose Al's homosexuality to the world—these are among the least well
kept secrets in the Queen canon. The dying message
loudly screams its own solution, the variations on sex-
confusion scattered through the book (such as Ellery's
mistaking Leslie for a man's name, and that terrible pun
about "one of Ellery's queerest cases") confirm the

point long before the climax, and the dinner sequence in Al's apartment makes the truth so obvious it hurts. Connected with these technical flaws is Ellery's ludicrous lecture to his father on the elementary facts of homosexuality, a subject with which I should think a thirty-year police veteran would be sufficiently conversant.[2] The reason for all this over-obviousness is that Queen is deliberately aiming the book at the great ignorant majority to whom homosexuals are simply fags, fairies or fruits.[3] Technically faulty as his approach is in whodunit terms, Queen deserves a great deal of credit not only for making the "pervert" in *The Last Woman* a person we can empathize with but for making his "perversion" one of the book's few decent acts.

"We didn't even know [in the early Thirties] that Queen had a homosexual connotation," Dannay told the British journalist Graham Lord late in 1970. "When we went on tour Manny [Lee] and I used to share a hotel room and with the name Queen it gave us some bad moments." Since the Thirties Queen not only improved his knowledge of the subject but contributed to legitimizing it as a theme for mystery fiction when in *EQMM* for November 1950 he published Philip MacDonald's "Love Lies Bleeding," still one of the best short mysteries ever written about a homosexual. Crime novels with homosexual themes became quite common in the Sixties (see Roderick Thorp's *The Detective,* and George Baxt's Pharoah Love trilogy), but Queen's treatment of the subject in *The Last Woman,* though debatable, is *sui generis.*

As if in counterpoint to its sexual originality, other elements of the novel form a veritable cornucopia of borrowings from earlier Queen stories. Ellery's momentary compulsion to "drop out" in the first scenes recalls the opening of *Cat of Many Tails*; the function of the two figures on the wedding cake echoes the first Queen short-short, "The Lonely Bride"; the negative clue in Johnny's wardrobe is vividly reminiscent of *The King Is Dead*; the murderer's use of his victim's clothes comes straight out of *The Spanish Cape Mystery*. But by now these allusions have become almost enjoyable in themselves, and we can relish the little variations, the way Queen fits together elements from half a dozen earlier works and rearranges them anew so that we recognize the sources yet never feel that he's trotting out the old merchandise once again. *The Last Woman* is far from Queen's best, but even after 41 years his reach happily exceeds his grasp.

After these three relatively weak novels Queen returned to near the top of his form in *A Fine and Private Place* (1971), which is the supreme manifestation of his tendency to build his recent novels around a leitmotif. In *The Player on the Other Side* it was a chess game, in *The House of Brass* it was greed for worthless things, in *The Last Woman in His Life* it was sex confusion. This time the leitmotif is the figure 9. Nino Importuna was born on the ninth day of the ninth month of 1899, whose digits add up to 27 which totals, and is divisible by and into, 9. Together with his younger brothers Julio and Marco, he resides on the top floors of the 9-story building at 99 East 99th Street and from there controls the vast Importuna industrial conglomerate, valued at half a billion dollars. The squat, bestial, 9-obsessed entrepreneur forces a girl one-third his age into marrying him—on the ninth day of the ninth month of 1962 whose digits total 18 which totals, and is divisible by and into, 9—and rewrites his will so that on their fifth anniversary she will become his sole legatee. Vir-

ginia Whyte Importuna falls in love with her husband's
much younger confidential secretary, Peter Ennis, and
exactly nine months before that fifth anniversary the
seed of death is sown. As the anniversary approaches, a
murderer who seems himself as 9-obsessed as Nino
strikes at the Importuna *famiglia*. And so the stage is
set for the entrance of Mr. Ellery Queen.

A Fine and Private Place is brim-full of the ingredi-
ents we have come to know as Queen hallmarks—the
self-enclosed chessboard milieu, the satanic manipulator,
the adversary's mocking notes to the investigators, the
false solution followed by the truth. But most Queenian
of all is the fantastic dozens upon dozens of variations
on the concept of nineness that Queen lovingly plants
in his pages. Most obvious of these are the many allusions to pregnancy, the growth of a fetus, and child-
birth—the entire crime, the murderer's brainchild, is
conceived and developed like a human baby. Perhaps
the least obvious 9-motif is that by beginning and ending
the novel with the same three words (words, as it happens, connoting fatherhood), Queen shapes the entire
book into a figure that curls back on itself: a 9 of sorts,
a fetus of sorts. I will not further spoil the pleasures of
nine-hunting in store for readers but will assure them
that the mind-blowing dazzlement of the most lavishly
involuted Queen novels blazes in full glory in *A Fine and
Private Place*.

As always in late Queen, the echo phenomenon is
distinctly noticeable. The Importuna *famiglia* is in some
respects evocative of the Van Horns in *Ten Days' Wonder,* in others of the Bendigos in *The King Is Dead*.
Nino's matrimonial finances recall Glory Guild's "ar-
rangement" in *Face to Face*; the rug and desk clues of
the first murder hark back respectively to the *Egyptian*

Cross and *Dutch Shoe* mysteries, and the note-scattering murderer to *The Finishing Stroke.* Once again Queen has taken full advantage of the right to borrow from himself without self-plagiarism.

If only the book's last twenty pages were as satisfying as what came before them! Unfortunately the solution is weakened by certain flaws built into the structure. For example, Queen here demonstrated a brilliant way of breaking the old rule that the murderer must be a major character, not a walk-on part; but the result is that there are literally no suspects on whom the wary reader can fasten and only one person who could possibly be the murderer. An even more damaging flaw is that the murderer's master plan requires of Ellery and his father at certain key points a whopping amount respectively of stupidity and failure to communicate— qualities with which each obligingly comes through at all the proper moments. If Richard Queen had done the natural thing and told Ellery about the New Milford motel, or if Ellery had read all the reports on the case, or had he stopped to think that if his Solution One were correct then the killer deliberately and for no reason gave Ellery the clue leading to himself, the manipulator's trap would have sprung on empty air. In other words (Raymond Chandler's words) the murderer in this book has God sitting in his lap.

But this is only to say that once again Queen's reach has exceeded his grasp. All carping aside, *A Fine and Private Place* must be ranked with *The Player on the Other Side* and *Face to Face* as one of Queen's three finest detective novels of the past fifteen years. And no one but Queen could have conceived it.

EPILOGUE

ON FRIDAY NIGHT, APRIL 2, 1971, MANFRED LEE DIED ON THE
way to the Waterbury hospital after suffering another
heart attack. His death made the lives of Queen's millions of readers the poorer as his work had made their
lives the richer.

His health had been poor during his last years, and
although he and I had exchanged a few letters we met
face-to-face only once, at the Mystery Writers of America annual dinner in New York City at the end of April
1970. When we were introduced to each other in the
lounge of the Biltmore Hotel, a young man sitting nearby suddenly jumped up like a jack-in-the-box and
whooped: "Manfred B. Lee! I think you're the greatest
writer that ever lived!" Lee peered owlishly at the
intruder and quipped: "That doesn't say much for your
taste, does it?" There was the essential Manny Lee—
genial, earthy, frank and unpretentious. I would have
given much to have known him better.

Fred Dannay has announced that he will carry on
with Ellery Queen and has told me that most of the plot
outline of Ellery's next case had been worked out prior

211

to Lee's death. But his own poor health, his full-time editorial and anthological duties, and the death of his own wife in the summer of 1972, have resulted in a long delay between novels. How much longer only time will tell. At present there are a total of six Queen stories that have not yet been assembled in book form, enough for one final collection if augmented by, say, the best of the radio plays. In chronological order the stories run as follows.

"Terror Town" (*Argosy*, 8/56; *EQMM* 8-9/58, as "The Motive") is not about Ellery but almost seems to be about Wrightsville masquerading under a different name. The small New England town of Northfield is deftly sketched as the background for a series of violent deaths, all on the exact same spot—the muddy gravesite where the first body, that of a farmer's son, had been discovered. The off-and-on romance between librarian Susan Marsh and deputy sheriff Linc Pearce slowly merges into the sequence of killings, to which the town reacts just as vilely as New York City had in *Cat of Many Tails* and Shinn Corners in *The Glass Village*. The solution, which is reached without deductions, exposes a murderer with delusions of divinity recalling *Ten Days' Wonder*. The crucial facts about the passage of title to a certain automobile are kept from the reader too long, and I can't quite believe that the police were unable even to tell what killed the first victim, but otherwise this is a good solid competent novelet. An hour-long film version entitled "Terror in Northfield" was aired on television's *Alfred Hitchcock Hour*, 10/11/63, with a script by Leigh Brackett (best known for her work on the screenplay of Howard Hawks' 1946 film *The Big Sleep*) and starring Dick York, Jacqueline Scott and R. G. Armstrong.

In the nine years separating "Terror Town" from
the next uncollected story, Queen had moved into his
highly stylized fourth period, and "Uncle from Australia" (*Diners' Club Magazine,* 6/65; *EQMM* 11/67) is a
typical fun-and-games short-short of this recent vintage.
Ellery interprets the dying message of the cockney-ac-
cented huncle from down hunder and determines which
of his three greedy relatives skewered him for the
inheritance. That the victim probably couldn't have
known the truth himself and that the reader will see it
literally as soon as the message is spoken are sufficient
reasons for ranking the tale rather far from Queen's best.

Ellery returns to Wrightsville in "Wedding Anniversary" (*EQMM* 9/67) just in time to witness the poisoning of his kindly host, the jeweler Ernst Bauenfel,
and to solve the puzzle of his death through another
Wonderlandesque dying message analysis. If the plot
evokes memories of that grand old radio play "The Last
Man Club," the early scenes leading up to Bauenfel's
death must be placed among the most touchingly human pages to be found in fourth-period Queen.

The minutes of three final sessions of the Puzzle
Club were printed in two of America's most famous and
high-paying magazines during the year of Manfred Lee's
death. In each of the stories Ellery is challenged to
solve an imaginary riddle devised by the other club
members. In "The Three Students" (*Playboy,* 3/71) he
must decide which of the titular trio (handily named
Adams, Barnes, and Carver) stole a valuable ring from
the university president's desk, and finds the answer in
a fact so specialized that the story must seem child's
play to those readers who know it and gibberish to
those who don't. "The Odd Man" (*Playboy,* 6/71)
requires him to tell his confreres which of their three

imagined suspects is a secret criminal when he is given virtually no information about them except their names and occupations. And in "The Honest Swindler" (*Saturday Evening Post,* Summer/71) he must explain how an old prospector could have spent five years on a fruitless uranium hunt and still have returned every penny of his backers' money.

To date, this is the end of the Queen canon. If Dannay alone writes further stories about Ellery, they may continue the hallmarks of Period Four, or we may see a new fifth period of works as highly personal in their own way as the late work of Picasso or Stravinsky. These matters are in the lap of the imponderables that shape our lives. For now at least, the story ends, the game is over, the ghost of Long John Silver has been exhibited for the last time, and Ellery Queen, author and detective, has entered the Valhalla of the immortals.

NOTES

INTRODUCTION

[1] The someone else was named Isabel Briggs Myers, and she seems to have abandoned the genre after two novels.

[2] Their Hollywood experiences led to two novels, *The Devil to Pay* (1937) and *The Four of Hearts* (1938), in which Ellery himself is working as a frustrated scenarist in the film capital. Studio head Jacques Butcher in these novels was modeled to a certain extent on Irving Thalberg. Although Dannay and Lee were never credited with the screenplay for any movie (most of their projects were shelved by the front office through no fault of theirs prior to filming), they worked on many scripts of the late Thirties, including one of the William Powell-Myrna Loy *Thin Man* stories.

[3] Those who have learned from Queen to read with infinite care may wonder how a 1915 Holmes novel crept into the life of a boy who, as we've seen earlier, did not encounter Holmes until 1917. In real life the book which the ten-year-old Danny raffled off was not *The Valley of Fear* but L. Frank Baum's *The Scarecrow of Oz*. But the editors at Little, Brown who read *The Golden Summer* thought the Oz book was too childish for a ten-year-old to be reading, so Dannay substituted the Holmes title.

[4] In 1956, in a last attempt to stir up some interest in *The Golden Summer*, Dannay devised a stratagem worthy of little Danny himself. He reprinted three chapters of the novel in *Ellery Queen's Mystery Magazine,* one each in the June, August and October numbers

215

for that year, the chapters being prefaced with a page of ecstatic commentary on *The Golden Summer* as a whole by mystery writers Anthony Boucher, Stanley Ellin and James Yaffe. The text of the stories was revised so as to keep readers from suspecting the true identity of Daniel Nathan; thus Ellery Herman the shoemaker becomes Old Man Herman. Coincidentally (or was it?), *EQMM* for October 1956 also contains "Tough Break," a story by Dannay's eldest son, Douglas, disguised under the byline Ryam Beck. Mary Beck was the maiden name of Dannay's first wife.

CHAPTER 1

[1] Fuller justice is done to this fascinating figure in a recent booklet by Jon Tuska et al., *Philo Vance: The Life and Times of S. S. Van Dine* (Bowling Green University Popular Press, 1971).

[2] According to McC in the Foreword to *The Roman Hat Mystery,* Ellery has married and is the father of an infant son!

[3] Don't try to figure out what year the story is supposed to be taking place. In a letter in Vol. I No. 2 of *The Queen Canon Bibliophile* (later *The Ellery Queen Review*), John Nieminski summarizes various arguments for the years 1923, '25, '26 and '28, each argument contradicting all the others. Nieminski concludes that "the whole thing is maddening."

[4] We never learn why the attorney Morehouse, who was searching for Janney between 10:30 and 10:40 a.m., failed to find him. Queen's objective of course was to deprive Morehouse of an alibi without enabling him to confirm or refute the alibi of Janney, but he could have

better obtained this objective by having the lawyer search for a bathroom instead of for a surgeon.

There is also one tiny flaw in the diagram of the hospital at the front of *Dutch Shoe*. Any careful reader will see that there must be a door connecting the main operating room and the west corridor: it is specifically referred to on pages 27 and 49 (of the first edition), and it is the only way Inspector Queen could have entered the anteroom from the amphitheater as he does on page 50. Yet on the printed diagram no such door appears.

CHAPTER 2

[1] Although the identity of Queen and Ross was not revealed until 1940, alert readers might have hit upon the truth by recalling the Foreword to *Roman Hat* with its reference to Ellery's first case, "the now-ancient Barnaby-Ross murder-case." There is also a building known as Barnaby's barn that figures prominently in Dannay's autobiographical novel *The Golden Summer*.

[2] The addition of Patience was clearly not in Queen's mind when he wrote X and Y, for as Patience herself points out in Z, there is not the slightest hint in the earlier books that Thumm ever had a daughter. The supposed ten-year hiatus between the prior cases and Z is another obvious afterthought, since innumerable details of X and Y prove that they are not set in the early Twenties. For instance, there is a reference in Act II Scene 9 of X to George Arliss' screen portrayal of *Disraeli* (1929), and an allusion in Act III Scene 2 of Y to the fictional detective Ellery Queen, who of course did not debut until 1929.

[3] Here's a sample of how Patience talks to her boy

friend: "But the only thing that differentiates us from the lower primates is the power of reasoning, and I don't see why the mere fact that a woman is biologically different from a man should prevent her from cultivating her mind."

[4]The murderer's identity is, however, both surprising and fairly clued, with one clue being planted as far back as *The Tragedy of Z* (*The XYZ Murders*, p. 492).

CHAPTER 3

[1]To cite a few imperfections, there is insufficient explanation of how the murderer acquired the knowledge and opportunity to initiate Solution One, and Solution Two is possible for him only because he had unmotivatedly removed his first victim's watch after killing him. Further, Queen does not know enough about the legal effects of the destruction of a will (e.g. the theory of dependent relative revocation) to make full use of the vanished-will problem he sets up. Finally, Queen fractures his scholarly image in Chapter 31 when he has Ellery quote the Latin proverb *Ne quid nimis* (nothing too much; moderation in all things) as *Ne quis nimis* (gibberish) and then translate it as "Know thyself!"

[2]The character of Horne was apparently based on the famous star of silent Westerns, William S. Hart. For a good account of Hart's career see Chapter 3 of William K. Everson, *A Pictorial History of the Western Film* (1969).

[3]Thus in Chapter 6 Ellery describes a Western movie in which Kit Horne, while galloping down a hillside, draws her pistol and shoots through the strands of

rope with which the villain is hanging the hero. Ellery insists that throughout the scene Kit, her revolver and the rope were all distinctly visible—although in reality no film director could capture all these elements in one take, without montage—and deduces on the basis of what he saw that she must have shot a real bullet in the film! He hedges his deduction slightly by conceding: "Nevertheless, I grant the possibility of a trick. . . ." The Inspector rightly retorts: "Darned decent of you."

CHAPTER 4

[1] Queen's first slick-paper sales were made in 1934, when both *Chinese Orange* and "The Mad Tea-Party" appeared in *Redbook,* but it took a year or so before the influence of the slicks on his work became apparent.

[2] Although neither the murderer nor anyone else in the book knows it, the plot hinges on the interaction of three laws: the simultaneous death statute, the law of intestate succession and the anti-lapse act. Without belaboring the legal technicalities, on the simultaneous death of his father and stepmother Ty Royle probably inherits one-fourth of the Tolland Stuart estate, which would remain beyond the killer's reach. On the simultaneous death of Ty and Bonnie, there would be no one left to inherit under the residuary clause of Tolland's will, the anti-lapse statute would be inapplicable, and the balance of the estate would go to the murderer by the law of intestacy. In other words, Queen made all the right legal moves, though purely by accident.

[3] I must admit, however, that after five readings I still can't understand how those cars in the garage could have been "perfectly dry" when Ellery examined them.

[4] The actual 1939 World Series was between the Yanks and the Cincinnati Reds, the first two games being played in New York on October 4 and 5, the final two in Cincinnati on the 7th and 8th. The Yankees won in four games. Queen's story, of course, was written so far in advance of the Series that no one can fairly accuse him of poor sports judgment.

[5] It's amusing to note that when Queen reprinted "Long Shot" in *EQMM*, March 1959, he changed the names of most of the movie stars who attend the big race: Crawford and Garbo are fused into Sophia Loren, Al Jolson is replaced by Bob Hope, Bob Burns by Rock Hudson, Joan Crawford the second time by Marilyn Monroe, and Carole Lombard by Jayne Mansfield. Only Clark Gable remains himself in both versions.

CHAPTER 5

[1] *Danger, Men Working* was co-authored by Queen and Lowell Brentano and closed after a few nights in Baltimore and Philadelphia. It was filmed abysmally in 1937, as we've seen, under the title *The Man Nobody Saw.*

CHAPTER 6

[1] Queen was the first editor and Anthony Boucher the first translator to present a Borges story to the American public: "The Garden of Forking Paths" in *EQMM* for August 1948.

[2] Except for certain periods in the first ten years of *EQMM,* this temperamental lack of sympathy with the

distinctive American tradition is noticeable in all of Queen's editorial work, and is further manifest in his consistent novelistic stance toward the "hardboiled" school from *The Door Between* (1937) to *The House of Brass* (1968). For these reasons I would argue that the most frequently quoted statement about Queen—Anthony Boucher's "Ellery Queen *is* the American detective story"—stands in need of considerable qualification.

[3] Readers of *101 Years' Entertainment* will recall that Holmes is represented therein not by a single story but by four separate deductions taken from four different tales and collectively entitled "The Science of Deduction." Through an oversight Queen's literary agent had secured permission from the Doyle estate to reprint only the first of the four passages, so that technically *101 Years'* was in infringement of Doyle's copyright. Shortly after *Misadventures* was published, Dannay discovered the error and brought it to Adrian's attention. Adrian, who intensely disliked the concept of *Misadventures* but had no independent legal grounds for taking action against it, threatened to sue for the *101 Years'* infringement unless *Misadventures* was voluntarily withdrawn from circulation. Since *101 Years'* was by far the bigger seller of the two, Queen had to comply.

[4] In his Introduction Queen pointed out the similarities between this book and a baby—a theme on which he elaborated in his most recent novel, *A Fine and Private Place* (1971).

[5] As the fifth entry in this series I would love to see a volume of the best uncollected stories of the late Cornell Woolrich, so many of whose finest tales Queen rescued from pulp oblivion and reprinted in *EQMM*. Among Woolrich's papers there was a title for an unwritten story which would be the perfect title for such a

collection: *First You Dream, Then You Die.*

CHAPTER 9

[1] There are many other differences between this Nikki and the Nikki of earlier days. We've already seen three separate accounts of Nikki's background, and *The Scarlet Letters* provides a fourth. Here she is a redhead who apparently spent her girlhood in Kansas City, unlike the Nikki of the radio plays and of the movie novelizations and of *There Was an Old Woman,* who all differed among themselves as well.

[2] The root cause of the story's breakdown is that Martha must *appear* to be an adulteress throughout the book although she must turn out virgin-pure at the end. If Queen had allowed an actual sexual relationship between Martha and Harrison, both the murder plot and the characters' credibility could have been salvaged. He wasn't writing for the Legion of Decency, and in fact his view of extra-marital sex in this book is fairly enlightened. ("I'm not going to deliver a sermon—I've seen worse crimes than adultery," Ellery remarks.) So his reasons for adopting such a restrictive approach to his characters' sexuality remain unclear.

CHAPTER 10

[1] For a fact-filled and terrifying survey of the McCarthy era, see Fred J. Cook, *The Nightmare Decade* (Random House, 1971).

[2] In the third chapter of *Double, Double* Shinn Corners is described as being deep in the farm country

southwest of Wrightsville, but a quick recheck has failed to turn up other allusions to the town.

[3] In his conversation with the Judge at the end of Chapter One, Johnny claims that he still believes in the traditional American shibboleths of God, the Constitution and the future of the republic. But the context makes it clear that he is not leveling with his uncle, and his true beliefs come out in his much franker dialogue with the Judge the following evening.

[4] Queen coined the term QBI in Chapter 3 of *Cat of Many Tails* which appeared in 1949, the same year his first short-shorts began to appear in *This Week*.

[5] One notable moment is while Jessie is questioning a black laundress she knows slightly. Suddenly she asks: "Do you mind if I call you Sadie?" The black woman's smoldering outrage at generations of white refusal to give blacks the dignity of Mr. or Mrs. and a last name is beautifully caught in her grim reply: "Not you I don't," a photoflash of racial realism that rivals the Harlem police-station scene in *Cat of Many Tails*.

CHAPTER 11

[1] Dannay told me that he conceived this novel after reading about the Dead Sea Scrolls, with their many parallels to the Gospel accounts of Jesus.

[2] The plot of this grisly pastiche must be read to be disbelieved. Its Spanish title, which looks as though it might be translated as "Jack the Stripper," apparently inspired Boucher's own short story "The Stripper" (*EQMM* 5/45).

CHAPTER 12

[1] In fact, holographic wills are not valid in any of the New England states, and are recognized in New York only if the testator is in military service.

[2] The casual remarks on homosexuality in *Cat of Many Tails* and *The Scarlet Letters* confirm that both Queen and his characters were familiar with the subject long before *The Last Woman.*

[3] Interesting technical point: why didn't Johnny-B use one of these common contemptuous synonyms for homosexual to identify his murderer? Ellery's Wonderlandesque analysis of the dying message fails to consider these possibilities.

AN ELLERY QUEEN CHECKLIST

PART I. FICTION

Section 1. Novels published as by Ellery Queen. I have listed the first American and English editions, the first unabridged paperback edition, subsequent paperback editions with distinctive features, and the current English uniform edition.   All titles are about the characters Ellery and Richard Queen except those marked with an asterisk.

The Roman Hat Mystery. Stokes, 1929. Gollancz, 1929. Pocket Book #77, 1940. Uniform ed.: Gollancz, 1969.

The French Powder Mystery. Stokes, 1930. Gollancz, 1930. Pocket Book #71, 1940. Uniform ed.: Gollancz, 1970.

The Dutch Shoe Mystery. Stokes, 1931. Gollancz, 1931. Pocket Book #202, 1943. Uniform ed.: Gollancz, 1970.

The Greek Coffin Mystery. Stokes, 1932. Gollancz, 1932. Pocket Book #179, 1942. Uniform ed.: Gollancz, 1971.

The Egyptian Cross Mystery. Stokes, 1932. Gollancz, 1933. Pocket Book #227, 1943. Uniform ed.: Gollancz, 1971.

The American Gun Mystery. Stokes, 1933. Gollancz, 1933. Dell pb #4, 1940. Mercury pb #164, 1951, as *Death at the Rodeo.* Uniform ed.: Gollancz, 1971.

The Siamese Twin Mystery. Stokes, 1933. Gollancz, 1934. Pocket Book #109, 1941. Uniform ed.: Gollancz, 1971.

The Chinese Orange Mystery. Stokes, 1934. Gollancz,

1934.   Pocket Book #17, 1939.   Uniform ed.:
Gollancz, 1972.

The Spanish Cape Mystery.   Stokes, 1935.   Gollancz,
1935.   Pocket Book #146, 1942.   Uniform ed.:
Gollancz, 1972.

Halfway House.   Stokes, 1936.   Gollancz, 1936.   Pocket
Book #259, 1944.   Uniform ed.: Gollancz, 1972.

The Door Between.   Stokes, 1937.   Gollancz, 1937.
Pocket Book #471, 1947.   Uniform ed.: Gollancz,
1972.

The Devil to Pay.   Stokes, 1938.   Gollancz, 1938.   Pocket Book #270, 1944.   Uniform ed.:   Gollancz,
1973.

The Four of Hearts.   Stokes, 1938.   Gollancz, 1939.
Pocket Book #245, 1944.   Uniform ed.: Gollancz,
1973.

The Dragon's Teeth.   Stokes, 1939.   Gollancz, 1939.
Pocket Book #459, 1947.   Pocket Book #2459,
1954, as *The Virgin Heiresses.*

Calamity Town.   Little Brown, 1942.   Gollancz, 1942.
(Due to a scheduling error the English is the true
first edition, preceding the U. S. edition by six or
seven weeks.)   Pocket Book #283, 1945.

There Was an Old Woman.   Little Brown, 1943.
Gollancz, 1944.   Pocket Book #326, 1945.   Pocket
Book #2326, 1956, as *The Quick and the Dead.*

The Murderer Is a Fox.   Little Brown, 1945.   Gollancz,
1945.   Pocket Book #517, 1948.

Ten Days' Wonder.   Little Brown, 1948.   Gollancz,
1948.   Pocket Book #740, 1950.   Signet pb
#Q4907, 1972 (with stills from Claude Chabrol's
film version of the novel).

Cat of Many Tails.   Little Brown, 1949.   Gollancz,
1949.   Pocket Book #822, 1951.   Bantam pb

#F3026, 1965 (with introduction by Anthony Boucher).

Double, Double. Little Brown, 1950. Gollancz, 1950. Pocket Book #874, 1952. Pocket Book #2874, 1958, as *The Case of the Seven Murders.*

The Origin of Evil. Little Brown, 1951. Gollancz, 1951. Pocket Book #926, 1953.

The King Is Dead. Little Brown, 1952. Gollancz, 1952. Pocket Book #1005, 1954.

The Scarlet Letters. Little Brown, 1953. Gollancz, 1953. Pocket Book #1049, 1955.

The Glass Village. Little Brown, 1954. Gollancz, 1954. Pocket Book #1082, 1955.

Inspector Queen's Own Case. Simon & Schuster, 1956. Gollancz, 1956. Pocket Book #1167, 1957.

The Finishing Stroke. Simon & Schuster, 1958. Gollancz, 1958. Pocket Book (Cardinal series) #C343, 1959.

The Player on the Other Side. Random House, 1963. Gollancz, 1963. Pocket Book #50487, 1965.

And On the Eighth Day. Random House, 1964. Gollancz, 1964. Pocket Book #50209, 1966.

The Fourth Side of the Triangle. Random House, 1965. Gollancz, 1965. Pocket Book #50508, 1967.

A Study in Terror. Lancer pb #73-469, 1966. Gollancz, 1967, as *Sherlock Holmes versus Jack the Ripper.* (Novelization of the film, with the addition of EQ and an original "framing story.")

Face to Face. New American Library, 1967. Gollancz, 1967. Signet pb #P3424, 1968.

The House of Brass. New American Library, 1968. Gollancz, 1968. Signet pb #T3831, 1969.

Cop Out. World, 1969. Gollancz, 1969. Signet pb #T4196, 1970.

The Last Woman in His Life. World, 1970. Gollancz,
  1970. Signet pb #T4580, 1971.
A Fine and Private Place. World, 1971. Gollancz, 1971.
  Signet pb #Q4978, 1972.

Section 2.   Short story collections published as by Ellery Queen.   All stories in all collections are about the
character Ellery Queen. The code designation after each
story refers to (a) the name, initials, or first syllable of
the magazine of original publication, and (b) the story's
chronological number among the Queen tales published
in that magazine.   Thus, for example, "Man Bites Dog,"
the earliest Queen story to appear in *Blue Book,* is *BB* 1.
A complete catalogue of Queen's magazine appearances
is printed in Section 6.

The Adventures of Ellery Queen.   Stokes, 1934.
  Gollancz, 1935. Pocket Book #99, 1941. Con-
  tents: The Adventure of the African Traveler (no
  prior magazine publication); The Adventure of the
  Hanging Acrobat (*Mys* 3); The Adventure of the
  One-Penny Black (*GD* 1); The Adventure of the
  Bearded Lady (*Mys* 5); The Adventure of the Three
  Lame Men (*Mys* 2); The Adventure of the Invisible
  Lover (*Mys* 6); The Adventure of the Teakwood
  Case (*Mys* 1); The Adventure of "The Two-Headed
  Dog" (*Mys* 4); The Adventure of the Glass-Domed
  Clock (*ML* 1); The Adventure of the Seven Black
  Cats (*Mys* 7); The Adventure of the Mad Tea-Party
  (*R* 1). Note that the earliest paperback edition of
  this collection (Bestseller pb #1, 1940), contains
  only six of the eleven stories in the original edition,
  namely The Mad Tea-Party, The Seven Black Cats,

The Hanging Acrobat, The "Two-Headed Dog," The Bearded Lady, and The Three Lame Men.

The New Adventures of Ellery Queen. Stokes, 1940. Gollancz, 1940. Pocket Book #134, 1941. Contents: The Lamp of God (*DS* 1); The Adventure of the Treasure Hunt (*DS* 2); The Adventure of the Hollow Dragon (*R* 2); The Adventure of the House of Darkness (*Am Mag* 1); The Adventure of the Bleeding Portrait (*Am Cav* 1); Man Bites Dog (*BB* 1); Long Shot (*BB* 2); Mind Over Matter (*BB* 3); Trojan Horse (*BB* 4). Note that the earliest paperback edition containing part of this collection was entitled *More Adventures of Ellery Queen* (Bestseller pb #3, 1940), and included The Lamp of God, from *New Adventures,* as well as four stories from the original *Adventures,* namely The Invisible Lover, The African Traveler, The Glass-Domed Clock, and The One-Penny Black.

The Case Book of Ellery Queen. Bestseller pb #59, 1945. This collection consists of The House of Darkness (from *New Adventures*), The Teakwood Case (from *Adventures*), The Hollow Dragon (from *New Adventures*), Long Shot and Mind Over Matter (both from *New Adventures*), and three previously unpublished Ellery Queen radio plays, which are discussed in Chapter Five.

Calendar of Crime. Little Brown, 1952. Gollancz, 1952. Pocket Book #960, 1953. Contents: The Inner Circle (*EQMM* 4); The President's Half Disme (*EQMM* 5); The Ides of Michael Magoon (*EQMM* 6); The Emperor's Dice (*EQMM* 8); The Gettysburg Bugle (*EQMM* 9); The Medical Finger (*EQMM* 10); The Fallen Angel (*EQMM* 11); The Needle's Eye (*EQMM* 12); The Three R's (*EQMM* 1); The Dead

Cat (*EQMM* 2); The Telltale Bottle (*EQMM* 3); The Dauphin's Doll (*EQMM* 7).

QBI: Queen's Bureau of Investigation. Little Brown, 1955.   Gollancz, 1955.   Pocket Book #1118, 1956.   Contents: Money Talks (*TW* 3); A Matter of Seconds (*TW* 16); The Three Widows (*TW* 2); "My Queer Dean!" (*TW* 15); Driver's Seat (*TW* 8); A Lump of Sugar (*TW* 5); Cold Money (*TW* 12); The Myna Birds (*TW* 14); A Question of Honor (*TW* 17); The Robber of Wrightsville (*T Fam* 1); Double Your Money (*TW* 10); Miser's Gold (*TW* 4); Snowball in July (*TW* 13); The Witch of Times Square (*TW* 6); The Gamblers' Club (*TW* 7); GI Story (*EQMM* 13); The Black Ledger (*TW* 11); Child Missing! (*TW* 9).

Queens Full.   Random House, 1965.   Gollancz, 1966. Signet pb #D2894, 1966.   Contents: The Death of Don Juan (*Arg* 4); E = Murder (*TW* 21); The Wrightsville Heirs (*BL* 1); Diamonds in Paradise (*EQMM* 14); The Case Against Carroll (*Arg* 2).

QED: Queen's Experiments in Detection. New American Library, 1968.   Gollancz, 1969.   Signet pb #T4120, 1970.   Contents: Mum Is the Word (*EQMM* 17); Object Lesson (*TW* 18); No Parking (*TW* 19); No Place to Live (*TW* 20); Miracles Do Happen (*EQMM* 16); The Lonely Bride (*TW* 1); Mystery at the Library of Congress (*Arg* 3); Dead Ringer (*DCM* 1); The Broken T (*TW* 22); Half a Clue (*TW* 23); Eve of the Wedding (*EQMM* 15); Last Man to Die (*TW* 24); Payoff (*Cav* 1); The Little Spy (*Cav* 2); The President Regrets (*DCM* 3); Abraham Lincoln's Clue (*MD* 1).

Section 3. Novels published as by Barnaby Ross. All
are about the character Drury Lane.

The Tragedy of X. Viking, 1932. Cassell, 1932. Stokes,
    1940, as by Ellery Queen.   Pocket Book #125,
    1941, as by Ellery Queen.
The Tragedy of Y. Viking, 1932. Cassell, 1932. Stokes,
    1941, as by Ellery Queen.   Pocket Book #313,
    1945, as by Ellery Queen.
The Tragedy of Z. Viking, 1933. Cassell, 1933. Little
    Brown, 1942, as by Ellery Queen. Pocket Book
    #355, 1946, as by Ellery Queen.
Drury Lane's Last Case. Viking, 1933. Cassell, 1933.
    Little Brown, 1946, as by Ellery Queen. Pocket
    Book #669, 1950, as by Ellery Queen.

Section 4.   Omnibus volumes published as by Ellery
Queen.

The Ellery Queen Omnibus. Gollancz, 1934. (*The
    French Powder Mystery, The Dutch Shoe Mystery,
    The Greek Coffin Mystery.*)
The Ellery Queen Omnibus. Grosset & Dunlap, 1936.
    (*The Roman Hat Mystery, The French Powder
    Mystery, The Egyptian Cross Mystery.*)
Ellery Queen's Big Book. Grosset & Dunlap, 1938. (*The
    Greek Coffin Mystery, The Siamese Twin Mystery.*)
Ellery Queen's Adventure Omnibus. Grosset & Dunlap,
    1941. (*The Adventures of Ellery Queen, The New
    Adventures of Ellery Queen.*)
Ellery Queen's Mystery Parade. World, 1944. (*The
    Greek Coffin Mystery, The Siamese Twin Mystery.*)
The Case Book of Ellery Queen. Gollancz, 1949. (*The

Adventures of Ellery Queen, The New Adventures of Ellery Queen.)

The Wrightsville Murders. Little Brown, 1956. (*Calamity Town, The Murderer Is a Fox, Ten Days' Wonder.*)

The Hollywood Murders. Lippincott, 1957. (*The Devil to Pay, The Four of Hearts, The Origin of Evil.*)

The New York Murders. Little Brown, 1958. (*Cat of Many Tails, The Scarlet Letters, The American Gun Mystery.*)

The XYZ Murders. Lippincott, 1961. (*The Tragedy of X, The Tragedy of Y, The Tragedy of Z.*)

The Bizarre Murders. Lippincott, 1962. (*The Siamese Twin Mystery, The Chinese Orange Mystery, The Spanish Cape Mystery.*)

Section 5. The autobiographical novel by Frederic Dannay and the key to all of the books in prior sections.

The Golden Summer, as by Daniel Nathan. Little Brown, 1953.

Section 6. Short stories and novelets published as by Ellery Queen. I have listed for each story the original magazine appearance, the first appearance in a collection of Queen's short fiction, and a cross-section of appearances in other magazines and anthologies. All stories are about the characters Ellery and/or Richard Queen except those marked with an asterisk.

AMERICAN CAVALCADE
1.   9/37   The Gramatan Mystery. (*New Adventures,*

as "The Adventure of the Bleeding Portrait.")

AMERICAN MAGAZINE

1. 2/35 The House of Darkness. (*New Adventures,*
as "The Adventure of the House of Darkness.") (Reprinted in *World's Great Detective Stories,* ed. Will Cuppy (World, 1943); *The Case Book of Ellery Queen* (Bestseller pb #59, 1945); *Murder for the Millions,* ed. Frank Owen (Frederick Fell, 1946).)

ARGOSY

1. 8/56 *Terror Town. (Uncollected.) (Reprinted in *Best Detective Stories of the Year,* ed. David C. Cooke (Dutton, 1957); and in *EQMM* 8-9/58 and *EQA* 1965, as "The Motive.")

2. 9/58 The Case Against Carroll. (*Queens Full.*) (Reprinted in *EQMM* 9/60; *EQA* 1970; *Ellery Queen's Best Bets* (Pyramid pb #N2775, 1972).)

3. 6/60 Enter Ellery Queen. (*QED,* as "Mystery at the Library of Congress.") (Reprinted in *EQMM* 2/63; *Crime Without Murder,* ed. Dorothy Salisbury Davis (Scribner, 1970).)

4. 5/62 The Death of Don Juan. (*Queens Full.*) (Reprinted in *Best Detective Stories of the Year,* ed. Anthony Boucher (Dutton, 1963); *EQMM* 8/64; *EQA* 1970 Midyear.)

BETTER LIVING

1. 1-2/56 The Wrightsville Heirs. (*Queens Full.*) (Reprinted in *EQMM* 11/57.)

BLUE BOOK

1.   6/39   Man Bites Dog. (*New Adventures.*) (Reprinted in *The Pocket Book of Great Detectives,* ed. Lee Wright (Pocket Book #103, 1941); *Sporting Blood,* ed. Queen (Little Brown, 1942); *The Kit Book,* ed. R. M. Barrows (Chicago: Consolidated Book Publishers, 1943).)

2.   9/39   The Long Shot. (*New Adventures,* as "Long Shot.") (Reprinted in *The Case Book of Ellery Queen* (Bestseller pb #59, 1945); *EQMM* 3/59.)

3.   10/39   Mind Over Matter. (*New Adventures.*) (Reprinted in *The Case Book of Ellery Queen* (Bestseller pb #59, 1945); *Dolls Are Murder,* ed. Harold Q. Masur (Lion pb #152, 1957); *EQMM* 9/62; *Best Detective Stories 2,* ed. Edmund Crispin (London: Faber, 1964); *Murder Most Foul,* ed. Harold Q. Masur (Walker, 1971).)

4.   12/39   The Trojan Horse. (*New Adventures,* as "Trojan Horse.") (Reprinted in *Sporting Blood,* ed. Queen (Little Brown, 1942).)

CAVALIER

1.   8/64   Crime Syndicate Payoff. (*QED,* as "Payoff.") (Reprinted in *Best Detective Stories of the Year,* ed. Anthony Boucher (Dutton, 1965); *EQMM* 7/66.)

2.   1/65   The Little Spy. (*QED.*) (Reprinted in *EQMM* 9/66; *Murder in Mind,* ed. Lawrence Treat (Dutton, 1967).)

DETECTIVE STORY

1. 11/35 House of Haunts. (*New Adventures,* as "The Lamp of God.") (Reprinted in *More Adventures of Ellery Queen* (Bestseller pb #3, 1940); in *All Fiction Detective Stories,* 1942; as Dell 10¢ Book #23, no date (c1950); and in *A Treasury of Great Mysteries,* ed. Howard Haycraft & John Beecroft (Simon & Schuster, 1957).)

2. 12/35 The Treasure Hunt. (*New Adventures,* as "The Adventure of the Treasure Hunt.") (Reprinted in *EQMM* Fall/41; *Saint Detective Magazine,* 6-7/53.)

DINERS' CLUB MAGAZINE

1. 3/65 Dead Ringer. (*QED.*) (Reprinted in *EQMM* 10/66.)

2. 6/65 Uncle from Australia. (Uncollected.) (Reprinted in *EQMM* 11/67.)

3. 9/65 The President Regrets. (*QED.*) (Reprinted in *EQMM* 7/67.)

ELLERY QUEEN'S MYSTERY MAGAZINE

1. 9/46 The Three R's. (*Calendar.*) (Reprinted in *Best Detective Stories of the Year,* ed. David C. Cooke (Dutton, 1947); *EQMM* 10/65.)

2. 10/46 The Dead Cat. (*Calendar.*) (Reprinted in *20 Great Tales of Murder,* ed. Helen McCloy & Brett Halliday (Random House, 1951); *EQMM* 11/65, as "The Hallowe'en Mystery.")

3. 11/46 The Telltale Bottle. (*Calendar.*) (Reprinted in *Eat, Drink, and Be Buried,* ed. Rex Stout

(Viking, 1956); *EQMM* 12/65, as "The Thanksgiving Day Mystery.")

4. 1/47 The Inner Circle. (*Calendar.*) (Reprinted in *20th Century Detective Stories,* ed. Queen (World, 1948); *A Choice of Murders,* ed. Dorothy Salisbury Davis (Scribner, 1958); *EQMM* 2/68.)

5. 2/47 The President's Half Disme. (*Calendar.*) (Reprinted in *Murder by Experts,* ed. Queen (Ziff-Davis, 1947); *Best Detective Stories of the Year,* ed. David C. Cooke (Dutton, 1948); *10 Great Mysteries,* ed. Howard Haycraft & John Beecroft (Doubleday, 1959); *Best of the Best Detective Stories* (Dutton, 1960); *EQMM* 3/65; *Merchants of Menace,* ed. Hillary Waugh (Doubleday, 1969).)

6. 3/47 The Ides of Michael Magoon. (*Calendar.*) (Reprinted in *Four and Twenty Bloodhounds,* ed. Anthony Boucher (Simon & Schuster, 1950); *EQMM* 4/65.)

7. 12/48 The Dauphin's Doll. (*Calendar.*) (Reprinted in *Best Detective Stories,* ed. Edmund Crispin (London: Faber, 1959); *EQMM* 1/68, as "With the Compliments of Comus"; *The Locked Room Reader,* ed. Hans Stefan Santesson (Random House, 1968).)

8. 4/51 The Emperor's Dice. (*Calendar.*) (Reprinted in *Best Detective Stories of the Year,* ed. David C. Cooke (Dutton, 1952); *EQMM* 5/65.)

9. 5/51 As Simple As ABC. (*Calendar,* as "The Gettysburg Bugle.") (Reprinted in *Butcher, Baker, Murder-Maker,* ed. George Harmon

Coxe (Knopf, 1954); *Three Times Three
Mystery Omnibus,* ed. Howard Haycraft &
John Beecroft (Doubleday, 1964); *EQMM*
6/65; *Dear Dead Days,* ed. Edward D. Hoch
(Walker, 1972).)

10.   6/51 The Medical Finger. (*Calendar.*) (Reprinted in *EQMM* 7/65.)

11.   7/51 The Fallen Angel. (*Calendar.*) (Reprinted in *EQMM* 8/65.)

12.   8/51 The Needle's Eye. (*Calendar.*) (Reprinted in *Crooks' Tour,* ed. Bruno Fischer (Dodd Mead, 1953); *EQA* 1963 Midyear; *EQMM* 9/65; *Ellery Queen's Shoot the Works!* (Pyramid pb #T2129, 1969).)

13.   8/54 GI Story. (*QBI.*) (Reprinted in *Best Detective Stories of the Year,* ed. David C. Cooke (Dutton, 1955); *EQA* 1967 Midyear; *EQMM* 5/70.)

14.   9/54 Diamonds in Paradise. (*Queens Full.*) (Reprinted in *Crime for Two,* ed. Frances & Richard Lockridge (Lippincott, 1955); *EQA* 1961; *Cream of the Crime,* ed. Hugh Pentecost (Holt, Rinehart & Winston, 1962); *Ellery Queen's 12* (Dell pb #2259, 1964).)

15.   8/55 Bride in Danger. (*QED,* as "Eve of the Wedding.") (Reprinted in *EQA* 1966 Midyear.)

16.   7/57 Miracles Do Happen. (*QED.*) (Reprinted in *20th Century Detective Stories,* ed. Queen (Popular Library pb #SP333, 1964); *The Crime-Solvers,* ed. Stewart H. Benedict (Dell pb #3078, 1966).)

17.   4/66 Mum Is the Word. (*QED.*) (Reprinted in *EQA* Spring-Summer 1973.)

18.   9/67 Wedding Anniversary. (Uncollected.)

GREAT DETECTIVE

1. 4/33 The One-Penny Black. (*Adventures*, as "The Adventure of the One-Penny Black.") (Reprinted in *My Best Mystery Story* (London: Faber, 1939); *More Adventures of Ellery Queen* (Bestseller pb #3, 1940); *Sporting Blood*, ed. Queen (Little Brown, 1942); *Maiden Murders*, intro. John Dickson Carr (Harper, 1952).)

MD

1. 6/65 Abraham Lincoln's Clue. (*QED*.) (Reprinted in *Best Detective Stories of the Year*, ed. Anthony Boucher (Dutton, 1966); *EQMM* 3/67; *Boucher's Choicest*, ed. Jeanne Bernkopf (Dutton, 1969).)

MYSTERY

1. 5/33 The Affair of the Gallant Bachelor. (*Adventures*, as "The Adventure of the Teakwood Case.") (Reprinted in *The Case Book of Ellery Queen* (Bestseller pb #59, 1945).)
2. 4/34 The Three Lame Men. (*Adventures*, as "The Adventure of the Three Lame Men.")
3. 5/34 The Girl on the Trapeze. (*Adventures*, as "The Adventure of the Hanging Acrobat.") (Reprinted in *Challenge to the Reader*, ed. Queen (Stokes, 1938).)
4. 6/34 The 'Two-Headed Dog'. (*Adventures*, as "The Adventure of 'The Two-Headed Dog'.")
5. 8/34 The Sinister Beard. (*Adventures*, as "The Adventure of the Bearded Lady.") (Reprinted in *The Fourth Mystery Companion*,

ed. A. L. Furman (Lantern Press, 1946).)

6.   9/34   Four Men Loved a Woman. (*Adventures,* as "The Adventure of the Invisible Lover.") (Reprinted in *More Adventures of Ellery Queen* (Bestseller pb #3, 1940).)

7.   10/34   The Black Cats Vanished. (*Adventures,* as "The Adventure of the Seven Black Cats.") (Reprinted in *Murder by the Dozen,* ed. Durbin Lee Horner (Dingwall-Rock, 1935).)

MYSTERY LEAGUE

1.   10/33   The Glass-Domed Clock. (*Adventures,* as "The Adventure of the   Glass-Domed Clock.")   (Reprinted in *More Adventures of Ellery Queen* (Bestseller pb #3, 1940).)

PLAYBOY

1.   3/71   The Three Students. (Uncollected.)
2.   6/71   The Odd Man. (Uncollected.)

REDBOOK

1.   10/34   The Mad Tea-Party. (*Adventures,* as "The Adventure of the Mad Tea-Party.") (Reprinted in *101 Years' Entertainment,* ed. Queen (Little Brown, 1941).)

2.   12/36   The Hollow Dragon. (*New Adventures,* as "The Adventure of the Hollow Dragon.") (Reprinted in *The Case Book of Ellery Queen* (Bestseller pb #59, 1945); *EQMM* 6/59; *Great Stories of Detection,* ed. R. C. Bull (London: Hutchinson, 1960).)

SATURDAY EVENING POST

1.   Sum-
mer/71 The Honest Swindler. (Uncollected.)

THIS WEEK

1. 12/4/49   The Lady Couldn't Explain. (*QED*, as "The Lonely Bride.") (Reprinted in *EQMM* 12/51; *EQA* 1960; *Ellery Queen's Lethal Black Book* (Dell pb #2261, 1965).)

2. 1/29/50   Murder Without Clues. (*QBI*, as "The Three Widows.") (Reprinted in *Best Detective Stories of the Year*, ed. David C. Cooke (Dutton, 1951); *EQMM* 1/52; *This Week's Short-Short Stories*, ed. Stewart Beach (Random House, 1953); *EQA* 1963.)

3. 4/2/50   The Sound of Blackmail. (*QBI*, as "Money Talks.") (Reprinted in *EQMM* 8/52; *This Week's Short-Short Stories*, ed. Stewart Beach (Random House, 1953); *EQA* Spring-Summer 1971.)

4. 6/18/50   Love Hunts a Hidden Treasure. (*QBI*, as "Miser's Gold.") (Reprinted in *EQMM* 4/64; *EQA* 1967; *Ellery Queen's Murder—in Spades!* (Pyramid pb #T2036, 1969); *EQMM* 11/71, as "Death of a Pawnbroker.")

5. 7/9/50   The Mystery of the 3 Dawn Riders. (*QBI*, as "A Lump of Sugar.") (Reprinted in *EQMM* 2/53; *EQA* 1961; *Ellery Queen's 12* (Dell pb #2259, 1964); *EQMM* 3/69, as "Murder in the Park"; *Ellery Queen's Minimysteries*, ed. Queen (World, 1969).)

6. 11/5/50   The Witch of Times Square. (*QBI*.) (Reprinted in *EQMM* 5/53; *EQA* 1965 Midyear; *Ellery Queen's Mystery Jack-*

pot (Pyramid pb #T2207, 1970).)

7.   1/7/51   The Gamblers' Club. (*QBI.*) (Reprinted in *EQMM* 3/55; *EQA* 1962.)

8.   3/25/51   Lady, You're Dead! (*QBI,* as "Driver's Seat.") (Reprinted in *EQMM* 11/55; *EQA* 1968 Midyear.)

9.   7/8/51   Kidnaped! (*QBI,* as "Child Missing.") (Reprinted in *EQMM* 6/58; *EQA* Fall-Winter 1971.)

10.   9/30/51   The Vanishing Wizard. (*QBI,* as "Double Your Money.") (Reprinted in *EQMM* 9/55; *EQA* 1968.)

11.   1/26/52   The Mysterious Black Ledger. *(QBI,* as "The Black Ledger.") (Reprinted in *EQMM* 12/55; *EQA* 1962.)

12.   3/20/52   Cold Money. (*QBI.*) (Reprinted in *EQMM* 1/56; *EQA* 1969.)

13.   8/31/52   The Phantom Train. (*QBI,* as "Snowball in July.") (Reprinted in *EQMM* 7/56; *EQA* 1969.)

14.   12/28/52   The Myna Bird Mystery. (*QBI,* as "The Myna Birds.") (Reprinted in *EQMM* 9/56 and *EQA* 1969 Midyear, as "Cut, Cut, Cut!")

15.   3/8/53   "My Queer Dean!" (*QBI.*) (Reprinted in *Best Detective Stories of the Year,* ed. David C. Cooke (Dutton, 1954); *EQMM* 11/56; *This Week's Stories of Mystery and Suspense,* ed. Stewart Beach (Random House, 1957); *The Comfortable Coffin,* ed. Richard S. Prather (Gold Medal pb #S1046, 1960); *EQA* 1971.)

16.   8/9/53   A Matter of Seconds. (*QBI.*) (Re-

printed in *EQMM* 1/57; *EQA* Spring-Summer 1972.)

17. 9/13/53   A Question of Honor. (*QBI.*) (Reprinted in *EQMM* 5/58; *Crimes Across the Sea*, ed. John Creasey (Harper, 1964).)

18. 9/11/55   The Blackboard Gangsters. (*QED*, as "Object Lesson.") (Reprinted in *For Love Or Money*, ed. Dorothy Gardiner (Doubleday, 1957), as "Kid Stuff"; *EQMM* 4/58; *EQA* Fall-Winter 1972; *Mirror Mirror Fatal Mirror*, ed. Hans Stefan Santesson (Doubleday, 1973).)

19. 3/18/56   Terror in a Penthouse. (*QED*, as "No Parking.")   (Reprinted in *EQMM* 2/58; *Wicked Women*, ed. Lee Wright (Pocket Book #1263, 1960); *EQA* 1964 Midyear; *Crimes and Misfortunes*, ed. J. Francis McComas (Random House, 1970).)

20. 6/10/56   The Man They All Hated. (*QED*, as "No Place to Live.") (Reprinted in *EQMM* 3/58; *EQA* 1964.)

21.   8/4/60   E = Murder. (*Queens Full.*) (Reprinted in *EQMM* 5/61; *With Malice Toward All*, ed. Robert L. Fish (Putnam, 1968).)

22. 7/27/63   Mystery in Neon Red. (*QED*, as "The Broken T.")   (Reprinted in *EQMM* 5/66.)

23. 8/25/63   Half a Clue to Murder. (*QED*, as "Half a Clue.") (Reprinted in *EQMM* 8/66.)

24. 11/3/63   Last Man to Die. (*QED.*) (Reprinted in *Best Detective Stories of the Year*,

ed. Anthony Boucher (Dutton, 1964);
EQMM 1/67.)

TODAY'S FAMILY

1. 2/53 The Accused. (*QBI,* as "The Robber of
Wrightsville.") (Reprinted in *EQMM* 12/54;
EQA 1966.)

STORIES WITHOUT INITIAL MAGAZINE PUBLICATION

1. The African Traveler. (*Adventures,* as "The
Adventure of the African Traveler.") (Re-
printed in *More Adventures of Ellery Queen*
(Bestseller pb #3, 1940); *Great American
Detective Stories,* ed. Anthony Boucher
(World, 1945); *14 Great Detective Stories,*
ed. Howard Haycraft (Modern Library,
1949).)

Section 7. Magazine appearances of Queen novels prior
to their book publication. All are condensations except
the one in *Mystery League,* which is uncut.

COSMOPOLITAN

1. 6/36 *Halfway House.*
2. 12/36 *The Door Between.*
3. 12/37 *The Devil to Pay.*
4. 10/38 *The Four of Hearts.*

MYSTERY LEAGUE

1. 10/33 *Drury Lane's Last Case.*

REDBOOK
1.   6/34   *The Chinese Orange Mystery.*
2.   4/35   *The Spanish Cape Mystery.*
3.   1/68   *The House of Brass.*

PART II. EDITORIAL AND CRITICAL WORK

Section 1. A checklist of contents of the four issues of *Mystery League* Magazine. All non-fiction is indented.

October 1933 issue (160 pp.)

Barnaby Ross, *Drury Lane's Last Case* (complete novel, published in book form as indicated in Part I Section 3 above).

Dashiell Hammett, "Nightshade" (short story later collected in *The Adventures of Sam Spade and Other Stories,* Queen ed. 1944).

Dorothy L. Sayers, "Suspicion" (short story later collected in *In the Teeth of the Evidence,* 1940, and anthologized by Queen in *101 Years' Entertainment,* 1941).

> "To the Queen's Taste"—gossip and criticism by Queen.

John Marvell, "Burlingame the Magnificent" (uncollected short story).

> "Secrets of Houdini"—an article by J. C. Cannell.

> "Puzzle Department"—a potpourri of brainteasers.

Ellery Queen, "The Glass-Domed Clock" (short story later collected in *The Adventures of Ellery Queen,*

1934).

> "Through the Looking Glass"—an editorial by Queen, whose title is perhaps his earliest use of a Lewis Carroll motif.

November 1933 issue (160 pp.)

Phoebe Atwood Taylor, *The Riddle of Volume Four* (complete novel published in book form as *Beginning with a Bash,* as by Alice Tilton, Collins 1938, Norton 1972).

G.D.H. & M.I. Cole, "The Owl at the Window" (a short story included under its original title "In a Telephone Cabinet" in the collection *Wilson's Holiday,* 1928, and later anthologized by Queen under its *Mystery League* title in *101 Years' Entertainment*).

John Marvell, "Watch Your Step" (uncollected short story).

> "Secrets of Houdini, Part II"—article by J. C. Cannell.
>
> "To the Queen's Taste"—more Queenian gossip and critique.

Henry Wade, "Payment in Full" (short story included in the collection *Policeman's Lot,* 1933).

> "Puzzle Department"—more brain-teasers.

Gavin Holt, *Drums Beat at Night* (Part I of a serial which was published in book form in England, Hodder & Stoughton 1932, but apparently never appeared in book form in the U. S. Gavin Holt is a pseudonym of Charles Rodda, 1891-   ).

December 1933 issue (160 pp.)

Brian Flynn, *The Spiked Lion* (complete novel which had earlier been published in book form in England, John Long 1933, and would soon appear here as well, Macrae Smith 1934).

Thomas Walsh, "Guns of Gannett" (uncollected short story).

"Secrets of Houdini, Part III"—article by J. C. Cannell.

John Marvell, "Burlingame Draws Two" (uncollected short story).

"To the Queen's Taste"—another helping of shoptalk.

Gerald Aswell, "The Fly" (uncollected short story).

"Puzzle Department"—more fun and games.

Gavin Holt, *Drums Beat at Night* (Part II of serial).

"The Reader's Corner"—letter column.

January 1934 issue (128 pp.)

B. G. Quin, *The Mystery of the Black Gate* (complete novel published in book form in England, Hutchinson 1930, but apparently never issued here).

Viola Brothers Shore, "The Mackenzie Case" (short story later anthologized by Queen in *101 Years' Entertainment*).

"Puzzle Department"—final assortment of brain-teasers.

"To the Queen's Taste"—final assemblage of commentary.

Charles G. Booth, "Orchid Lady" (uncollected short story).

Gavin Holt, *Drums Beat at Night* (third and final installment of serial).

Section 2A. "Thematic" anthologies edited by Queen. I have listed the first American edition, the first English edition where there is one, subsequent editions with distinctive features, and all unabridged paperback editions known to me.

Challenge to the Reader. Stokes, 1938.

101 Years' Entertainment: The Great Detective Stories, 1841-1941. Little Brown, 1941. Modern Library, 1946, with the four Sherlock Holmes excerpts in the original edition replaced by a Nick Carter story, for reasons explained in footnote 3 to Chapter Six.

Sporting Blood: The Great Sports Detective Stories. Little Brown, 1942. Faber, 1946, as *Sporting Detective Stories.*

The Female of the Species: The Great Women Detectives and Criminals. Little Brown, 1943. Faber, 1947, as *Ladies in Crime: A Collection of Detective Stories by English and American Writers.*

The Misadventures of Sherlock Holmes. Little Brown, 1944.

Best Stories from Ellery Queen's Mystery Magazine. Detective Book Club, 1944.

Rogues' Gallery: The Great Criminals of Modern Fiction. Little Brown, 1945. Faber, 1947.

To the Queen's Taste: The First Supplement to 101 Years' Entertainment, Consisting of the Best Stories Published in the First Five Years of Ellery Queen's Mystery Magazine. Little Brown, 1946. Faber, 1949.

Murder by Experts. Ziff-Davis, 1947. Sampson Low, 1950.

20th Century Detective Stories. World, 1948. Includes the first version of *Queen's Quorum.* The second edition of the anthology, Popular Library pb #SP333, 1964, omits the *Quorum* and replaces eight of the stories from the original edition with newer tales.

The Literature of Crime: Stories by World-Famous Authors. Little Brown, 1950. Cassell, 1952. Pan pb #X12, 1957, as *Ellery Queen's Book of Mystery Stories.*

Poetic Justice: 23 Stories of Crime, Mystery and Detection by World-Famous Poets from Geoffrey Chaucer to Dylan Thomas. New American Library, 1967. Signet pb #Q4269, 1970.

Minimysteries: 70 Short-Short Stories of Crime, Mystery and Detection. World, 1969.

Section 2B. Annual compilations of best stories from *EQMM* edited by Queen. I have listed the first American and English editions, subsequent editions with distinctive features, and all paperback editions known to me.

The Queen's Awards, 1946. Little Brown, 1946. Gollancz, 1948.

The Queen's Awards, 1947. Little Brown, 1947. Gollancz, 1949.

The Queen's Awards, 1948. Little Brown, 1948. Gollancz, 1950.

The Queen's Awards, 1949. Little Brown, 1949. Gollancz, 1951.

The Queen's Awards, Fifth Series. Little Brown, 1950. Gollancz, 1952. Black's Readers Service, n.d., as *The Lady Killer and Other Stories.* Ace pb #D493, 1961.

The Queen's Awards, Sixth Series. Little Brown, 1951. Gollancz, 1953. Black's Readers Service, n.d., as *The Enemy and Other Stories.*

The Queen's Awards, Seventh Series. Little Brown,

1952. Gollancz, 1954. Black's Readers Service, n.d., as *Always Trust a Cop and Other Stories.*

The Queen's Awards, Eighth Series. Little Brown, 1953. Gollancz, 1955. Perma pb #M3015, 1955. Black's Readers Service, n.d., as *Born Killer and Other Stories.*

Ellery Queen's Awards, Ninth Series. Little Brown, 1954. Collins, 1956.

Ellery Queen's Awards, Tenth Series. Little Brown, 1955. Collins, 1957. Perma pb #M3076, 1957.

Ellery Queen's Awards, Eleventh Series. Simon & Schuster, 1956. Collins, 1958.

Ellery Queen's Awards, Twelfth Series. Simon & Schuster, 1957. Collins, 1959.

Ellery Queen's Thirteenth Annual: A Selection of New Stories from Ellery Queen's Mystery Magazine. Random House, 1958. Collins, 1960, as *Ellery Queen's Choice: Thirteenth Series.*

Ellery Queen's 14th Mystery Annual. Random House, 1959. Collins, 1961, as *Ellery Queen's Choice: Fourteenth Series.*

Ellery Queen's 15th Mystery Annual. Random House, 1960. Gollancz, 1961.

Ellery Queen's 16th Mystery Annual. Random House, 1961. Gollancz, 1962. Popular Library pb #K14, 1962.

To Be Read Before Midnight. Random House, 1962. Gollancz, 1963. Popular Library pb #SP237, 1963.

Ellery Queen's Mystery Mix #18. Random House, 1963. Gollancz, 1964. Popular Library pb #M2065, 1964. (Nine stories from this anthology reprinted as *The Most Wanted Man in the World.* New English Library pb, 1968.)

Ellery Queen's Double Dozen. Random House, 1964.

Gollancz, 1965, as *Ellery Queen's 19th Mystery Annual.* Popular Library pb #M2082, 1965. (Nine stories from this anthology reprinted as *Death Scene.* New English Library pb, 1968. Another ten reprinted as *L As in Loot.* New English Library pb, 1969.)

Ellery Queen's 20th Anniversary Annual. Random House, 1965. Gollancz, 1966. Popular Library pb #75-1205, 1966. (Eight stories from this anthology reprinted as *A Craving for Violence.* New English Library pb, 1969.)

Ellery Queen's Crime Carousel. New American Library, 1966. Gollancz, 1967. Signet pb #P3267, 1967.

Ellery Queen's All-Star Lineup. New American Library, 1967. Gollancz, 1968, as *Ellery Queen's 22nd Mystery Annual.* Signet pb #T3698, 1968.

Ellery Queen's Mystery Parade. New American Library, 1968. Gollancz, 1969. Signet pb #Q3893, 1969.

Ellery Queen's Murder Menu. World, 1969. Gollancz, 1969.

Ellery Queen's Grand Slam. World, 1970. Gollancz, 1971. Popular Library pb #445-00304-095, 1971.

Ellery Queen's Headliners. World, 1971. Gollancz, 1972.

Ellery Queen's Mystery Bag. World, 1972. Gollancz, 1973. Manor pb #12153, 1973.

Ellery Queen's Crookbook. Random House, 1974.

Section 2C. Anthologies culled directly from the titles listed in Section 2B.

The Quintessence of Queen, edited by Anthony Boucher. Random House, 1962. Gollancz, 1963, as *A*

Magnum of Mysteries.   Both editions subtitled: *Best Prize Stories from 12 Years of Ellery Queen's Mystery Magazine.*

The Golden 13: 13 First Prize Winners from Ellery Queen's Mystery Magazine. World, 1971. Gollancz, 1972. Popular Library pb #445-00316-095, 1972.

Section 2D.   Collections of stories from *EQMM* rearranged in anthology/magazine format.   The starred title includes five brand-new stories.

Ellery Queen's 1960 Anthology. Davis pb, 1959.
Ellery Queen's 1961 Anthology. Davis pb, 1960.
Ellery Queen's 1962 Anthology. Davis pb, 1961.
Ellery Queen's 1963 Anthology. Davis pb, 1962.
Ellery Queen's Anthology, 1963 Mid-Year Edition. Davis pb, 1963.
Ellery Queen's 1964 Anthology. Davis pb, 1963.
Ellery Queen's Anthology, 1964 Mid-Year Edition. Davis pb, 1964.
Ellery Queen's 1965 Anthology. Davis pb, 1964.
Ellery Queen's Anthology, 1965 Mid-Year Edition. Davis pb, 1965.
Ellery Queen's 1966 Anthology. Davis pb, 1965.
Ellery Queen's Anthology, 1966 Mid-Year Edition. Davis pb, 1966.
Ellery Queen's 1967 Anthology. Davis pb, 1966.
Ellery Queen's Anthology, 1967 Mid-Year Edition. Davis pb, 1967.
Ellery Queen's 1968 Anthology. Davis pb, 1967.
Ellery Queen's Anthology, 1968 Mid-Year Edition. Davis pb, 1968.
Ellery Queen's 1969 Anthology. Davis pb, 1968.

Ellery Queen's Anthology, 1969 Mid-Year Edition. Davis pb, 1969.

Ellery Queen's 1970 Anthology. Davis pb, 1969.

Ellery Queen's Anthology, 1970 Mid-Year Edition. Davis pb, 1970.

Ellery Queen's 1971 Anthology. Davis pb, 1970.

Ellery Queen's Anthology, Spring-Summer 1971. Davis pb, 1971.

Ellery Queen's Anthology, Fall-Winter 1971. Davis pb, 1971.

Ellery Queen's Anthology, Spring-Summer 1972. Davis pb, 1972.

Ellery Queen's Anthology, Fall-Winter 1972. Davis pb, 1972.

Ellery Queen's Anthology, Spring-Summer 1973. Davis pb, 1973.

Ellery Queen's Anthology, Fall-Winter 1973. Davis pb, 1973.

Section 2E. Anthologies culled directly from the titles listed in Section 2D.

Ellery Queen's 12. Dell pb #2259, 1964.

Ellery Queen's Lethal Black Book. Dell pb #2261, 1965.

Ellery Queen's Murder—In Spades! Pyramid pb #T2036, 1969.

Ellery Queen's Shoot the Works! Pyramid pb #T2129, 1969.

Ellery Queen's Mystery Jackpot. Pyramid pb #T2207, 1970.

Ellery Queen's Best Bets. Pyramid pb #N2775, 1972.

Section 3. Collections of others' short fiction edited by Queen. I have listed all known American editions. None of these collections has been published in England.

Dashiell Hammett, *The Adventures of Sam Spade and Other Stories.* Bestseller pb #50, 1944. World, 1945. (Five of the seven stories in this collection reprinted as *A Man Called Spade and Other Stories.* Dell pb #90, 1945; #411, 1950. The complete collection reprinted as *They Can Only Hang You Once and Other Stories.* Mercury pb #131, 1949.)

Dashiell Hammett, *The Continental Op.* Bestseller pb #62, 1945. Dell pb #129, 1946.

Dashiell Hammett, *The Return of the Continental Op.* Jonathan pb #17, 1945. Dell pb #154, 1946.

Dashiell Hammett, *Hammett Homicides.* Bestseller pb #81, 1946. Dell pb #226, 1947.

Dashiell Hammett, *Dead Yellow Women.* Jonathan pb #29, 1947. Dell pb #308, 1948.

Dashiell Hammett, *Nightmare Town.* Mercury pb #120, 1948. Dell pb #379, 1949.

Dashiell Hammett, *The Creeping Siamese.* Jonathan pb #48, 1950. Dell pb #538, 1951.

Dashiell Hammett, *Woman in the Dark.* Jonathan pb #59, 1952.

Dashiell Hammett, *A Man Named Thin and Other Stories.* Mercury pb #233, 1962.

Stuart Palmer, *The Riddles of Hildegarde Withers.* Jonathan pb #26, 1947.

John Dickson Carr, *Dr. Fell, Detective, and Other Stories.* Mercury pb #110, 1947.

Roy Vickers, *The Department of Dead Ends.* Bestseller pb #91, 1947.

Margery Allingham, *The Case Book of Mr. Campion.*

Mercury pb #112, 1947.

O. Henry, *Cops and Robbers.* Bestseller pb #94, 1948.

Stuart Palmer, *The Monkey Murder and Other Stories.* Bestseller pb #128, 1950.

Erle Stanley Gardner, *The Case of the Murderer's Bride and Other Stories.* Davis pb, 1969.

Lawrence Treat, *P As In Police.* Davis pb, 1970.

Edward D. Hoch, *The Spy and the Thief.* Davis pb, 1971.

Michael Gilbert, *Amateur in Violence.* David pb, 1973.

Section 4.   Critical and bibliographic books written by Queen.

The Detective Short Story: A Bibliograpy.   Little Brown, 1942.   Reprinted with new Introduction, Biblo & Tannen, 1969.

Queen's Quorum: A History of the Detective-Crime Short Story As Revealed by the 100 Most Important Books Published in This Field Since 1845. Little Brown, 1951. Gollancz, 1953. New edition (including Supplements through 1967), Biblo & Tannen, 1969.

In the Queens' Parlor, And Other Leaves from the Editors' Notebook.   Simon & Schuster, 1957. Gollancz, 1957. Biblo & Tannen, 1969.

PART III. ASSOCIATION ITEMS

Section 1. Novelizations of films and radio plays about Ellery and dramatizations of novels about him. No work herein was written by Queen.

Movie Novelizations
Ellery Queen, Master Detective. Grosset & Dunlap, 1941. Pyramid pb #R1799, 1968, as *The Vanishing Corpse.*

The Penthouse Mystery. Grosset & Dunlap, 1941. Pyramid pb #R1810, 1968.

The Perfect Crime. Grosset & Dunlap, 1942. Pyramid pb #R1814, 1968.

Radio-Play "Novelettizations"
The Last Man Club. Whitman, 1940. Included in *The Last Man Club,* Pyramid pb #R1835, 1968.

The Murdered Millionaire. Whitman, 1942. Included in *The Last Man Club,* Pyramid pb #R1835, 1968.

Dramatization of Novel
Ellery Queen's The Four of Hearts Mystery, dramatized by William Rand. Chicago: Dramatic Pub. Co., 1949. (William Rand is a pseudonym of William Roos who is half of the husband-wife mystery-writing team of Kelley Roos.)

Section 2. Juvenile mysteries signed as by Ellery Queen, Jr., although none in fact were written by Queen.

The Black Dog Mystery. Stokes, 1941. Collins, 1942.

The Golden Eagle Mystery. Stokes, 1942. Collins, 1943.

The Green Turtle Mystery. Lippincott, 1944. Collins, 1945.

The Red Chipmunk Mystery. Lippincott, 1946. Collins, 1948.

The Brown Fox Mystery. Little Brown, 1948. Collins, 1951.

The White Elephant Mystery. Little Brown, 1950. Hodder & Stoughton, 1951.

The Yellow Cat Mystery. Little Brown, 1952.

The Blue Herring Mystery. Little Brown, 1954.

The Mystery of the Merry Magician. Golden Press, 1961.

The Mystery of the Vanished Victim. Golden Press, 1962.

The Purple Bird Mystery. Putnam, 1966.

Section 3.   True Crime collections signed as by Ellery Queen. The articles in these collections were written by Manfred Lee based on research materials supplied by the magazines that commissioned the pieces.

Ellery Queen's International Case Book. Dell pb #2260, 1964.

The Woman in the Case. Bantam pb #F3160, 1966. Corgi pb, 1967, as *Deadlier Than the Male*.

Section 4.   Paperback novels signed as by Ellery Queen.

Pocket Books series
Dead Man's Tale.   Pocket Book #6117, 1961.   Four Square pb, 1967.

Death Spins the Platter. *Pocket Book* #6126, 1962.

Murder with a Past. Pocket Book #4700, 1963.

Wife Or Death. Pocket Book #4703, 1963. Four Square pb, 1966.

Kill As Directed. Pocket Book #4704, 1963.

The Golden Goose. Pocket Book #4705, 1964. Four Square pb, 1967.

The Four Johns. Pocket Book #4706, 1964.

Blow Hot, Blow Cold. Pocket Book #45007, 1964.

The Last Score. Pocket Book #50486, 1964.

Beware the Young Stranger. Pocket Book #50489, 1965.

The Copper Frame. Pocket Book #50490, 1965. Four Square pb, 1968.

A Room to Die In. Pocket Book #50492, 1965.

The Killer Touch. Pocket Book #50494, 1965.

The Devil's Cook. Pocket Book #50495, 1966.

The Madman Theory. Pocket Book #50496, 1966.

Tim Corrigan series (Popular Library)

Where Is Bianca? Popular Library pb #50-477, 1966. Four Square pb, 1966.

Who Spies, Who Kills? Popular Library pb #60-2111, 1966. Four Square pb, 1967.

Why So Dead? Popular Library pb #60-2122, 1966. Four Square pb, 1966.

How Goes the Murder? Popular Library pb #60-2168, 1967.

Which Way to Die? Popular Library pb #60-2235, 1967.

What's in the Dark? Popular Library pb #60-2269, 1968. Gollancz, 1970, as *When Fell the Night.*

Dell series

Losers, Weepers. Dell pb #5034, 1966.

Shoot the Scene. Dell pb #7845, 1966.
Kiss and Kill. Dell pb #4567, 1969.

Lancer series

Guess Who's Coming to Kill You? Lancer pb #73-802, 1968.
*The Campus Murders. Lancer pb #74-527, 1969.
*The Black Hearts Murder. Lancer pb #74640-075, 1970.
*The Blue Movie Murders. Lancer pb #75277-095, 1972. Gollancz, 1973.
    NOTE: Starred titles are in the "Troubleshooter" series.

Section 5. Historical novels signed as by Barnaby Ross. The identity between this byline and Queen's early pseudonym misled some library sources into attributing some or all of these titles to Dannay and Lee, although in fact the cousins had nothing to do with any of them.

Quintin Chivas. Trident/Simon & Schuster, 1961. Pocket Book #6141, 1962.
The Scrolls of Lysis. Trident/Simon & Schuster, 1962. Perma pb #M5083, 1963. Alvin Redman, 1964.
The Duke of Chaos. Pocket Book #6232, 1964.
The Cree from Minataree. Pocket Book #50200, 1964.
Strange Kinship. Pocket Book #50493, 1965.
The Passionate Queen. Pocket Book #50497, 1966.

Section 6. A selective checklist of writings about Queen.

Amis, Kingsley. "My Favorite Sleuths." *Playboy,*

12/66.   (Includes a brief critique of Queen.)

Bainbridge, John. "Ellery Queen: Crime Made Him Famous And His Authors Rich." *Life*, 11/22/43. (Lengthy profile of Dannay and Lee.)

Barzun, Jacques, and Wendell Hertig Taylor. *A Catalogue of Crime: Being a Reader's Guide to the Literature of Mystery, Detection and Related Genres.* Harper & Row, 1971. (Queen is discussed on pp. 351-353, 370-371, 541-546, 607-608.)

Boucher, Anthony. *Ellery Queen: A Double Profile.* Little Brown, 1951. (A 12-page pamphlet published on the occasion of Queen's 25th novel, *The Origin of Evil.*)

Boucher, Anthony. "There Was No Mystery in What the Crime Editor Was After." *New York Times Book Review*, 2/26/61; *Ellery Queen's Mystery Magazine*, 6/61. (Essay on Queen as an editor.)

"A Century of Thrills and Chills: Ellery Queen Meets the Critics." *Wilson Library Bulletin*, 4/42. (Transcript of a radio discussion with Dannay, Lee, Howard Haycraft and others, broadcast on *Speaking of Books*, 11/25/41.)

Christopher, J. R. "The Mystery of Social Reaction: Two Novels by Ellery Queen." *The Armchair Detective*, 10/72. (Essay on *The Glass Village* and *Cop Out.*)

Connor, Edward. "The Four Ellery Queens." *Films in Review*, 6-7/60. Revised version: "The Films of Ellery Queen." *The Queen Canon Bibliophile*, 4/71. (Critical discussion of the Queen novels as filmed.)

The Ellery Queen Review (formerly *The Queen Canon Bibliophile*). A mimeographed journal devoted to Queen and his works, edited by Rev. Robert E.

Washer (82 East Eighth St., Oneida Castle, N.Y. 13421), and apparently terminated after eight issues.

Erisman, Fred. " 'Where We Plan to Go': The Southwest in Utopian Fiction." *Southwestern American Literature,* 4/71. (Includes discussion of *And On the Eighth Day.*)

Haycraft, Howard. *Murder for Pleasure: The Life and Times of the Detective Story.* Appleton-Century, 1941. (Queen is discussed on pp. 173-179.)

Lord, Graham. *London Sunday Express,* 12/13/70. (Interview with Dannay.)

Mooney, Joan M. *The American Detective Story: A Study in Popular Fiction.* (Ph.D. dissertation, University of Minnesota 1968, published in five installments in *The Armchair Detective,* 1/70-1/71, as "Best-Selling American Detective Fiction." Includes lengthy discussions of Queen.)

Nevins, Francis M., Jr., ed. *The Mystery Writer's Art.* Bowling Green University Popular Press, 1971. (Queen is discussed by many of the almost two dozen contributors to this anthology.)

Parker, Dorothy. *Esquire,* 1/59. (Review of Queen's threesome *The New York Murders.*)

Prescott, Peter S. *Look,* 4/21/70. (Interview with Dannay and Lee, not printed in all copies of the issue.)

The Queen Canon Bibliophile; see *The Ellery Queen Review.*

Routley, Erik. *The Puritan Pleasures of the Detective Story.* Gollancz (London), 1972. (Queen is discussed on pp. 193-195.)

Scott, Sutherland. *Blood in Their Ink: The March of the Modern Mystery Novel.* Stanley Paul (London), 1953. (Queen is discussed on pp. 51-55.)

Shenker, Israel. *New York Times*, 2/22/69. (Interview with Dannay and Lee on the occasion of their 40th anniversary as mystery writers.)

A Silver Anniversary Tribute to Ellery Queen from Authors, Critics, Editors and Famous Fans. Little Brown, 1954. (A 31-page pamphlet published to celebrate Queen's 25th year in the mystery field.)

Symons, Julian. *Mortal Consequences: A History from the Detective Story to the Crime Novel.* Harper & Row, 1972. (Queen is discussed on pp. 121-122.)

Tomasson, Robert E. *New York Times*, 4/5/71. (Obituary notice on the death of Manfred Lee.)

Unsigned. "A Case of Double Identity." *MD*, 12/67. (Lengthy profile of Dannay and Lee, Dannay's choice for the best reportage on Queen.)

Unsigned. "Ellery Queen Builds Collection of Rare Detective Short Stories." *Publishers' Weekly*, 11/20/43. (Illustrated article on Queen as a bibliophile.)

Unsigned. "Mysterious Masked Author." *Publishers' Weekly*, 10/10/36. (Brief news item revealing for the first time the identity of Queen.)

Unsigned. "Queen, Ellery." *Current Biography, 1940.* (Biographical profile, with checklist of earlier periodical materials on Queen.)

INDEX